Gender

Gender

Harriet Bradley

polity

First published in 2007 by Polity Press

Reprinted in 2008

Polity Press
65 Bridge Street
Cambridge CB2 1UR, UK

Polity Press
350 Main Street
Malden, MA 02148, USA

ISBN-13: 978-07456-2376-4
ISBN-13: 978-07456-2377-1 (pb)

A catalogue record for this book is available from the British Library.

Typeset in 10.5 on 12 pt Sabon
by SNP Best-set Typesetter Ltd, Hong Kong
Printed and bound in the United States by Odyssey Press Inc.,
Gonic, New Hampshire

The publisher has used its best endeavours to ensure that the URLs for external websites referred to in this book are correct and active at the time of going to press. However, the publisher has no responsibility for the websites and can make no guarantee that a site will remain live or that the content is or will remain appropriate.

Every effort has been made to trace all copyright holders, but if any have been inadvertently overlooked the publishers will be pleased to include any necessary credits in any subsequent reprint or edition.

For further information on Polity, visit our website: www.polity.co.uk

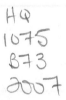

Contents

For Ian, Irving and Steve

Three very different men who proved
that the 'pleasures and dangers' of
masculinity can bring joy to women

Acknowledgements

Thanks are due to Polity staff for their forbearance during the long time it has taken me to produce this book. Thanks, too, to Bristol University and its Sociology Department for resourcing me through a sabbatical year following my term as Dean, which allowed me to complete it at last. Hugs and kisses to Ruth and Vala, co-warriors for gender justice. Thanks to Ruth Levitas for guidance on reading about feminist Utopias. Research carried out with Ruth Levitas, Steve Fenton, Jackie Guy, Ranji Devadason and Geraldine Healy has been crucial in shaping this book and the themes within it; working with them all provided huge intellectual stimulus. Geraldine's extraordinary energy and productivity has helped me push my own to the limits! The research drawn on in the book was funded by the NHS and the ESRC. I have learned much from working with undergraduates and postgraduates on gender analysis over the years and discussions with them continue to mould and enlarge my thinking. Finally, my gratitude to all the people I know or have interviewed whose stories have fed into my vignettes. If they recognize bits of themselves in my fictionalized portraits, I hope they will feel pleased and flattered: I have found them interesting and important enough to want to use them as illustrations of the contemporary 'doing' of gender. However, the interpretations of their *petits récits* are of course mine not theirs, as are the ideas developed in the rest of this book, for which I must bear the sole responsibility.

Finally many thanks to Steve Gillen for his patience with my distraction when writing the book, especially the frantic last stages. As usual, he has kept me sane.

Introduction

This book presents an account of the major debates around and usages of the sociological concept of gender. Very generally, gender refers to the relations between women and men. Writing in 1996 I defined it in the following way, which I still find a useful starting point:

> Gender refers to the varied and complex arrangements between men and women, encompassing the organisation of reproduction, the sexual divisions of labour and cultural definitions of femininity and masculinity. (1996: 205)

However, as we shall see, gender is quite a hotly contested concept. It is also, as Glover and Kaplan aptly put it, 'a busy term' (2000: ix), meaning that it is very widely used, in many differing contexts, so that its usages are continually evolving and its meaning is quite slippery. Part of the 'busyness' and 'slipperiness' arises from the fact that this is a highly politically charged concept. Its use is inextricably bound up with the centuries-long struggles over power between men and women.

Since the 1970s, gender has become both an important topic of academic study in its own right and a major category to be used in analysis within the social sciences and humanities. So prevalent is its use that many universities now have courses and programmes in Gender Studies, which often developed from the Women's Studies courses that emerged under the influence of the 'second-wave' feminism of the 1970s and 1980s. Courses on gender have a strong appeal to many students because the issues they deal with are so obviously relevant to the lives of young women and men. While the initial students and researchers were mainly women, increasingly men have been drawn to this area of study, especially since Gender Studies' options now deal with men and masculinity as well as women and femininity.

In popular usage, the notion of gender is also common, especially in the mass media. Terms like the 'genderquake', the 'gender gap' (first used about the continuing pay differential between men and women, now increasingly in relation to girls' better performance than boys in school examinations) or 'gender-bending' are coined by journalists and used to highlight changes in existing relations between the sexes in the contemporary world. Most large organizations – from corporations to universities to trade unions – have formal equal opportunities policies which outlaw discrimination on the basis of gender, as well as race, religion and sexual orientation.

Like many key social science concepts, the term 'gender' is both dense and contested. It has been written about and argued about exhaustively. Since Ann Oakley wrote her very influential book *Sex, Gender and Society* in 1972, often taken to represent the first major feminist reutilization of the existing grammatical term, millions of pages have been written about it. It would not be possible in a short text like this to explore in detail the full history of the term's usage and all the twists and turns of the debates around it that have occurred over the past three and a half decades. There are in existence a number of books on feminism which perform that task in a helpful and accessible fashion.[1] Here, rather, I have chosen to focus on how the term is currently utilized and to put my own particular spin on the meaning and importance of gender

---

[1]   I would recommend in particular Rosemarie Tong, *Feminist Thought* (Allen and Unwin, 1989); Sylvia Walby, *Theorizing Patriarchy* (Blackwell, 1990); Valerie Bryson, *Feminist Debates* (Macmillan, 1999); Jane Freedman, *Feminism* (Open University Press, 2001).

in our social world. As a sociologist, I have also focused on sociological debates and literature. That is not to denigrate the excellent work on gender being carried out in other areas such as culture, literature and politics. However, I think there is a need at this stage to reassert the need for a vigorous, creative sociology of gender, given the tendency for Gender Studies to drift into more abstract realms.

The book takes the form of a series of short chapters which set out key issues and dilemmas. The first three chapters deal with gender on a fairly abstract and general level. Chapter 1 looks at definitions and the attempts to conceptualize gender. Chapters 2 and 3 lay out the major theoretical perspectives within which the concept has been deployed, linking them to the two major contemporary competing frameworks of modernity and postmodernity. Since my own belief is that the most valuable way to explore any concept is by looking at specific social contexts in which it is seen to be operating, chapters 4, 5 and 6 look at gender relations in action in three different contemporary areas: production, reproduction and consumption. These three sociological terms can be taken to represent what we more popularly think of as work, family and leisure. The terms are taken from Marx, but this book is in no way confined to Marxist ideas. Rather, I have chosen these terms because they seem to me to provide a reasonably inclusive framework for thinking about the process of gendering *in everyday life*. Of course, they do not cover everything! Again, I have had to be selective, and regret all the good work I've had no space to explore. Finally, the Conclusion sets out a possible future for the analysis of gender relations, revolving especially round the concepts of 'power', 'intersectionality', 'identity' and 'Utopia'.

A number of propositions underpin the discussion in this book. First, gender is a social construct; it is a category used by human beings as a way of dividing up the world they perceive around them and making sense of it. Since the distinction between women and men is very basic to all societies, this way of categorizing social relations is one that has a very long history. However, being a social construct, gender is not something fixed, but something that varies according to time, place and culture. What it means to be a woman and a man is not the same now as it was in Ancient Egypt or in medieval

Europe; nor are the relations today between the sexes the same in Britain, in Saudi Arabia and in India.

My second proposition is that gender as a construct is politically deployed. That is, the usage of the term has been persistently bound up with power relations between women and men. For example, I have pointed out above that the growth in interest in gender as an academic concept arose from the rebirth of feminism in the 1970s, which itself was a political movement that sought to help women achieve equality with men. Although the close link with feminist politics and activism has been broken, at least in the UK, I shall argue that the way the term is employed still has political implications.

Thirdly, gender must be seen as lived experience. Although the term 'gender' is indeed a construct, it refers to aspects of our lives that are all too real. It is important to state this, as there is a counter-view of the world, espoused by some adherents of post-structuralism and postmodernism, which wants to see the whole of social reality as a kind of fiction, created by human beings out of words. While, for the social realist, an object, such as a flower, a cat, a chair, a university, exists as a material entity to which different cultures give different names, for theorists of discourse, the words and constructs that human beings devise actually constitute and make up the world. The flower, cat, chair and university are as they are because that is how we have named them. This is an intricate philosophical debate which will be considered briefly in chapter 3. But since the dispute between these two positions is probably ultimately irresolvable (which came first, the chicken or the egg? the word or the thing?), I do not intend to waste too much time on it. The position I espouse in this book is one that I have set out in a series of other publications (Bradley 1996; 1999a and b; Bradley and Fenton 1999; Fenton and Bradley 2002): that gender is at the same time both a material and a cultural phenomenon. It refers both to the lived experiences of men and women in relation to each other and to the ideas we develop to make sense of these relations and to frame them. Material experiences inform cultural meanings, which in turn influence the way lived relations change and develop.

To say that gender has a material existence, however, is not to give it the status of a 'thing' (like, say, a chair or a university) to which we can fix a label and which has a stable physical existence. Gender is more than a fixed category or label for individuals. Thus a simple statement such as 'Harriet is a woman' or 'Stephen is a man' tells us nothing about their gender beyond a basic grammatical assignment or an identification of their accepted sex. Such a usage of gender is of limited utility except as a 'variable' in social analysis (where, for example, we may look at 'voting patterns broken down by age and gender/sex'). Gender only becomes a meaningful term when we consider the relationship *between* Harriet and Stephen and the broader relations in which they live. Gender is a social phenomenon, not merely an attribute of individuals. As I stated at the start of this Introduction, gender as explored in this book is a set of sociological relationships. However, like all sociological phenomena, gender impacts on the experience of each one of us as individuals. That is what I mean by lived experience.

Because I want to emphasize strongly that gender is lived experience, I have included in between the main chapters of this book a series of vignettes, or illustrative sketches, exploring the way that gender is lived out in people's lives. These vignettes are set in a different typeface from the main chapters, so can be easily identified. Some are narratives or personal stories of individuals, including myself: others illustrate a series of dilemmas and possibilities that individuals may face. This technique illustrates a fourth proposition, which is that 'the personal is political'. This was a favourite proposition of second-wave feminists as they sought to bring what had formerly been seen as private matters (such as housework or domestic violence) on to the political agenda. I use this proposition to show that the political relations of gender, disparities of power between women and men, affect us all in every aspect of our lives, *whether we realize it or not*. This is what the second-wave feminists tried to address by the process they called consciousness-raising: small groups of women, often friends or workmates, met together regularly to discuss what being a woman meant to them, to share the experiences and problems they faced in their everyday lives. This later became the model for similar men's groups.

Finally, I stress that gender is a very diffuse and all-embracing concept. Unlike some social science concepts (such as class, democracy, deviance) gender does not relate to a single aspect or sphere of human activity. Gender affects every aspect of our personal lives. Whether we identify as a man or a woman determines how we look, how we talk, what we eat and drink, what we wear, our leisure activities, what jobs we do, how our time is deployed, how other people relate to us. Similarly, as I shall argue in the second half of this book, all the institutions which make up our society (marriage, families, schools, workplaces, clubs, pubs, political organizations) are themselves *gendered* and are locations in which the *gendering* of individuals and relationships takes place. Thus, while the study of class, for example, focuses on the economic sphere (issues of occupation, income and resources), the study of gender is multifaceted, leading to the proliferation of research and writing mentioned above. One can conduct a study of gender in relation to virtually any social or cultural phenomenon. Ulrich Beck (1992) rightly described gender as 'omni-present'. As Jan Morris said in the autobiography, *Conundrum*, in which she described her experience as a transsexual crossing from male to female: 'There seems to be no aspect of existence, no moment of the day, no contact, no arrangement, no response, which is not different for men and women' (quoted in Abbott 2000: 140).

While I was writing this book, I had the good fortune to visit India as a guest at a Women's Studies Network Conference convened by the British Council in Delhi. This gave me a chance to look at gender issues from a new perspective, listening to the concerns of women living in a very different cultural and socio-economic context. What I learned from them has informed the way I have written this book. Literally, a new window on the world was opened which affected my 'way of seeing' (Berger 1972). Thus, I have tried to incorporate material from India into the discussion as a counter to the ethnocentrism of which Anglo-American feminism has often been accused. The points that I have made above are at play in considering how gender is experienced in India.

Gender is a social construct and the rules of gender relations operate very differently in India from how they do in

Europe (for example, all the time I was in Delhi, I never saw a woman driving a car). Gender is politically shaped: the state in India currently has a key role in redefining gender rules pressured by a very active and focused feminist movement. While I was writing this book, a Women's Party of India was formed which contested the 2004 elections in the state of Maharashta, although it did not win any seats. The Indian feminists also draw very strongly on CEDAW, the Convention on the Elimination of All Forms of Discrimination Against Women, an internationally approved agreement on equal rights. CEDAW is used in India and in many other countries in Asia, the Middle East and Africa to give legitimacy to feminist movements. In Britain, where the climate of equality is more developed, feminists have not needed such a tool. Gender is lived experience and puts terrible constraints as well as opportunities in our way. The Indian women spoke with passion about the 'missing girls' of India as manifested in the adverse sex ratio in many states, caused in part by female foeticide and infanticide. The personal is political. Just as British feminists had done in the 1980s, Indian women were campaigning to raise awareness of the severe problems in their country of widespread violence against women and to break the silence around domestic violence.

Here in Britain the study of gender is well established in our colleges and universities, although increasingly this occurs through the processes of *gender mainstreaming*: that is, incorporating gender broadly throughout disciplinary curricula rather than through special women's studies and gender studies centres or courses, though some of these still exist. Gender has been recognized as a respectable academic study, while at the political level the New Labour government has developed a number of policies designed to help women and open up opportunities to them. We can certainly say that we are living in a gender-aware society, in contrast to the position described to me by women in India. I have described this current situation as constituting 'a climate of equality' (Bradley 1999a). However, as this book is designed to show, that does not mean that battles around gender and its meanings are over. Beneath the surface of the climate of equality still lie major divergences of gendered power.

IN AND OUT OF THE FRAME: A PERSONAL HISTORY OF GENDER

Her voice was ever soft,
Gentle and low – an excellent thing in woman.
(Shakespeare, *King Lear*)

I have given suck, and know
How tender 'tis to love the babe that milks me.
(Shakespeare, *Macbeth*)

That's a woman's life – waitin' and waitin'. (John Galsworthy, *Strife*)

Although I have the body of a woman, I have the heart and stomach of a king. (Queen Elizabeth I)

Men's love is of men's life a thing apart
'Tis woman's whole existence. (Lord Byron, *Don Juan*)

I was brought up in the 1940s and '50s, a time when the separation of women's and men's experience – social patterns of gender difference, though such terminology would not have been used at the time – was taken for granted and thus unquestioned. My father went out to work, running an office to support his wife and three children. My mother had been a schoolteacher until she gave birth to me – the oldest of the three. After that, she became a full-time domestic worker, doing the shopping, cleaning and washing and cooking elaborate meals for the rest of us. When we were short of money, she would take in lodgers or 'night-stop visitors' for whom she provided bed and board. Most of my friends' families had similar arrangements; this was the heyday of the 'traditional' or male breadwinner family, at least among the middle classes. I went to a single-sex grammar school, as did my brother and sister. In many ways my adolescence was comparable to that of middle-class girls in parts of Asia and the Middle East today; I grew up in a segregated world of girls and girl culture. Though I had a younger brother, boys of my own age seemed a different species. I knew that at school they did 'boy things', such as woodwork and metalwork, sports like rugby, soccer and cricket. I was scared of having to talk to one as I had no idea what went on in their minds: obviously they would not be interested in pets and ponies, romantic fiction and gorgeous pop singers like Cliff Richard, Adam Faith and Billy Fury! Later, when I went to university, I envied those whom I met who had had the luck to attend a mixed comprehensive school and had grown up at ease with the 'opposite sex'. That term, commonly used then (as in 'how to attract the opposite sex'), seemed perfectly to sum up the bipolar world which I inhabited. Boys were everything that girls were not. This was the frame for gender relations in the 1950s.

Like my girlfriends, I took it for granted that in the future I would get married and look after children, unless – horrid fate – I became a 'spinster' or 'old maid' getting 'left on the shelf'. The academically oriented school I attended made a big thing about 'careers for girls', and distinguished old girls would come to speech days to talk about their work as scientists, civil servants or politicians. But this all flowed over our heads. Some of our teachers were not married and we pitied them in a condescending sort of way. It was even whispered in the playground that two of them were lesbians, a cause of much giggling and speculation. Like many girls, I had fantasies of 'what I might do when I grew up': become an actress, a writer, even a teacher. But I did not think of these activities in terms of earning a living or supporting myself or having a career. It was just that it seemed that as an adult you had to do something, at least until marriage. As Sylvia Walby writes in *Gender Transformations* (1997), women at the time were oriented towards a domestic future as an unquestioned fate.

As I grew older and teenage sexual angst set in, I became gradually convinced that I was so plain and shy that I would never find a boyfriend or husband: at this point it began to occur to me that my fate might indeed be to be left on the shelf and I began to imagine how it would be possible to be an adult woman and not to be a wife and mother. Being at the age of 16 deeply soaked in French literature – Balzac, Molière, Stendhal, Proust – I had become familiar with the idea of the 'bluestocking' and some vague vision of myself as an intellectual began to emerge, since, while not being pretty, athletic or artistic, I was normally top of the class. But even then my fantasies took gendered, if highly literary, forms: I would run off to Paris, starve in a garret (very romantic!) and struggle to become a novelist; if successful I would then set up a 'salon'. Poets, musicians and philosophers would attend and I would gain reflected glory from their wit and wisdom. This was a fantasy that persisted long into my adult life. Less acknowledged, but nevertheless present in my consciousness, was a version of the 'ugly duckling' theme very popular in children's and romantic fiction: I would throw off my teenage pudge and gawkiness and some man would recognize the beauty of my soul and sweep me off my feet!

What is strange looking back on that epoch is how completely unchallenged and taken for granted this bipolar world of the sexes seemed. Men had to work; women had babies. Nor did this difference manifest itself in any way as a form of 'inequality': the nearest I came to this was a vague sense of 'unfairness'. Why did my sister and I have to help with the washing up, while my brother was excused as it was more important for him to do his homework? Why did I have to clear up the playroom? I would have liked to have been born a boy, especially when I was pre-teen. At that stage I was a tomboy, keen on climbing trees, fishing in rockpools, scrambling up rocks and playing at soldiers. Yet, having been born a girl, one's fate was determined. Anatomy was indeed destiny.

I went to university to study English in the late 1960s and there I discovered the more enjoyable sides of being a girl: sex, dancing and rock 'n' roll. Although absorbed in these activities and all the excitement and revolutionary fervour of the student protest movement, some inkling of gendered inequality was beginning to dawn upon me. The lecturers always seemed to treat the male students as more serious and important than us girls. Young men had the freedom to ask us out, while we had to sit in the hall of residence desperately hoping the phone would ring for us on Fridays and Saturdays. Young men had the liberty to roam about, while we women were policed by hall wardens 'in loco parentis' (we could enter their rooms in the male halls, but they were not allowed to venture beyond the common room in ours!). The 'double standard' reigned strong. It was acceptable, indeed desirable, for a young man to gain some sexual experience, so he would be a skilful initiator of his wife. But girls who had 'sex before marriage' risked being labelled sluts or slags.

Fascinating research into the lives of female students in the post-war decades carried out by Carol Dyhouse (2006) reveals how girls who became pregnant (and this was not a rare occurrence) often had to leave university, abandoning their degrees. I remember going to see my doctor to ask to be prescribed the pill when I started my relationship with my future husband, only to be told that she could not condone such immorality. It was back to the Durex, then, until the Family Planning Association came to our rescue. It would be hard for present-day young women, perhaps, to understand all the stress and embarrassment this caused. We had to inhabit, then, a world of sexual secrecy, confiding only in our best friends. And was it fair that our hearts were so often broken, causing us to lie weeping on our narrow student bedsteads while they set jauntily off to the sports field, apparently impervious to Cupid's arrows, just as Byron had noted?

These vague disquiets were, indeed, echoed in my engagement with literature, as exemplified in the quotations at the start of this section. Lear's comment on Cordelia's quiet voice, often quoted approvingly by my grandfather, seemed the attitude of a patriarch proved foolish: on the other hand, the noble and wifely Cordelia was clearly the heroine compared to her hateful but ambitious sisters Regan and Goneril. Lady Macbeth's acknowledgement of her femininity was followed by a rejection of softness as a challenge to her faltering husband. But one would not want to be Lady Macbeth. Elizabeth the First, virgin queen of ambiguous sexuality, was an easier figure to identify with: like me, she had clearly wanted to be a boy, and she had embraced the masculine role of sovereign with voracity, stringing the men along and out-manoeuvring them all along the line. And what passion and fire I breathed into Madge's line from Galsworthy's play about striking male factory workers, *Strife*, as a student actress: 'Waitin' and waitin'.' Why were we doomed to passivity while men got all the drama?

These feelings of injustice and disadvantage, however, remained inchoate until, in 1978, I embarked on a second degree as a (not very) mature student. By then I had married, trained and worked as an English teacher, suffered health problems and held off from having a child because it didn't somehow feel right. I valued the freedom I had begun to attain and my marriage was beginning to falter. I was ripe for feminism to hit me, and it did! I was studying sociology because I had discovered Marxism during my PGCE year and had developed a passionate interest in work relations, class and politics. But by the end of my PhD period, gender had become just as strong a passion. Like so many women of that time, my active involvement in the Women's Liberation Movement evolved alongside an academic identification as a Marxist feminist. My marriage had collapsed and now I was going at last to develop that career commended to me on school speech days. There was a world to win! It was a time of crux, such as that described by Carol Gilligan in *The Birth of Pleasure*, her retelling of the myth of Cupid and Psyche: 'In moments of epiphany – moments of sudden, radical illuminations – we see through the categories that have blinded our vision. These are the moments when we step out of the frame' (2002: 207). As Gilligan says, stepping out of the frame is a frightening experience as we lose our bearings, 'find ourselves without a map' (ibid.: 159). But it also offers us extraordinary freedom to make our own roads and step over boundaries. From now on, whatever might befall me, I owed it to womankind to turn my back on passivity. Feminism had taught me that we had 'the right to choose': the right to be an active human being and not merely a reflector of male glory. While this was a moment of personal epiphany, it is important to emphasize that this was the kind of experience shared by many women of my generation and similar educational backgrounds. Gender change, like gender identity, is a social phenomenon.

In Britain, we have moved on considerably from that segregated but naturalized gender order in which I grew up. But 'women's liberation' has not reached all women either in Britain or, more notably, across the globe. This is what a rural woman in India told a researcher about life for women in her village:

> Men in our families are like the sun, they have a light of their own. Women are like satellites without any light of their own. They shine only if and when the sun's light touches them. This is why women have to constantly compete with each other for a bigger share of sunlight, because without this light, there is no life. (Bhasin 2000: 23)

One of the hopes for the study of gender has always been that, through voicing such insights, women (and men) will be able to move forward to a point where they, too, will be able to step outside their own frames of inequality and acceptance and take us forward to a new world of opportunity, understanding and respect.

1
What's in a Name? Meanings and Usages of Gender

The concept of gender as it is utilized in social science thinking today is relatively new. But the word has a much longer history. Various dictionaries offer the earlier meanings of the word. First, it is a grammatical term, used to categorize nouns as male, female or neuter. Interestingly, the Collins dictionary states that this can be 'actual or ascribed', which gives an immediate clue as to the way gender categories have been so central to ways of portraying the world. In the English language, nouns are normally gendered only when they actually refer to biological sex difference: man and woman, stag and hind, dog and bitch. But many languages, including the two great classical and formative languages of European civilization, Latin and Greek, assign gender values to all nouns. This is a basic way in which humans have tended to divide up and categorize the reality we perceive.

The grammatical use of the term seems to have led to two other former usages: one is as a synonym for sex (an issue in gender analysis today); and in another, 'to gender' meant to beget or procreate (we might use 'engender' today). All three of these linked usages can be seen as relatively technical: there are no disputes about their meaning and they are a standard part of a grammarian's vocabulary.

The academic use of the term which we are discussing here is largely a product of the Women's Studies movement of the 1970s and 1980s. The consciousness of women's disadvantage and oppression, as uncovered by the second-wave feminist political movement which sprang up on the heels of the social ferment of the 1960s, spawned an academic arm. Many of the young women who were active in the Women's Liberation Movement (WLM) were graduates, some of them starting out on academic careers (see Banks 1981; Bradley 2003; Coote and Campbell 1982; Oakley 1981). Quickly they discerned the absence of women's experience in the gamut of academic disciplines, from history to literature, from sociology to psychology. The infant Women's Studies movement, which sprang up first in North America and then in Britain, sought to recover the lost story of women and 'add women in' to social and cultural research. To do this, however, they needed to develop their own theoretical framework and set of related concepts.

It is not quite clear who first used the word gender in this context. Glover and Kaplan (2000) suggest that it was employed in the 1960s in the then burgeoning area of sexology and the psychology of sex. One book that sprang from this tradition, psychologist Robert Stoller's *Sex and Gender: On the Development of Masculinity and Femininity* (1968), is cited by them as the first study to formulate fully the distinction between sex and gender that was commonly used by the feminist writers of the 1970s. Ann Oakley is usually credited with having introduced the distinction to feminism in her extraordinarily influential 1972 text *Sex, Gender and Society*. She herself drew on Stoller's work in her account: 'gender' refers to the socio-cultural aspects of being a man or woman – that is, how society sets the rules for masculinity and femininity – while sex refers to 'the base of biological sex differences ("male" and "female") on which they were erected' (Andermahr et al. 2000). Thus, put simply, gender is cultural and socially constructed, sex natural and biological. Interestingly, in India, where there is only one existing word to cover sex and gender – *linga* – feminists have used qualifying adjectives to cover this distinction: *praakritik linga* (biological sex) and *saamajik linga* (social sex) (Bhasin 2003).

While Stoller used these terms analytically to show how differences between male and female psychology came about, it was Oakley, along with other early feminist writers such as

Kate Millett (1971), Juliet Mitchell (1971) and Gayle Rubin (1975), who linked the concept of gender to a theory of inequality and oppression of women. This was the theory of *patriarchy*, a social system of male dominance (Bradley 1989; Walby 1990) which became for a time the main theoretical framework of gender analysis and which will be discussed more fully in the next chapter. Rubin also coined the term 'sex/gender system' to describe such a social system, because, as an anthropologist, she pointed out that it was not necessarily the case that men were the dominant sex; it would also be possible to have a 'matriarchy' as an alternative form of sex/gender system. Theoretically, this is logical, although anthropologists have disagreed as to whether any known existing society could actually be described as matriarchal, even though some are matrilocal (where households form around women) (Bamberger 1974; Coontz and Henderson 1986). In an influential paper, Sherry Ortner (1974) claimed that all known societies were characterized by male dominance.

The distinction that Oakley and others made between gender and sex was crucial to the feminist case as a way to contest the view, still widely held today, that gender differences are 'natural', arising from genital and genetic differences, and thus inevitable and impossible to change. Such a position, for example, underlay functionalist approaches to the study of gender roles, such as that of Parsons and Bales (1956). Gender role theory had been the dominant sociological perspective in studying relations between women and men before the advent of second-wave feminism. Parsons and Bales suggested that within the family in a capitalist industrial society there was a need for role specialization, as different social functions required different personality characteristics. *Instrumental* roles, carried out by men, involved functioning in the cut-throat world of economic competition. Thus men needed to be aggressive, ruthless and intellectual. By contrast, the family also needed women to carry out *expressive* roles of caring and nurturing, looking after children and providing for people's physical and emotional needs. The idea that these sets of roles were mutually incompatible provided the grounds for justifying the type of family that was dominant in the United States in the 1950s: the 'traditional' or breadwinner/

housewife family. Underpinning this account was a biologistic view that women's reproductive role and hormones made them 'natural' carers. Others, especially the socio-biologists, suggested that men's primordial role as 'hunters' and their male physique and hormones (testosterone) made them 'naturally' aggressive and competitive.

This 'naturalist' view of masculinity and femininity as a biological 'given' was challenged by the sex/gender distinction. While not denying the 'sexual dimorphism' of the human species (the bodily and physiological differences between women and men), the feminists stated that since gender was a cultural phenomenon, gendered forms of behaviour were learned – and thus could be unlearned. A large part of Oakley's book is taken up with discussing the great range of variations in men's and women's social roles and in ideas about masculinity and femininity in different societies, past and present. She appropriated another key term from functionalist theory – 'socialization' – to explore how this comes about, developing a fuller account of this in another influential book, *Subject Woman* (1981). For the functionalists, socialization consists of the processes by which we learn how to become human, by learning from various sources (the family, school, the media) the rules and norms of appropriate behaviour. Oakley extended this idea to explore processes of gender socialization, showing how in families, schools and workplaces, and through literature and the mass media, girls and boys were taught appropriate behaviour for their gender. All these approaches can be summed up in Simone de Beauvoir's famous dictum: 'One is not born, one becomes a woman' (1973: 301). Or a man.

The sex/gender distinction was central to many early feminist studies throughout the 1980s. A useful summary of this approach comes from the historian Joan Scott: 'gender is a social category imposed on a sexed body' (1988: 18). But, as she noted, increasingly this distinction between socio-cultural gender and biological sex has been contested. Once again, this contestation can be seen to arise from the politics of gender and sexuality.

One of the first challenges came from feminist biologists such as Lynda Birke (1986), who argued that sex and biology should themselves not be seen as fixed and static. Birke argues that the human body changes in interaction with the social environment. For example, our body size and shape are different from those of our British ancestors because of dietary change and different physical regimes: a look at clothes in costume museums will quickly confirm the smaller physique of sixteenth-, seventeenth- and eighteenth-century men and women. We could not cram our large modern hands and feet into their dainty gloves and slippers! In a television history programme, Dan Snow suggested that in the late seventeenth century the average height of British soldiers was five foot three (*Battlefield Britain*, BBC 2, 10 September 2004). The implication of these arguments is that a sharp distinction between nature and culture is not tenable, as the 'natural', too, is in part socially constructed. Thus the gender/sex distinction starts to collapse.

In support of this position, feminists have drawn on the work of French historian and philosopher Michel Foucault, whose important study, *The History of Sexuality* (1980), highlighted the way in which different sexual categories and identities developed in different centuries, largely because of the work of medical scientists, psychologists and other experts. According to Foucault, the notion of 'the homosexual' as a form of fixed sexual identity did not appear until the nineteenth century; before then, the practices we now call 'homosexual' were just part of an array of sexual activities in which men and women might engage. Thus for Foucault sexuality, too, is a construction.

These ideas were taken up and developed by those interested in the natural sciences as a way to challenge naturalistic forms of thinking within them: it is still the case that much scientific and psychological thinking tends to see masculinity and femininity as biologically determined (and thus unavoidable). For example, there have been controversial claims that a 'homosexual gene' has been identified. In fact, two major current scientific developments in bioscience – the human genome project (which seeks to identify the determining function of each gene) and neuroscience (which uses complex technology to scan the brain and demonstrate how stimulating particular parts results in certain responses, outcomes and behaviours) – offer the prospect of providing a biological explanation for all human characteristics and behaviours.

Using such knowledge, we could design the perfect human being! It is easy to see how such sensational pieces of Big Science can capture the public imagination. In my experience, very many first-year undergraduates espouse some elements of such biological explanations of male and female behaviour. Thus, we can understand the political importance for feminists working in the natural sciences of attempting to challenge naturalistic views of nature by using the constructionist position.

This position has since been pushed a stage further by those who argue, under the influence of French philosopher Jacques Derrida, that all forms of binary categorization (which, as we pointed out earlier, have been very central to western thinking) are in themselves oppressive, since they put limits on what we are expected and thus able to do. To call somebody a 'woman' or a 'man', or to call them 'black' or 'white', is to compel them to *act* and *be* in certain ways (Haraway 1990). This philosophical doctrine of *deconstructionism* (the breaking down of binary categories) was very attractive to a new generation of feminists who were influenced by the ideas of postmodernism and post-structuralism (which will be discussed further in chapter 3). Thinking in terms of binary categories was seen by feminists to be part and parcel of an oppressive, patriarchal, western scientific mode of thinking often labelled the 'mainstream' or 'malestream'. New perspectives of thought, such as feminism, gay and lesbian theory or postcolonial theory, saw themselves as challenging such orthodoxies of scientific academic discourses.

Subsequently many postmodern feminists, most notably Judith Butler (1990; 1993), have argued that the distinction between sex and gender is no longer sustainable and should be collapsed. Butler sees no difference between sex and gender, as they are inextricably linked and both, in her view, are created in tandem through daily acts of 'playing out' male or female identity. Butler argues that we should understand gender/sex in terms of *performativity*: in our daily lives we repeatedly 'do gender', act out being a man or woman in ways that give the illusion of stability and fixity: 'Gender is the repeated stylisation of the body, a set of repeated acts within a highly regulatory frame that congeal over time to produce the appearance of substance, of a natural sort of being' (1990:

33). As a lesbian, Butler argues that the route to gender liberation is through challenging the rules of performance to create
'transgressive' gender activities and identities. Thus she advocates drag and cross-dressing, adopting individualized and
mixed forms of sexual identity, as ways in which we can break
down binary thinking on gender. We will explore this further
in chapter 3.

The existence of 'third sex' categories is indeed an important way in which to challenge the view of the sexes as inherently 'opposite' and distinct that I discussed earlier. Some
individuals are born with genital features of both sexes or
with indeterminate sexual features (hermaphrodites). Others
choose to disalign their gender and their sexuality from their
genital and bodily characteristics (transvestites, gays and lesbians). Others undergo bodily changes to alter their sexual or
gender identities (eunuchs, transsexuals). Some cultures openly
acknowledge a third sex, the 'berdache' or popularly termed
'ladyboys' of countries like Brazil and Thailand. On a more
mundane level, many women display patterns of behaviour
that are popularly identified as masculine, while many men
display attributes described as feminine. For example, there
is a current debate about whether men and women adopt
different styles of behaviour when they become managers.
Men are said to be more authoritarian, more aggressive and
ruthless in their behaviour and to favour bureaucracy and
hierarchy. Women are said to possess a softer, more caring
and consultative style, encouraging democracy and participation. But in fact it is easy enough to identify examples of
autocratic, ruthless women and caring, consultative male
managers. While we may associate these styles as typically
masculine and feminine, it is clear that men and women can
choose to employ either of these approaches or indeed a mix
of both.

Butler and her followers have thus revealed the complexity
and fluidity of sex and gender categories. Many contemporary
feminists, therefore, see no use in making a sharp distinction
between sex and gender, since in this view we create the illu-
sions of fixed gender identities through means of embodied
actions. For example, when we engage in a heterosexual sex
act, we are simultaneously affirming our gender identities as
women or men. In contemporary western societies gender

identities are so deeply imbued with heterosexual meanings as to be virtually indistinguishable. The cultural and social processes which create gender are tied up with our physical beings.

While this has been a very influential position, some feminists see it as being politically problematic. The complete deconstruction of the gender/sex distinction reopens the possibility of anti-feminists explaining gender differences in terms of biology. While Butler's ideas about transgressive gender acts have appealed to artists and performers, like Annie Sprinkle and Grace, whose acts include the manipulation and parading of sexuality and gender identity (Annie openly displays her vagina to her audience, Grace has grown a moustache), they have little resonance for the majority of people who are happy to accept a given sexual identity and to enjoy the experiences of conventionally sexed/gendered bodies.

My own view is that, while Butler's work poses an important corrective to views of gender as a fixed identity, the obstinacy of bodies and genital difference is underplayed in this type of theory. Moreover, battles to show that gender is socially constructed are far from won. The sex/gender distinction remains a vital instrument for explaining the construction of difference. It is instructive to see that this position is shared by many Indian feminists, such as Bhasin. Where society's gender awareness is very low, collapsing the social back into the biological is a dangerous strategy. So in this book I take gender to be something different from either biological sex or sexuality and the subsequent discussion is grounded in this distinction. We might paraphrase and expand on de Beauvoir: one is born with a body that is immediately ascribed a male or female identity (usually on the basis of fairly unambiguous physiological evidence, the possession of a penis or a vagina), but one becomes a man or a woman through social interactions within a set of cultural understandings about femininity and masculinity.

However, one very important contribution of recent thinking about gender is the recognition of how individual women and men are actively involved in 'doing gender'. Our identities as gendered and sexual beings are not simply imposed on us, but are something which we are constantly engaged in creating and recreating, even at quite a basic physical level.

Consider, for example, how much work and effort girls and women put into creating the bodily appearance of being feminine. Writers on adolescence rightly stress the enormous amount of labour teenage girls put into presenting themselves as maturing sexual beings: learning about make-up and trying it out, experimenting with hairstyles, trying out different fashions, learning how to walk in high heels, moderating their voices to be 'sexy', decking themselves up for discos and parties, decorating their bodies with piercings and tattoos, shaving bodily hair, improving skin tone with all sorts of creams and potions. As radical feminist Andrea Dworkin puts it:

> In our culture, not one part of a woman's body is left untouched, unaltered. No feature or extremity is spared the art, or pain, of improvement. . . . From head to toe, every feature of a woman's face, every section of her body is subject to modification, alteration. The alteration is an ongoing, repetitive process. It is vital to the economy, the major substance of male-female differentiation, the most immediate physical and psychological reality of being a woman. From the age of 11 and 12 until she dies a woman will spend a large part of her time, money and energy on binding, plucking, painting and deodorising. (Dworkin, quoted in Bordo 1993: 21)

Similarly, boys and men labour (if perhaps not quite so consciously) to develop an adult masculinity by repetitive action to enhance muscularity and macho appeal. The 'new men', with their cosmetics, interest in fashion-wear and exercise and gym routines, are only exemplifying a more consumerist version of what David Jackson so tellingly describes in his account of how young boys, through constant activity, build up their superiority (over girls) in sport. As a rather small boy with 'delicate' limbs, he had to strive the harder to accomplish the masculine physical ideal:

> What seemed like innate physical superiority to girls in sporting matters like learning to throw balls becomes critically exposed as the result of very different social practices and power relationships. . . . Whereas my sisters had been trained for domestic labour, childcare, homemaking and servicing other people (including me), with very little time, positive

context and motivation for the sporting activities I took for granted almost every day of my life, I had learned to throw with concentrated strength and accuracy through hundreds of hours of informal practice.

I developed the muscles in my throwing arm through frequent games of cricket up on the Bumps (the grassy headland sticking out between the beaches where I lived) and mastering the quick deadly throw at the stumps (only we used a wastepaper basket or chalk marks on an old air-raid shelter wall). Looking back now from my very different vantage point I can reconstruct one brief moment in my life, somewhere between the ages of eight and ten, as a time of compulsive stone throwing. It seems to me now that I had to have a stone in my hand, firing away at road signs, advertising hoardings, even occasionally blackbirds. . . . Because of my culturally learned view of my body as inadequate, I urgently wanted to see it in a new way – as a potential 'instrument of power' – and to develop a virile physical presence that would help me hold my own in the street and playground. So I was ready to strive for a swaggering physical presence and put in hours and hours of routine practice to try and achieve such an end. (Jackson 1990: 208–9)

Note how in both Dworkin's and Jackson's account the repetitive, everyday nature of the behaviour is stressed, bearing out Butler's account of gender as a 'set of repeated acts within a highly regulatory frame'.

We refer to this process of doing gender as *gendering*. This active term has now largely superseded the older concept of gender socialization discussed above. Both the feminist and functionalist theories of socialization came under attack for being too deterministic, presenting individuals as passively shaped by the processes that surrounded them. If that were the case, how did change in social rules and roles ever occur? Why do some individual men reject the heterosexual norm and the 'macho' aggressive style that Connell (1987) has termed 'hegemonic masculinity'? Why do some women carry a tomboy style past their childhood, turn their backs on domesticity and declare their disinterest in having babies? What leads some people to conform to gender orthodoxies and some to rebel? While some of the old insights from socialization are useful in showing where ideas of normality come from and in revealing the pressures we are under as individuals to be 'normal', the more active idea of gendering allows us to explore how individuals develop as agents in interaction with their environment.

Gendering can be seen to operate at three levels (which social scientists like to call the micro, meso and macro level). The first involves the patterns of individual behaviour and interaction described above. The second is the institutional level, which is extremely important. Joan Acker, who has made important contributions to the study of gendering in organizations, offers a useful definition: 'To say that an organisation, or any other analytic unit, is gendered means that advantage and disadvantage, exploitation and control, action and emotion, meaning and identity are patterned through and in terms of a distinction between male and female, masculine and feminine' (Acker 1990: 146).

However liberated and gender-aware we may be as individuals, institutions such as schools and workplaces operate with quite rigid rules, conventions and expectations about gender, which place restraints on people and which they find difficult to resist without being penalized. The rules of some institutions (such as boarding schools, prisons and sports clubs) can actually promote a considerable degree of gender segregation and the development of the 'separate worlds' described earlier.

Finally, these institutional processes feed into the development of gendered structures at the macro, or societal, level. The choices people make and the rules governing social interaction and social institutions come together and coagulate into gendered structures such as the sexual division of labour which are remarkably robust and operate across a whole society. Indeed, as we shall see in later chapters, structures of gender have some remarkable similarities across the globe, for example in terms of the domestic division of labour.

This brings us to address the prevailing and longstanding issue in sociology concerning the relationship between agency and structure. As individual agents, we are at least relatively free to choose our course of action, while at the same time being constrained by the structures and cultures which are our contexts. However, these contexts are in themselves variable: for example, the rules of gender-appropriate dress vary in different societies and even in different subcultures within societies. Moreover, the degree to which different groups of people are free to challenge rules is very variable. If we stick with gendered dress codes, in Britain women are free to choose virtually any style of dress, from ultra-feminine blouses and skirts to masculine pinstripes. English men, on the other hand, cannot choose to wear dresses or skirts without ridicule, except in very special circumstances (fancy-dress parties, sarongs on the beach) or unless they are people whose charisma and power puts them above normal rules (Boy George and David Beckham). Scottish men can choose between 'trews' or kilts. In Arab countries, however, women are prohibited from wearing male garments. In India, middle-class urban women can wear western-style clothes, including trousers, but in Indian villages women must wear traditional women's attire (saris, shalwar kameez). This example illustrates the variability of rules of gender; but the constant is that every society has different dress rules for women and men.

In the second half of this book we shall consider processes of gendering in three aspects of our daily lives: production, reproduction and consumption. We shall consider how the three levels outlined above – individual actions, institutional rules and broader social structures – operate in the perpetuation of gender differences and inequalities. In doing so we will highlight the ubiquity of gender and the grip it has over our behaviour and life chances, whether it is acknowledged or not. But, as the discussion above illustrates, we have to be aware of variations of gender, especially in terms of how gender processes are affected by differences of class, ethnicity, religion and nation.

The interaction of gender and class was a particular concern of some of the early second-wave theorizing around gender because of the close link with Marxist sociology. A discussion of these types of theory in chapter 2 is preceded by an account of the intermeshing of class and gender in processes of socialization and gendering.

Gendering and Class: Growing up Girl, Growing up Boy

I remember one day walking along the beach with 12-year-old Lucien, when he turned to me seriously and asked, 'Harriet, how do I cope at school with being different?'

It was a heart-wrenching question to answer, as I remembered myself the horrors of being different at school, and a period when I used to hide in the lavatories over break in order not to be seen being alone. That is why so many parents worry about school and whether their child is fitting in, and why young boys are often told, especially by fathers, that they must learn to fight in order to defend themselves against teasing and bullying. In telling Lucien that in the long run being different was a source of strength and that he would eventually find friends of his own kind, I knew that in advising nonconformity I would not be helping to ease the pains of early adolescence.

Jake Shears, of the gay and lesbian band Scissor Sisters, described to a journalist the difficult period he went through when he decided to 'come out' as gay at the age of 15:

> He lived away from home for a time and had a terrible time at state school – he wore makeup and dresses, and became a target for the hatred of his mostly Mormon

classmates. 'I don't know what I was thinking' he says of his early exit from the closet. 'I probably wouldn't recommend it to every gay fifteen-year-old, but what doesn't kill you makes you stronger.' (McLean 2004: 24)

Among the various forces of gender socialization we encounter in our lifetimes, it is likely that the family has the longest-lasting and deepest effect: but I am convinced that the pressure from peer culture is the most intense we ever experience. This is especially true for boys. Carol Gilligan suggests that boys, at around the age of 5, are pressurized to conceal parts of themselves which are not seen as tough, masculine and manly. They must suppress interests in things assigned as 'girlie' or 'sissie', learn to hide sensitive feelings if they are not later to be stigmatized as 'poofs'. Girls, on the other hand, are left much freer from gender imperatives, being allowed to be tomboys, to run with boys and wear male clothing – at least until early adolescence, when Gilligan suggests that they in turn become initiated into the rules of femininity, a time at which the 'vicious games of inclusion and exclusion' become common (2002: 91). Certainly, my own period of misery commenced when I was about 13.

Tom is quite a typical boy: he moved rapidly from dedication as a youngster to the Teenage Ninja Mutant Turtles, to a passion for football and a determination to become a professional player. The craze for sport then partly gave way to a devotion to noisy and increasingly obscure types of popular music, with its accoutrements of rebellion, long hair and a Kurt Cobain t-shirt. Tom, however, got his teenage rebellion over reasonably early: there were rows and fights at home, troubles and suspensions at school, over-enthusiastic drinking bouts, but in his late teens he was knuckling down and putting his energies into school work. His younger brother Simon, meanwhile, had never become a real sports fan, despite being fit, lithe and an able athlete. His passion was for all things technological: from cars to cameras, from computers to cell-phones.

Before Tom's sudden surge to maturity, he and his brother had fought and scrapped constantly and sometimes quite viciously, kicking, punching, wrestling. Let out of a car, they would take off, looking for the nearest bit of grass to run over, wall to climb or ball to kick. In this restless young male energy, they were united in a contemptuous disinterest in anything they saw as 'girlie'. Avoidance of girls continued until the dawning of a sniggering and secretive pubescence, with whispered phone conversations to nameless sweethearts. However, these ghostly girlfriends seemed, ultimately, less important than Tom's rock band or Simon's latest Playstation console.

Tom and Simon come from a middle-class background, with parents who can support them in their schooling and whose considerable reserves of 'cultural capital' have been lent to the boys' upbringing. By contrast, Gary grew up in a deprived inner-city housing estate, known for its levels of crime, its poor schools and its serious heroin problem. Brought up by a determined single mother, who wanted to save him from the fate of his drug-addicted father, Gary seemed to get off to a good start: he had a talent for sport, played for a local youth rugby team, loved bikes and cars and was reasonably steady, if not very gifted, in his early school years. A photo of him at around 9 or 10, with his sister Cindy, shows them both smiling, clean-cut and bright-eyed. But as he hit adolescence, Gary fell into a very familiar pattern among young men of his background, bunking off school, losing interest in classwork, getting into minor trouble with the police. By the time he was 16 he had dropped out of school, failed to stick to any of the youth training programmes his social workers had started him on, was hanging around with a crowd of 'bad lads' and had been in the courts a number of times. His mother fought hard to gain help for him, but became increasingly disillusioned with his persistent recidivism, although she blamed his problems largely on the company he kept rather than his own inclinations. Linda McDowell, in her study of young working-class men (2003), similarly notes that, as individuals, their hopes and aspirations were orthodox, and it was only when in groups that 'laddishness' and 'having a laff' tended to assert itself. Finally, Gary left home to live in his girlfriend's parents' house. His mother hopes he will keep off hard drugs, but the prospects for an easily influenced young man in his environment do not look good.

These examples illustrate the importance of seeing gender as classed. Tom, Simon and Gary are all following well-established trajectories of young masculinity, but in contexts which are highly class-specific and which will lead them to very different types of adult manhood. Gary exemplifies a brand of tough, physical masculinity common in working-class environments. Like McDowell's respondents, Gary finds himself in an epoch where skilled manual jobs (mechanic, builder's labourer and so forth) are in short supply. His mother says he can take anything to pieces and put it back together again successfully; but, unless accompanied by paper qualifications and a conformist demeanour, such skills increasingly go unwanted. McDowell describes this in terms of 'redundant masculinities' (2003). Thus Gary looks headed for a young manhood of unemployment, temporary casual labour, trouble with the law and possible spells in prison. By contrast, Tom and Simon, who are successful at school and tell me 'all the really bright people' in their classes are boys, are headed for university and professional careers: science, law, finance or computing, perhaps. They are no less masculine than Gary, but the context which has shaped their childhood and youth has channelled them to the assertive type of middle-class manhood, fitting them to be rulers of men. Articulate and confident, they are headed towards the new types of managerial and entrepreneurial masculine roles which have been usefully described by Collinson and Hearn in *Men as Managers, Managers as Men* (1996).

I think Gilligan is right that the weight of gender socialization through peer pressure is much heavier for boys, at least in the early days, and that the rules of young masculinity are more powerfully enforced. At least until their teens, little girls like Cindy or like Heather, the daughter of two university lecturers, are free to try out and play with different types of gender roles. As a pre-teen, Heather's most popular clothing was a t-shirt and jeans; but she also liked to dress up in feminine dresses for special outings and parties and has had a long obsession with jewellery and decoration. Becoming a teenager, she entered the realm of fashion, and started wearing puffball skirts, asymmetrically cut dresses. Cindy too has a passion for shopping. When they were younger Cindy and Heather both liked to dress up as fairies and princesses, as so many little girls do, but were also at home riding bicycles and clambering on playground equipment. A little girl has a wide range of choice of activities facing her. Heather's particular passions are animals, books and computers: but the computer games she plays are very different from the war-games favoured by Tom and Simon. Instead, she plays card games, designs costumes (a hi-tech version of cut-out paper dolls), towns or castles and processes animal pictures from her digital camera to make slide shows.

Both Cindy from her inner-city estate and Heather brought up by professional parents are 'good girls' who enjoy school and work hard. But at the transfer to secondary school not only does the process of gendering begin to kick in, so also does class differential. Cindy attends the same poor-performing school as Gary did and has on one or two occasions got into 'bad company' and become alienated from school. Happily, her mother has managed so far to keep her on track. Cindy has had boyfriends, but nothing major. But at the age of 15 she is soon likely to face the pressures of teenage sexuality which, as many studies have documented, lead girls to lose interest in school attainment (Griffin 1985; Wolpe 1988). By contrast, Heather is protected. She attends a single-sex grammar school which is high in the league tables and has so far not ventured into the world of boys and dating.

It would be incorrect to say that girls are not pressured; but Walkerdine et al., in *Growing Up Girl* (2001), from which the title of this section is taken, point to the way that pressures are distinguished by class. Middle-class girls, they argue, have been subject to the most change. They are now being brought up to be *like their fathers*, that is, to be academically and professionally successful, rather than following the domestic model of my own mother's generation. They are constantly pressured to succeed at school and beyond, which may cause extreme anxiety in those not academically inclined. Not to do well in your exams is to be branded a failure. By contrast, the pressure on working-class girls is to do better than parents, *not to be like their fathers*. However, the anxiety may not be so acute, as the working-class parents' main priority, Walkerdine et al. claim, is the child's happiness rather than success. Therefore, school failure may be accepted pragmatically, as may teenage pregnancy. By contrast, teenage pregnancy is strongly vetoed amongst middle-class girls: if they do get pregnant, they are more likely to have it terminated. Three-quarters of girls from working-class backgrounds who become pregnant in their teens keep their babies, as opposed to 25 per cent of middle-class girls.

It is almost inevitable, then, that Heather will find her way to university and there commence to grapple how to 'juggle' career, sexuality and marriage, which is now an overriding concern of middle-class young adult femininity, as we shall see in later chapters. Cindy's future is less certain. She may succeed in school and go on to a local college, possibly following a vocational course of some kind (beautician, catering, childcare). Or she may follow in her mother's footsteps and become pregnant early, bringing up a child or two before returning to work. She is more likely than Heather to adopt the traditional female two-phase working-life pattern. Whichever of these courses she takes, her labour market options will be more promising than her brother Gary's: there are plenty of low-paid service jobs for young women, qualified or unqualified, to take up. Problems for Cindy are more likely to come from relationships than from work: she may become one of the young women who get sucked into the teenage world of drugs and casual sex. If she continues, as seems more likely, to follow in the quest for 'respectability', which Bev Skeggs saw as a dominant motif in her study of young working-class women (1997), she may avoid this stage and find a steady boyfriend to settle with. But Cindy is growing up in a locality where most of the young men are following the same trajectory as Gary. It takes strength of character to tackle this dilemma: do I stay with my roots, my family and friends and find myself slipping into insecurity and poverty? Or do I break out of this world into the middle-class one where I may remain forever an outsider? The work of Walkerdine (1990) and Mahony and Zmroczek (1997) has highlighted the psychological traumas experienced by those who must 'pass' in an alien class milieu.

Tom, Simon, Gary, Cindy and Heather are following well-defined gendered pathways. But as we have seen, these pathways are highly class-specific. For people in their age group, the struggles to resist prevailing orthodoxies of gender and class are intense. Of course, there are those who break out and succeed against the odds. But for many, the class and gender patterning acquired in childhood and adolescence will follow them a long way into adulthood.

I remember some other words of Lucien's, when he was a small child, under Gilligan's milestone age of 5. Snuggling up to me on the sofa, he raised large serious eyes to me and said, 'I think I love you'. How difficult would he find it today at 17 to say those words even to his mother and father, let alone some strange older woman! It is not a 'boy thing' (or even a 'man thing') to make an open display of feeling. Only when grown-up Lucien has identified a person with whom he wants to establish a partnership (probably heterosexual) will he feel enabled to utter such words again. And so it is, as Gilligan argues, that the rules of masculinity and femininity put limits on the full achievement of humanity, for all of us, whether we grow up boy or grow up girl.

2
Gender and Modernity

So far, I have argued that the academic use of the term 'gender' was politically informed, having been developed in tandem with the activities of the feminist movement which sought equality between women and men. Extending this analysis, we can also state that the development of theorization about gender, like any other social science concept (Weber 1949), is shaped by the political and intellectual contexts of the time. In this and the next chapter I shall be examining two intellectual 'moments' which have strongly influenced the way thinking about gender within social sciences has evolved. The shorthand terms for these moments are *modernity* and *postmodernity*. This chapter gives a brief overview of the way theories of gender developed in the intellectual epoch sociologists currently characterize as modernity.

The politics of modernity

As stated before, the interest in gender spread in the 1970s as part of the second-wave feminist movement. But it was also influenced by other events which formed its context. The 1960s and 1970s witnessed in Britain a major expansion of higher education, which brought a new kind of young person first into the body of students and then into jobs as lecturers and teachers. Many young people from working-class back-grounds were the first members of their families to go to university; far more women were going into higher education, instead of into secretarial college, finishing school or straight into work. This new generation of young people with university experience started to challenge academic and political orthodoxies. Many were swept up into the mass protests against the American war in Vietnam (the 1960s equivalent of Iraq) and subsequently into broader movements calling for greater democracy within and outwith the universities. They marched, demonstrated and occupied buildings, and in Paris their counterparts ripped up paving stones and took control of areas of the city. In America four protesting students were shot dead and several others injured by the National Guard at Kent State University in Ohio. Others were more attracted by the cultural movement known by its adherents as the 'alternative' or 'counter-culture', whose members were popularly characterized as 'hippies' or 'drop-outs', and who pioneered new lifestyles based on communal living, drugs, sexual experimentation and 'psychedelic' music. All this ferment fed into the academic agenda, where Marxism and other radical approaches became the order of the day.

Marxism in particular appealed to the many young men from working-class and lower-middle-class backgrounds who had benefited from the expansion of mass education. This was the generation of radicals who included future politicians such as Jack Straw, a future Home Secretary, Peter Hain, known for his work on poverty and Third World development before becoming an active adherent of New Labour, and David Triesman, General Secretary of the Labour Party in 2001–3 and now a member of the House of Lords. Bill Clinton confessed to sampling marijuana at Oxford, though he famously 'did not inhale'. Most, however, did! Many of these young radicals then moved to academic jobs in sociology, social policy and other social sciences.

In the UK in the late 1960s and early '70s Marxism was the nub of radical sociological thinking. It was debated and analysed even by those who rejected it, such as Frank Parkin in his critical text *Marxism and Class Theory* (1979), which set out an alternative form of class analysis drawing on the work of Max Weber. It is not surprising that feminists developed their account of gender inequality in response to ideas about class and capitalism. A brand of analysis variously known as Marxist feminism or materialist feminism became one of the major theoretical perspectives in the second-wave study of feminism. In Britain, its major early exponents included Michelle Barrett, Veronica Beechey and Miriam Glucksmann. In America, the work of Heidi Hartmann and Iris Young was especially important. Christine Delphy was an influential French contributor.

Marxist feminist thought took many forms, engendered many debates and still helps shape the analysis of gender. In later chapters we will look at the work of Miriam Glucks-mann, which deals with the 'total social organization of labour', a new way of developing some of Marx's ideas. However, it is not my intention here to enter into a discussion of the details of this wealth of literature. Readers will find useful accounts of these theoretical debates in Barrett (1980), Marshall (1994) and Tong (1989), among others. Here, I shall focus on the general way in which the Marxist feminists understood gender and utilized it for analysis.

Marxism, feminism and gender

For the Marxist feminists of the 1970s, gender was viewed primarily as a system of inequality and oppression. In this it was analogous to one of the key concepts of Marxist sociology: class. Class was seen as a relation of inherent exploitation between, in capitalist societies, the property-owning capitalists or bourgeoisie and the propertyless proletariat or working class, who were forced to sell their labour to capitalist employers to survive. This relationship, by which labour power (capacity to labour) is appropriated by the bourgeoisie and used to generate a profit, is what Marx conceptualized as 'exploitation' and is the kernel of Marxist class theory. The stress on property at a time (the mid-nineteenth century) when married women in Britain had no entitlement to their own wealth or income led Marx's collaborator, Friedrich Engels (1972), to claim that in the family 'the man was the bourgeois and the woman the proletariat'. Within the patriarchal family system, in which the man had absolute rights over his wife and children, he appropriated the labour of female members to cook, clean and sew. This was the basis, for Engels, of gender oppression. Engels also believed that the route to equality for women was through wage labour, which would free them from dependence on fathers and husbands and from unpaid virtual 'slave' labour in the home.

Things obviously have altered vastly since Engels wrote *The Origin of the Family* in 1884, not least because of the passing of a number of pieces of legislation which gave rights to women. The Married Women's Property Act of 1882 brought a potential end to the propertyless status of wives by allowing them rights to retain and keep their own property separate. However, it is interesting to reflect that in societies where women do not have the right to work, as in certain parts of Arabia and Asia, Engels's analysis may still apply. Paid work outside the home, offering both the right to enter the public sphere and the ability to acquire an independent source of income, may start to challenge the patriarchal dominance of husband, brothers or father. Indeed, Bhachu's research on Sikhs in Britain (1991) revealed that when young women started to be involved in paid work it had an immediate effect on the domestic arrangement of the family, with women gaining more freedom of choice.

While Engels's work drew attention to the family as the main site of women's oppression, the analysis of the Marxist feminists of the second wave was particularly drawn to the sphere of production. This was because of the centrality in Marxist theory of the concepts of labour (the work of production and social reproduction) and labour power (the capacity to labour). The ability of capitalists to squeeze the worker into producing more goods for the same payment (what we now call 'work intensification') is what enables them to produce profits. Thus a major concern of Marxist feminism was to study the *labour* and *labour power* of women, how it was employed, where it was employed and how it differed from that of men. This led to theoretical debates about the lower value put on women's labour and about the way domestic labour performed by women contributed to the maintenance of the capitalist system. Empirically, the earliest research studies by feminists in the UK tended to focus on women's work, either as wage labour (for example, Sally Westwood's participant study of hosiery workers (1984) and Anna Pollert's (1981) account of women in a tobacco factory) or as domestic labour and carers (Ann Oakley's pioneering text *Housewife* (1974) or Pauline Hunt's study of gender and class consciousness within families (1980)).

The strategy of Marxist feminists in approaching gender was to see it as a system of oppressive relations and view it in relation to capitalism. Sometimes this meant developing theories of how gender relations fitted within capitalist social organization; sometimes it involved the elaboration of a parallel system, often referred to as *patriarchy*, which coexisted with and interlocked with capitalism. This was the popular 'dual systems theory' which was elaborated, for example, by Hartmann (1986) and Walby (1986; 1990). Gender relations, in this view, were a form of inequality and oppression parallel with class, though, as in the case of class, such inequalities could be removed by the institution of a truly socialist regime.

I have concentrated on Marxism here because it exemplifies well the structure of thinking which we know as 'modernism'. This is a type of thinking which has its ancestry in the Enlightenment era of the late eighteenth century. The hallmark of the Enlightenment was its view of human reason as a key instrument by which the problems of society could be understood, tackled and ameliorated. The power of reason would shed light on darkness and enable mankind to progress towards better, more just and orderly social forms and institutions. Human nature, too, could be trained and developed to enable people to live more nobly and harmoniously with their fellows, according to the doctrine known as *the perfectibility of man*. As compared to the previous era of thinking, which was heavily theological in tenor and tended to explain events in terms of the 'will of God' (think of the Muslim view of life and the mantra, *inshallah*), there was a strongly secular and humanistic impulse to Enlightenment thought. Enlightenment ideas heavily influenced the evolution of sociology, early sociologists such as Comte, St Simon, Mill and Spencer being leading lights of the movement. Their legacy was inherited by Marx, Weber and Durkheim, the 'Big Three' contributors to the development of sociology in its classic manifestation. They shared the humanistic belief that understanding the world could lead to social change. All provided evolutionary accounts of social development, historical typologies of society and, in the case of Marx and Durkheim, accounts of how societies might progress towards justice and democracy. This optimistic, almost Utopian, strand was not shared by the more sceptical Max Weber, whose visions of the future presaged oppressive and bureaucratic totalitarian states. Nevertheless, he shared with the other two the idea that societies were orderly and logical enough for a future to be deduced from understanding the present. It is that view of societies as logically ordered, regular structures which characterizes modernist theory and which was to be challenged by postmodern and post-structuralist thinkers such as Lyotard, Foucault and Derrida (see chapter 3). In the case of Marx and Durkheim, the idea of 'regular structures' or 'patterns of behaviour' was extended further, developing the image of society as a 'system' in which each part contributed to the coherent functioning of the whole.

The modernist thinkers gave scant attention to gender, as is indicated by the usage of terms like 'mankind' and 'man' in the preceding paragraph. This was a typical feature of the vocabulary of the Enlightenment. However, it can be argued that feminism was also an inevitable product of Enlightenment and modernism. Enlightenment concern over 'the rights of man' pointed inexorably to the question 'and what about women?' Enlightenment thinkers Mill and Wollstonecraft wrote about the rights of women. As liberalism emerged in the nineteenth century as the most popular version of modernist political thought, it was almost impossible for those committed to freedom and individuality not to turn to the plight of women, whose social status was seen by the liberal feminists of the mid-nineteenth century as being analogous to that of the slaves the liberals were so keen to free. Thus, as political theorist Diana Coole argues (1998), the 'liberation of women' can be seen as an ideal inherent within liberalism and so a product of the Enlightenment project and modernist emancipatory ideas. This of course fits with the tendency in modernist thinking to see a positive movement in social evolution ('progress') towards a better society founded upon reason. In the feminist ideal this would be a society where women and men would be equal partners, to the benefit of both sexes.

Wollstonecraft's work (1975 [1792]) is particularly interesting, since she argued that being deprived of rights and, consequently, dependent on men led to a kind of deformation in the human potential of women, especially those from the privileged classes. They were forced to adopt a personality of being docile, innocent, sexually dormant, obedient and soft, immersed in trivial and frivolous activities designed to make them attractive to men. Finding a husband was the be-all and end-all for such women, reflecting the quotation from Byron: '...'tis women's whole existence'. This is a powerful early example of a sociological account of the construction of gender identity. Men, too, lose out in this process, as these limited, charming, childlike women cannot be equal intellectual companions in their lives. A gripping dramatization of these gendered processes is played out in George Eliot's great novel *Middlemarch*. The heroic and attractive Dr Lydgate, whom the reader immediately identifies as a fitting mate for the highly intelligent Dorothea Brooke, is in fact enraptured by the pretty but shallow Rosamond Vincy. Eliot painfully portrays his growing disillusionment and bitter realization that Rosamond's superficiality prevents her from reciprocating his passionate emotional engagement and that she cares for little beyond clothing, appearance and consumption. Dorothea, the enlightened woman (reflecting some elements of George Eliot herself), is the one who cares about poverty, progress and human well-being; but she is herself trapped in a sterile marriage with the dusty academic Edward Casaubon. While she yearns to engage with his intellectual work, he will only treat her as a kind of filing clerk.

Modernism and the second wave

The modes of thinking characteristic of modernism were dominant when second-wave feminism developed in the 1970s and early '80s. Thus, feminists took on the idea of societies as orderly systems, whose structures could be studied and analysed by a mixture of empirical study and conceptual logic. Feminist academic work involved building models of sex oppression and inequality and the accumulation of research studies showing how life experience was differentiated by gender and how these differences were the basis of gender inequality and gender disadvantage.

As I have stated, in Britain much of this second-wave research and theory was informed by Marxist ideas. However, there are other approaches associated with the modernist stance in gender analysis. It was common during the 1980s and '90s to group these approaches into three broad perspectives: Marxist/materialist feminism; radical feminism; and liberal or equal rights feminism. Subsequently, commentators pointed out that these categories were rather crude and that it is often not possible to fit any writer or any text neatly into one of these three boxes (see Barrett and Phillips 1992; Bryson 1999; Tong 1989). This is quite correct: many scholars drew ideas from all three approaches. For example, as we shall see, the work of Sylvia Walby synthesizes many ideas characteristically associated with each perspective. And how would one ever pigeonhole the ground-breaking and influential studies of Ann Oakley? Nonetheless, if we see this threefold classification as an example of Weberian 'ideal types', models by which to benchmark actual phenomena, then I think the typology is worth preserving, as each identified approach does display a distinct 'take' on gender.

As we saw above, Marxist feminists saw gender as a relationship of oppression, but one which depended on what Marxists saw as the primary basis of social inequality, the economic relations of class. By contrast, the radical perspective, which Bryson (1999) usefully labels 'woman-centred', saw gender as the primal source of social inequality, going right back to the simplest tribal societies, from which all other forms of social inequality derived. The sexual division of labour predated any form of class division. Nor did they see production alone as the main site of gender difference: reproductive relations, the family and sexuality were the starting point for male domination over women. While this has some resemblance to Engels's arguments, radical feminists did not see paid employment as a simple route away from gender oppression, because the family was not conceived in the materialist framework of labour and labour power alone. Violent, physical and emotional aspects of gender relations were highlighted as well, for example in Shulamith Firestone's challenging and anxiety-provoking statement 'love . . . is the pivot of women's oppression today' (Firestone 1971: 142). Firestone argued that until the nuclear family was abolished, or at the least drastically reconfigured, women would remain in thrall to men. Women's role as child-bearers and rearers forced them into dependency on men, especially during the gestation period. It is perhaps not surprising that radical feminists were often caricatured as 'man-haters'.

The radical approach to gender was most influential in the United States, where, because of the strength of commitment to capitalism as the fulfilment of the 'American Dream', Marxist thinking was less respectable within academia. It also found favour in the social democracies of Scandinavia, where class inequalities were considered to be less severe, but where gender segregation was still marked. Among its best-known practitioners, who tended to combine research and public activism, were Andrea Dworkin, Catharine MacKinnon, Dale Spender and Germaine Greer.

These writers and those influenced by them pushed into new areas which had been less important to the materialists, such as rape, domestic violence and pornography. Activism around these issues was a major part of second-wave achievement, with the setting up of organizations such as Women's Aid and Rape Crisis Centres. These became a crucial part of the 'gender agenda' hitherto hardly acknowledged. Another major issue highlighted by Spender was the gendering of language: 'made by men', it did not contain words for women to express their emotions or speak of sex-specific experience. Vernacular words for sexual intercourse, for example, describe the act from the point of view of the penetrative male: banging, shafting, screwing, poking, fucking. Within the tyranny of this phallocentric language, women can only read the universe through the male gaze. Mary Daly (1978) attempted to rectify this by developing a new 'gynocentric' language, drawing on the long tradition of women's spirituality and mysticism. In a strategy later utilized within Queer Theory, pejorative words used about women – witch, bitch, hag, shrew – were reappropriated to express female values, strengths and power.

Beyond the activist contribution, however, perhaps the most abiding influence of the radical or woman-centred approach was its development of the concept of patriarchy, exemplified in Kate Millett's ground-breaking *Sexual Politics* (1971). Patriarchy was described by Millett as a system of male domination over women that was embedded in all the institutions of modern society. Through the structures of patriarchy, men held power over women and devalued their social activities and contributions. Not only were social institutions such as families, schools, churches and work organizations seen as patriarchal, but, as Spender and Daly were to emphasize, the very structures of language, ideas and thought were also shaped by men: they were 'phallocentric'. This is what became known as the 'malestream', which was to be challenged persistently by feminist academics. Heterosexual normativity was also seen as a major mainstay of male power, suppressing a range of other possibilities for attachment and partnership (homosexuality, bisexuality, passionate friendships, celibacy) which were seen as potentially undermining patriarchal control.

Thus the thrust of the radical approach was to extend the analysis of gender beyond the realm of labour. However, it shared with Marxism some key distinguishing marks of modernist thinking: the portrayal of societies as structured, displaying patterned regularities of interaction; the assertion of gender as a central organizing principle of social life; a stress on the collective nature of human existence and of collectivities as the potential basis for political mobilization (be it class revolution or militant sisterhood); a belief that rational analysis could uncover the causes of oppression and thus be the basis of social reform; and an optimistic view of the future potential for equality and the 'just society'.

The two latter traits were shared with liberal feminism, or 'Equal Rights' feminism as Olive Banks (1981) called it in an influential text. However, this approach, with its roots way back in the nineteenth-century liberalism discussed earlier in the chapter, differed from the other two perspectives in the way it conceptualized gender. Gender was not in this analysis a feature of social structure or a system of oppressive relationships. For the liberal tendency, gender was a form of discrimination relating to ascribed biogenetic differences of the sexes.

Indeed, 'the sexes' or 'the woman question', rather than 'gender', had been the preferred terminology of Victorian women's rights activists. This discrimination was fostered by the behaviour of individuals, rather than being institutionally embedded. It arose from ignorance and prejudice (along with economic self-interest) and could be combated through education, political campaigning and legal reform. Valerie Bryson (1999) refers to it as 'common-sense' feminism, as it was much easier for non-academics to accept. Indeed, it has been labelled 'the acceptable face of feminism'. Indicatively, first-year undergraduates have little difficulty in identifying with its tenets, while the structural approaches of Marxist and radical feminism are often perceived as 'over-stated', 'taking it a bit too far'. While critics of the position see its faith in the power of education and the law as naive and its analysis of gender as limited, we should not underestimate the power and scope of liberalism. Liberal activists have headed the fight for women's rights and made great headway in the political channels in individual western countries and, subsequently, internationally through institutions such as the United Nations, the Beijing Convention and the Commission for Human Rights.

Equally, within social science theory the influence of modernist thinking remains powerful, despite the challenges of postmodernism which will be reviewed in the next chapter. The view of gender as a regular set of relations between men and women embedded into social structures and institutions informs social science research across a range of disciplines. Modernist feminist thinking was responsible for developing the concept of gender, bringing issues of gender disadvantage and inequity into the public arena and making it a central concern of the academic agenda. Gender and related concepts, such as patriarchy, gender segregation, domestic labour, domestic violence and heterosexual normativity, are now a respected part of the social science conceptual toolkit. To illustrate this, I will conclude this chapter with discussion of the work of two highly influential contributors to gender analysis – Sylvia Walby and Ray Connell – whose work exemplifies the strengths and interests of the modernist approach and is highly influential on the thinking of others.

Sylvia Walby and the theory of patriarchy

Walby's work on gender has developed through a series of well-regarded books, *Patriarchy at Work* (1986), *Theorizing Patriarchy* (1990) and *Gender Transformations* (1997), which have made her one of the best-known British feminist scholars. Bringing together elements of Marxist, radical and liberal feminism, she developed an account of patriarchy as a set of interlocking structures that perpetuate male dominance. These consist of paid work, the domestic division of labour, sexuality, the state and other institutions of civil society, especially culture and male violence. They combine to form a system of patriarchal relations, which coexist and interact within a system of capitalist relations. Walby was thus a proponent of the 'dual systems' theory; that is, she did not visualize the social order as a single interlocking system in which all the parts fitted together neatly. Rather, she argued that these two systems, although sometimes working together in harmony (for example, keeping women in low-paid jobs, as cheap labour serves to reinforce male superiority alongside capitalist profits), could also be in tension. For example, capitalism's tendency to suck women into the labour force, especially at times of labour shortage such as during the two world wars, was at odds with men's desire to keep women under their control by confining them to housework. By viewing these two 'systems' as connecting but not coterminous, Walby was able to allow both class and gender relations a degree of freedom to change independently of each other.

One criticism that has been persistently levelled at the concept of patriarchy is that it implies that men are always and everywhere dominant, allowing no room for alternative power relations between the sexes. Seeking to counter this, Walby developed an interesting account of a change in the nature of gendered power relations between the nineteenth and late twentieth century, speaking of a switch from 'private' to 'public' patriarchy. Private patriarchy involved the control of individual women by their menfolk within the family; their powerlessness in the private sphere was reinforced by the limited access permitted them to the public domains of employment, political activity and government. The twentieth century witnessed a gradual erosion of male domination in the family, as ideals of equality have been backed by legal reforms granting women entitlement to fair shares of family resources and strong parental rights by virtue of their maternal role. However, this has not brought true gender equality, as relations between men and women in the public sphere remain skewed. Men retain positions of power in authority within the labour market, in political and other institutions and in the majority of cultural and social institutions such as the arts and media, religious bodies and the military. Within these public arenas, women remain confined to subordinate and secondary roles, in a way which serves to proclaim the social superiority of men.

In *Gender Transformations*, Walby takes this analysis one stage further by abandoning the use of patriarchy and replacing it with the more open-ended concept of gender regime. She uses this term to illuminate recent shifts in gender relations in the post-war period. The gender regime of the early twentieth century was one in which women were socialized and trained to fulfil a domestic role. Their lives were focused around their potential as wives and mothers, so that employment was seen merely as a prelude to marriage (and indeed, in the 1930s many organizations operated a 'marriage bar', requiring women to leave when they got wed or when they had children). However, by the end of the twentieth century, the expectation that both partners in a couple should work, along with the opening up of higher education and a range of professional opportunities to women, had freed women from this domestic fate, allowing them to compete with men in the public sphere, if not on quite equal terms. In her current work, Walby is seeking to link this account of a changing gender regime to alterations in the nature of capitalism, as it moves to a phase of heightened global linkage and competition, accompanied in western societies by a switch away from manufacture and industrial production to service-based and knowledge-based forms of profit accumulation.

Walby's work can be criticized for being overly monolithic and not taking sufficient account of differences in the fortunes of different groups of women, but nevertheless the 'dual systems' approach may have paved the way for further exploration of the 'intersectionality' of the various forms of social division with gender (class, ethnicity, age and sexual orientation among others), while her account of 'gender transformations' refutes the claims of critics that the analysis of patriarchy is inherently ahistoric and insensitive to change.

Robert Connell: 'hegemonic masculinity' and 'emphasized femininity'

The Australian sociologist Robert Connell is perhaps the best-known contemporary theorist of masculinity. His ideas evolved as part of a movement to broaden out the work of feminist scholars on gender by turning the attention to issues surrounding men and masculinity. What was at the time called 'the new men's studies' developed in the 1980s as concerned men pointed out that, in the words of Terrell Carver (1996), 'gender is not a synonym for women'. While Connell has over the years drawn on a broad range of influences, including some of the ideas of postmodernism and post-structuralism, his core strategy, set out in *Gender and Power* (1987), was classically modernist. He pointed to three sets of structures which produced inequalities of gender: the division of labour, power and cathexis. By the latter he meant the structure of feelings and emotions which is prevalent in society, especially in relation to sexual relationships. Historically, men had gained the upper hand in these three areas of social life: they held the top jobs and predominated in the best-paid and most highly respected occupations; they had a virtual monopoly of decision-making positions, and 'men in suits' ('male, pale and stale') occupied a majority of top political posts, as well as other positions of authority and leadership; they had set the rules of sexual engagement in a way that made women emotionally dependent upon them.

Like Walby, Connell offered a strongly structural account of gender. He suggested that these three interlinked structures came together to produce particular 'gender orders' or 'gender regimes'. However, he emphasized very strongly that these should not be seen as any kind of fixed and inexorable system. In this sense, the discussion of the structures of a gender order or regime is different from the Marxian analysis of the capitalist system, in which the economic base (made up of relations of production and forces of production) determines all the rest of society (the 'superstructure'). As Connell states, in none of these three sets of structures 'is there an ultimate determinant, a "generative nucleus" from which the rest of the pattern of gender relations springs' (1987: 116).

This is important, because, as we shall see, one of the major criticisms aimed by postmodernists at modernist thinking was its deterministic nature. Postmodernists reject all approaches which suggest that society is built upon a specified foundation, from which all other facets of social life can be deduced; and they particularly rebut the metaphor of societies as 'system', since this implies the idea of closure. In a system, the parts work together to produce a functioning whole and new elements cannot easily be introduced into it without disrupting the functioning. Thus the notion of a 'social system' is difficult to combine with an idea of social relations as fluid and changing. What both Walby and Connell have tried to do is produce a version of structure which is flexible and allows for change.

Concerned not to develop a monolithic account of gender interactions, Connell is renowned for having developed the idea of a number of different forms of masculinity and femininity, different ways of being a man or a woman, and, in addition, that these plural gender identities were framed in relation to what he termed *hegemonic masculinity*. By this he meant the most widely accepted form of being a man in any given society. In contemporary context, this is the form of masculinity we refer to as 'macho': tough, competitive, self-reliant, controlling, aggressive and fiercely heterosexual. Connell states that 'hegemonic masculinity is always constructed in relation to various subordinated masculinities as well as in relation to women' (1987: 183). Subordinated forms of masculinity could include homosexuality, ethnically differentiated masculinities and the more empathetic and softer forms of heterosexual masculinity such as the 'New Man' (see the vignette that follows this chapter). While Connell believes that there is no single form of femininity which is dominant, he speaks of 'emphasized femininity', which is the counterpoint of hegemonic masculinity, defined by its oppositeness to the masculine: emphasized femininity is soft, submissive, sexually coy, alluring or flirtatious, concerned with domesticity and preoccupied with bodily appearance (similar to the deformed female personality described by Wollstonecraft). As discussed earlier, this is the form of gender relations which poses the sexes as 'opposite'. To be a man is to be 'not-like-a-woman', to be a woman is to be 'not-like-a-man'.

The strength of Connell's work, it seems to me, is that, like Walby's work, it offers a strong set of propositions, or models of gender relations, against which to test and match our own understandings of the world, with which we can agree or disagree. Both authors offer a view of gender relations as historically specific and changing. Both avoid a deterministic account of gender, while suggesting what are the most important sites of gendered inequalities. Both provide an explanatory framework for male dominance, but one that does not preclude the recognition of shifts in the balance of power. Connell's view of plural masculinities informs the vignette that follows, discussing contemporary ways of being a man. After that, in chapter 3, I shall turn to the new approaches to the study of gender which gained prominence in the 1990s and challenged the legitimacy of thought based on the traditions of the Enlightenment: post-structuralism and postmodernism.

'WHAT'S IT ALL ABOUT?' BEING A MAN IN THE TWENTY-FIRST CENTURY

Heterosexual masculinity is predominantly defined through the exclusion and oppression of those actors by whom it feels threatened (mainly women and homosexuals). It strengthens and buttresses its internally cracked position through jeering at what it most fears and takes refuge in the apparent solidarity and support of other heterosexual men. (Jackson 1998: 80)

Jackson's account of masculinity is compelling. We have already discussed the pressures that push men and women into channelling their behaviour into the limits set out by whatever are the acceptable norms of masculinity and femininity, and noted that these pressures are at the most intense in adolescence, the time of burgeoning, if tentative, sexuality. But, as I argued, these pressures fall more heavily on young males, at least in our western societies. While peer opinion may favour what Connell calls 'emphasized femininity' it has not been too difficult for some young women to resist and adopt a much more masculine persona: butch, tomboy, biker girl. While these modes of being a girl may not find favour with potential boyfriends, they are not socially stigmatized and may even carry a certain cachet: 'hard girls' may be admired in school or on the street. But for a boy to be 'soft', a 'sissie', brings general social disapprobation and can make relationships difficult with family (especially fathers) and friends.

Vic Seidler (1985; 1997), taking a psychoanalytic perspective, points out how young boys are forced to separate themselves at an early age from their primary attachment and early identification with their mothers (in a way which, of course, is inapplicable to girls). To do this they must distance themselves from all kinds of 'girl things' and girl feelings. This involves a type of psychological violence towards their own selves, which might mark them for life, and indeed Seidler sees masculine heterosexual identity as inherently fragile. To maintain it, men have over the ages involved themselves in characteristic activities that mark them out from women: big game hunting, fighting, warfare, sexual predation, rape, physical sports and games, journeys of exploration, handling large animals, feats of endurance. These forms of masculine behaviour, well documented in a majority of societies and historical periods, have become seen as increasingly problematic and even counter-productive in an age where the need for physical strength to earn a living is dwindling and where technology reduces society's dependence on muscle. Is masculinity becoming redundant, to borrow Linda McDowell's (2003) phrase? Are there more constructive ways in which men can establish their gender identities?

Early adherents of the Men's Studies movement, such as Kimmel (1987), Brod (1987) and Connell (1987), pioneered research into changing forms of masculinity, especially since the advent of industrialism. In Britain the Victorian upper-class and middle-class model of 'manliness' was fostered by the new 'public schools', the armed forces and the institutions of imperialism:

> If you can keep your head when all about you
> Are losing theirs . . .
> . . . you'll be a man, my son!

Rudyard Kipling's well-known poem 'If' sets out a model for late Victorian manhood. A man must be strong, self-reliant, loyal, adventurous but not foolhardy, in control of himself and his emotions, a potential leader of other men. This was the masculine ethos which public schools such as Thomas Arnold's Rugby sought to instil in their pupils, through a regime of classical education, discipline, sport and religion, the ideal of 'muscular Christianity'. The boys were training to be leaders of men: politicians, soldiers and sailors, administrators of the empire. Service to the nation was a long-term goal. It was jested that the Battle of Waterloo was won on the playing fields of Eton.

Kipling himself attended a public school for the sons of military officers and wrote about it in his collection of short stories, *Stalky and Co.* Interestingly, his trio of heroes, Stalky, M'Turk and Beetle (the bespectacled Beetle was based on the young Kipling), are hardly the models of virtue implied by the model of muscular Christianity or by the noble sentiments of 'If'. These adolescents swear, break bounds, drink, crawl off into the bushes for a furtive smoke, play awful tricks on their enemies (sticking a dead cat in the rafters of a rival dormitory) and flirt with the local shopkeeper's daughter. Not so unlike modern adolescents. Nonetheless, the underlying and final impression is that Stalky and co. will go out to keep the empire safe for Britain. In a telling scene in one of the stories, 'The Flag of their Country', an evangelist for the imperial ideal comes to the college to give a lecture. His openly patriotic rhetoric is listened to with growing disgust by the silent ranks of boys whose own fathers are mostly in active service. At the end of his peroration he shakes out a Union flag, expecting a wave of rapturous applause:

> They looked in silence. They had certainly seen the thing before – down at the coastguard station, or through a telescope, half-mast high when a brig went ashore on Braunton Sands; above the roof of the Golf Club and in Keyte's window, where a certain kind of striped sweetmeat bore it in paper on each box. But the college never displayed it; it was no part of the scheme of their lives; the Head had never alluded to it; their fathers had not declared it unto them. It was a matter shut up, sacred and

apart. What in the name of everything caddish, was he driving at, who waved that horror before their eyes?

Kipling speaks of the deep 'reserve' of boys, their reluctance to expose the 'secret places of their souls', any private dreams of glory to even their closest friends. Being a man is about carrying out the duties of toughness, sacrifice and service, not voicing them or sentimentalizing them. To be a man is to act.

The ideals of masculinity are, however, very specific to context. Venezuelan explorer Charles Brewer-Carias spent some time in the Amazonian rainforest with the Acuana tribe. When he arrived, the men asked him to show them how to make a can of baked beans or sardines. When he explained he could not do it, they were astonished and contemptuous. 'You do not know how to make your own food?' Nor did he know how to weave a hammock or build a hut, what plants were edible, which were useful for medicine, and so forth. The Acuana told him, 'You are like a child among us.' When he had spent some time among them and had begun to share in their bushcraft, they commented that he was becoming a man at last. For the rainforest people, masculinity implied knowledge and control of their environment, independence, the ability to survive.[1]

So what does it mean to be a man in Britain in the early twenty-first century? There has been talk of a 'crisis of masculinity' (Brittan 1989; Kimmel 1987); women's demands for freedom and equality have left men confused about their role. The breadwinner/dependent housewife model of the family is in decline. How can a man prove his masculinity (and superiority) in such circumstances?

One answer provided by those working in the Men's Studies movement is that new models of masculinity have emerged in response to economic and cultural

---

[1]   This example was drawn from Ray Mears's *Bushcraft*, shown on BBC 2, 23 September 2004.

changes, including the rise of feminism. Perhaps the most notable of these was the 'New Man' (Chapman and Rutherford 1988). The New Man was a softer, caring creature. He was photographed holding a baby, or posing in finely tailored fashion garments. The latter point emphasized the role of consumer industries and advertising in the genesis of the idea of the New Man. He was deeply body-conscious: fashionable clothing and expensive toiletries were replacing home-knitted sweaters (made by adoring mothers) and a manly indifference to sweaty socks and smelly rugby jerseys. Sociologically, the New Man was committed to shared parenting and understanding the needs of his female partner, whether it was for sensitive sex (lots of foreplay) or help with the washing up. New Men were seen pushing trolleys in the local supermarket and taking their children to play in the park. Harry Christian (1994), criticizing the idea of the New Man, but affirming the rise of 'non-sexist men', argued that such men often had their behaviour and attitudes moulded by strong women who had been involved in their socialization: a bevy of sisters, a breadwinner mother, a partner influenced by feminism.

However, the idea of the feminized man became problematized as both men and women seemed to reject this model. Non-sexist men complained that women did not appreciate them and continued to fall for 'Traditional Men', despite their violent and sexist ways. The vastly popular heroine Bridget Jones fell initially for the dastardly Hugh Grant character (her boss) before realizing the worth of Colin Firth (Mark Darcy/Mr Darcy). But Jane Austen's original Mr Darcy was hardly a New Man, given his arrogance, aloofness and misogyny. Consequently, the media identified more firmly masculine models as prevalent; the 'New Lad' was a drinker of lager, reader of *Viz* and soft porn magazines and relentless pursuer of women: the Lad reborn, but with an ironic postmodern twist. The New Dad was a hybrid of the New Lad and the New Man, caring but tough, exemplified by Robert Carlyle's character in *The Full Monty*, with his passionate devotion to his son and attempt to restore the respect of his estranged wife. But it is significant that Carlyle had risen to fame in *Trainspotters* and *Cracker*, playing violent and delinquent men.

The media preoccupation with the New Man, New Lad and New Dad can be taken to symbolize the anxieties and confusions about masculinity in the late twentieth and early twenty-first centuries. Where previously, masculinity was taken for granted (however much inner agony men may have suffered), the norms of male behaviour were now unclear. Perhaps nothing illustrates this more than the changing public portrayal of men in the armed forces. In the past, soldiers, sailors and pilots were symbols of male strength and endurance, and the psychological traumas experienced by fighters in the first and second world wars were concealed behind the walls of family privacy and in asylums and hospitals. In contrast, men in the first and second Gulf wars were shown crying, detailing the horrors of war and receiving trauma counselling. In his novel, *Birdsong*, Sebastian Faulks captured the public imagination by describing the First World War within this new frame.

What the study of masculinity and the moral panic about the 'crisis of masculinity' and 'failing boys' has established is that male gender identity is as fluid and variable as female gender identity. We can reword Denise Riley's (1988) question to women, 'Am I that Name?' for men. Does this word 'Man' make any sense to me? What kind of man am I?

There are, of course, as many ways to be a man as to be a woman, but we can highlight some themes through contemporary examples. Leroy is typical of the kind of man who is seen to be 'failing', an exemplar of 'masculinity out of control'. A young man from a respectable, devoutly Christian Caribbean family, Leroy nevertheless has become enmeshed in 'ghetto culture', criminality and drug-taking. A promising sporting career offered him money, status and esteem, but it was abruptly curtailed by an injury. Lacking qualifications, Leroy drifted into a series of unskilled, casual jobs, which were all too clearly leading him nowhere. Low self-esteem and a sense of hopelessness led him to take crack cocaine, and the habit, while offering instant solace, sucked him quickly into a self-destructive lifestyle.

Like many young black Caribbean men, Leroy has several children, all by different mothers. Fathering a child is a potent marker of masculine sexuality in the ghetto culture. But while being a 'baby-father' gives status among similar males, it paradoxically only compounds Leroy's sense of failing as a man, as he is unable to be a 'proper father' or breadwinner for his sons and daughters. This sense of failed masculinity is compensated for among this group of young males by a variety of strategies, gang membership and assertive aggression in the street being a common mode. But Leroy is not a violent person; instead he props up his male esteem with more low-key strategies: flirtation and pulling the girls, goal-scoring for park football teams and, above all, being 'cool' on the street, using his skill and charm in blagging money for his next pipe of crack. While he is able, as a strong and good-looking young man, to survive on the street, it is hard to see a positive future for Leroy as he grows older. His lack of qualifications or substantial work experience, combined with a disorderly curriculum vitae and some short spells in prison, make it very difficult for him to build a career. A life of crime, prolonged periods of incarceration or death from overdose, disease or street violence seem likely fates for the Leroys of this world. Disaffected and disengaged young men of his sort can be found in the deprived working-class areas of America, Britain and, increasingly, in other countries such as France and Germany. They represent to society an uneasy sense of young masculinity gone out of control. Indeed, as I write this book, nightly fires and riots in the banlieues around Paris are bearing witness to the frustration of young unemployed men, especially from minority ethnic backgrounds, and to society's inability to find ways to re-engage them.

Very different are the stories of two young men of about the same age as Leroy, and of similar ethnic background. Nathan has taken the conventional road of being a 'breadwinner', with a wife who is currently not working and four young children. Nathan works long hours at a building society to support his family. He is hard-working and a committed churchgoer. Like Leroy, he loves to play football on Saturdays. He is very ambitious and frustrated at the time it is taking him to move up the career ladder, but makes it clear that his first priority is to care for his wife and children, whom he says 'he loves to bits'. Nathan could be seen as something of a 'New Man' since he helps with cooking and cleaning when he gets home and is involved with his children, putting them to bed and reading bedtime stories even when he arrives from work late and exhausted.

Halford is also very ambitious, but has a more flamboyant and freewheeling personality than Nathan. Halford has numerous irons in the fire; he has been successful within a major IT company, having reached a higher position than any colleague of his ethnic background. He is also a musician and DJ, a committed traveller and an enthusiastic student, who has collected a clutch of degrees: 'I always say when you stop learning you may as well be dead.' He spends a lot of time at the gym. Halford represents a successful type of contemporary masculinity, the dynamic young man who works hard and plays hard, but has something of the 'good citizen' about him as well. Yet he himself acknowledged how easily his gregariousness could have tipped him over into being like Leroy, especially when there was a period of family disruption in his late teens: 'People always say why didn't you go off the rails, because I was at college and those are meant to be the wildest times of your life, right?' But Halford believes the discipline he learned in his family as a young boy saw him through the difficult times.

Leroy, Nathan and Halford represent three modes of contemporary masculine being: the disaffected, criminalized urban young man; the conventional family man and main breadwinner; and the highflying singleton. These correspond to the three types of masculinity identified among working-class boys by Mairtin Mac an Ghaill in his study of schooling (1994): the Macho Lads, the Academic Achievers and the New Enterprisers. Nathan and Halford attribute their success to a religious background and strong discipline in the family (though both these factors were present in Leroy's home as well). But although they have been 'winners' in the contemporary game of masculinity, their lives are not free of strain. To support his family, Nathan had to sacrifice his own desire to complete a degree in business studies, which he believes could help him make a desired career shift into marketing. He has to work very long hours, making it difficult for him to see as much of his family as he would like. Even though he has had several promotions, in 2002 he was only earning £14,000 a year on which to bring up his four children, whose success and happiness he believes will depend on how he thrives.

Earning more than £50,000 in 2002, Halford can count himself lucky, but he too struggles with the culture of working long hours which sucks in so many ambitious young men. Having initially dropped out from school, he has since submitted himself to a punishing regime, perpetually upgrading his qualifications so that he can move on up the ladder. Moreover, he feels that he has had to struggle persistently against racism and stereotyping – first at school, now within his organization – which holds him back from realizing his full capacities. Although he presents himself as a carefree bachelor, there is some sense in which he would be happy to find his 'Miss Right' to support him. Marks of esteem, such as being given a company car when he goes on training courses, seem important to him as a way of proving his merit. America, with a promise of a less discriminatory culture, is a lure, but would mean severing relations with his existing family and friends. There is a sense that he has a long journey in front of him.

'A young man ain't got nothin' in the world these days', sang The Who's Roger Daltrey back in the 1970s. The song seemed wrong for its times, as the 1960s and '70s were generally a good time for youth, with prospects opening up for young working-class men – within the music world, in highly-paid sport, opportunities for upward mobility in the expanding professions. However, with the subsequent decline in heavy industry, the words now ring true:

> Long ago in the old days
> When a young man was a strong man
> All the people stood back
> When a young man walked by!

As brain is increasingly more marketable than brawn, men have certainly lost some of their past employment advantage over women. Masculinity for some men has always been fragile, an achievement of effort and struggle; but in a world in which many jobs have been 'feminized' young men face a difficult search for alternative forms of masculine assertion. Increasingly, too, young women are prepared to countenance a life without a permanent male partner. It is not easy being a man in the contemporary world. It is likely, then, that the search for new models of masculinity will continue in the next decades. There may be a need for men to accept a more androgynous world, in which their desire to distinguish themselves from women becomes less dominant.

However, there is a danger that consciousness of gendered power disparities may lead masculinity in itself, rather than specific forms of masculine behaviour, to be viewed negatively. We may have reached an inversion of the pre-feminist epoch in which masculinity was seen as the norm, unquestioned and accepted. Feminist study of gender brought masculinity onto the research agenda; but it is important not to lose sight of Connell's insight: 'I disagree profoundly with the idea that masculinity is an impoverished character structure. It is a richness, a plenitude. The trouble is that the specific richness of hegemonic masculinity is oppressive, being founded on and enforcing the subordination of women' (1983: 22).

The challenge for us all, men and women alike, is to work to find ways in which to allow the richer aspects of masculinity to flourish but to eliminate some of the destructive practices which characterize unfettered masculine behaviour.

3
Gender and Postmodernity

There occurred in the early 1990s a quite dramatic shift in the feminist approach to the analysis of gender. We can refer to this as a 'postmodern turn'. According to Barrett and Phillips (1992), in one of the earliest commentaries on this development, this effectively amounted to a 'paradigm' shift – that is, a complete change in the way theorists began to understand what gender is (ontology) and how gender should be studied (epistemology). What Barrett and Phillips describe as a shift from 1970s' to 1990s' feminism resulted in part from the build-up of critical thinking about some basic feminist premises and concepts (such as the theory of patriarchy) during the 1980s. According to Kuhn (1970), a paradigm shift in scientific thinking occurs when the weight of evidence that there are some central problems with the existing theoretical framework becomes too great to be ignored. That is what the advocates of postmodernism believe has happened to gender analysis. However, as we shall see, there is no unanimity over this. Many believe that the insights of modernity on gender remain vital and that the revelatory and progressive thrust of feminist work is in danger of being lost in the 'postmodern moment'.

Indeed, if the watchword of modernist feminism was 'enlightenment', the core impulse of postmodernism is 'deconstruction'. Increasingly, feminist theorists turned their attention away from issues about gender inequalities in the world around them and began to question and unpick their own assumptions. In the words of Patricia Waugh: 'Feminism of late ... has developed a self-reflexive mode, questioning its own legitimating procedures in a manner which seems to bring it close to a Postmodernism which has absorbed the lessons of post-structuralism' (Waugh 1992: 120).

According to Waugh, this reflexivity has led feminists to discern a contradiction at the heart of their thinking: namely, that the quest for equality, which is the political heart of feminism, is based on the notion of a distinct and separate gendered identity. This in turn is the foundation of a common movement among women, the solidarity of sisterhood built on shared experience. But this idea of women as 'different' from men in some common way is similar, Waugh suggests, to the patriarchal ideology which legitimates different treatment of the sexes through the proposition of 'essential' and 'natural' gender difference. Moreover, it is not at all evident that all women do share a common identity. Throughout the 1980s women from various ethnic minority backgrounds increasingly argued that white feminism did not speak to or for them and that they did not feel included in the notion of 'sisterhood': their experiences, they stated, were too different from those of white middle-class women.

These ideas of 'difference' and 'essentialism' are central issues in the postmodernist case against modernism. Before looking in more detail at the key features of a postmodern approach to gender, however, I want to offer an account of the political context which led to this major shift in thinking.

The politics of postmodernity

In the last chapter I linked the development of gender as an academic topic to the growth of the movement of radical protest in the 1960s. It is perhaps more difficult to make a firm link between postmodern feminism and particular political events, partly because, as we shall see, postmodernism is a very diffuse and diverse body of thought. However, I have no doubt that one crucial contextual influence was the break-up of the Soviet bloc at the end of the 1980s, especially that key symbolic event, the fall of the Berlin Wall in 1989. The pulling down of the wall brought together two previously sundered social formations, one successfully capitalist, one (quasi?) socialist, into the new unified German Republic, breaching the frontline confrontation between these two combative ideological and political systems. This triumph of capitalism posed a major challenge to radical political thinking and appeared fatally to damage the legitimacy of Marxist theorizing. Many western Marxist intellectuals sought a new radical home. Along with this blow to Marxism there was engendered a general scepticism to the kind of 'grand theories' or 'big ideas' which the Marxist theory of socialist revolution perfectly exemplified. This is demonstrated in what is seen as the key initial text of postmodernity, Jean-François Lyotard's *The Postmodern Condition* (1984), in which he explicitly defines postmodernism as 'scepticism towards Grand Narratives'.

The 1980s were also notable for the political and moral ascendancy of the New Right, spearheaded by Ronald Reagan and Margaret Thatcher, and the accompanying deployment on a global basis of neo-liberal economic policies. The idea that there was, in fact, no credible or sustainable alternative to capitalism also bred a climate of disillusion and disenchantment, given that the radicals remained deeply critical of capitalism and acutely aware of its divisive and exploitative nature: the gap between rich and poor people within western societies and the gap between the richest and poorest nations on a world scale continued to grow through the 1980s and 1990s. Ordinary people during this period felt disempowered, as I discovered during the mid-1980s when I was interviewing working people in Newcastle and Sunderland for a project on gender and trade unions. This feeling of rather helpless powerlessness spread, I think, to academics and contributed to the kind of pessimistic, almost nihilistic, accounts of social relations produced by the influential French thinker Michel Foucault and his followers. Foucault elaborated a vision of extraordinarily powerful systems of domination, orchestrated by the state, facilitated by the 'scientific' ideas of various expert groups (such as clinicians, psychiatrists, social reformers), but in which we were all to some extent complicit, in that power, in Foucault's view, was 'capillary'; that is, it flowed through the whole of the social body to the very fingertips and toes which were ordinary people. This pessimism, it seems to me, fuelled the deconstructionist thrust which led postmodernist and post-structuralist academics to interrogate critically their own concepts and ways of thinking. As Kemp and Squires summarize it, there is a move from the old central question of second-wave feminism, 'what is to be done?', to 'the more reflexive "what is the basis of my claim to knowledge?" and "who is the 'I' that makes such a claim?"' (1997: 8).

I identify two other contextual factors which helped promote the postmodern turn, one much remarked on, the other less so. One relates to the external environment, the other to trends within academe. The first was the rise during the 1980s, to be consolidated after the Soviet collapse, of various well-organized bodies promoting 'identity politics' – that is, a type of politics based on the claims of specific subgroups in society, for example, disabled people, gays, bisexuals and lesbians, or radical Islamists. Sociologists conceptualize this in terms of the increasing salience of 'new social movements' as against the old class-based politics of the labour movement. This was accompanied by a diminishing use, both in the sphere of political action and in the academy, of the notion of class. Notably, in sociology, where class had so long been almost the most central concept, its position was gradually superseded by analytic interest in gender, ethnicity and other forms of social difference (see Bradley 1996). In this scenario, class became no more than one of a long list of sources of division and inequality, rather than the basic organizing principle of society Marxists had proclaimed it to be. A particularly important result of these processes of change was a burgeoning body of literature in the 1980s in which feminists of minority ethnic origin, under the banner of 'black feminism', attacked white feminists for their ethnocentricism, racism and colonialist assumptions (for example Amos and Parmar 1984; Carby 1982; Mama 1984). Such writings challenged the notions of sisterhood and unity within feminism, and pointed to the need to consider 'difference' and divisions within the category of 'women'. These writings were a major contribution to the build-up of explanatory anomalies leading to the paradigm shift noted by Barrett and Phillips.

The second factor was that during this period, academic feminists had to a great extent achieved one of their goals: that is, getting the idea of gender accepted as a key part of the curriculum within the social sciences and humanities. It would have been an odd sociology department that did not, in the 1990s, offer a course or package of courses on gender and feminist research. One can state that from the mid-1980s the analysis of gender was increasingly mainstreamed, that is, that it had at last entered into the 'malestream'. The pioneers of Women's Studies no longer bore the sole responsibility for addressing the activist question 'What is to be done?' about gender inequalities and were able to turn to more complex and academic debates. There was, in effect, a separation between the campaigning and the philosophical and reflective aspects of second-wave feminism. This almost inevitably led gender theorists to draw on the ideas of the currently modish intellectual perspectives. Enter postmodernism!

What is postmodernism?

There is no simple answer to this frequently posed question. This is in part because postmodernism is not really a specific theory or set of theories so much as an intellectual *mood* or *climate*, a type of collective state of mind. Many different things contributed to this state of mind. There were influences from literary theory, from art and from architecture. In literature, postmodern writing was said to be the successor to 'high modernism' – that is, the complex and rather esoteric work produced by writers such as T. S. Eliot, Ezra Pound and James Joyce. These texts were possessed of a high seriousness and an attempt to tease out the inner truths of humanity (the analogy to modernist sociology comes in here). They were replaced by more accessible, playful and popular writings, which were often self-referential, with the author playing a part in them or providing a commentary. The novels of Paul Auster or of Alain de Botton would be good examples. Similarly, in architecture, while modernist buildings pay strict attention to function, postmodern artefacts are more playful, designed to appeal broadly to all sorts of people, often parodic

of past building styles. Christopher Jencks's books on postmodernism present images of hotels in Disneyland and Las
Vegas, built in the style of Egyptian pyramids or Roman
temples (1986; 1991). The theme of self-reflexivity, which we
have already associated with feminism's postmodern turn, is
a common one here; postmodernism's mood is a knowing,
slightly ironic self-awareness.

In the academic turn to postmodernism, as already mentioned, the rejection of grand theories, or 'metanarratives',
was a starting principle. In his key text, Lyotard argued for
the abandonment of 'totalizing' theories, those that attempted
to build models of societies as integrated, functioning systems,
and their replacement with a myriad of partial and locally
based 'small' narratives. The most social science could aspire
to was the description of particular processes of social interaction within a specific context. Here the term 'postmodern'
links to the idea of 'post-structuralism', that is, an approach
which denies the validity of the concept of structure as a valid
metaphor for societies and social life. The term originated
within linguistic theory, as a critique of prevailing theories
which claimed that languages were based upon some kind of
fundamental structural principles which governed usage and
meaning. The post-structuralist view is that languages and
societies are random, fluid, even chaotic, rather than governed
by discernible organizing principles.

Lyotard set out some basic theoretical principles which
have been upheld by adherents of postmodernism, but the
ideas of a number of other theorists, who would not necessarily describe themselves as postmodernists or even post-
structuralists, have contributed to the popularity of the
perspective. In particular, major influences on the development of postmodern and post-structural feminism have been
Jacques Derrida, Michel Foucault and Jacques Lacan, three
French social theorists whose work predates the postmodern
turn. Barrett concisely explains why:

> Feminist theory has been able to take up a number of issues
> outside that classically 'materialist' perspective. . . . Post-
> structuralist theories, notably Derridean deconstructive read-
> ing, Lacanian psychoanalysis and Foucault's emphasis on the
> material body and the discourses of power, have proved very

important in this. Feminists have appropriated these theories rather than others for good reasons: these theorists address the issues of sexuality, subjectivity and textuality that feminists have put at the top of the agenda. . . . It is clear that the classic materialist presuppositions are increasingly harder to apply usefully. (1992: 20)

Derrida is particularly connected with the approach known as deconstruction, which involves unpicking many of the tenets of western thought, in particular the characteristic binary patterns of scientific and rational thinking. Binaries are particularly relevant to the analysis of gender, given that it rests upon the crucial oppositions of man/woman, masculine/feminine, nature/culture, public/private, heterosexual/homosexual, and so on. Post-structural feminists such as Butler, whose work was discussed in chapter 1, argued that modernist feminists had accepted these distinctions as unproblematic, whereas they actually needed to be questioned, challenged and dissolved. Derrida makes play of the 'excluded' middle: all those shades of experience that do not fit the polar opposites. Thus, people are pressured into accepting one or other of binary terms, to be either a man or a woman, to display either masculine or feminine attributes, when in fact individual experience may locate them at one of a myriad of points along a continuum. Much play is made here of the various forms of ambiguous sexuality we discussed in chapter 1.

Moreover, the binaries imply fixity, whereas individuals may change and move over time; for example, they may fluctuate between homosexual and heterosexual behaviours. In addition, any singly posited binary identity, as being, say, a man or a woman, is cross-cut or intersected by other sources of identity. The attack on notions of fixed identities became an important part of the postmodern feminist critique, and is well expressed in a famous quotation from Donna Haraway's influential piece 'A manifesto for cyborgs' ('cyborg' of course being a metaphor for transcendence of binaries as it describes an organism which is part human, part machine): 'A Chicana or a US black woman has not been able to speak as a woman or as a black person or as Chicano. The category "woman" negated all non-white women; "black" negated all non-black people, as well as all black women' (1990: 197).

This idea of the 'non-fixity' of individual identities or subjectivities chimes well with the work of Foucault, who has perhaps been the most important theoretical influence not just on feminism but within large areas of social science over the past decades. One of the most important aspects of Foucault's attack on western rationality and science was his criticism of all approaches which portrayed human subjects in terms of an autonomous, self-directing core self, which stayed stable throughout a lifetime of social vicissitudes. Examples of this concept, which are commonly adhered to, are the notions of 'the rational actor', 'economic man' or the 'master of the soul'. The reader will note that these kinds of 'historic agents' are described in masculine terms, which is one of the reasons feminists were so taken by Foucault's 'decentring' of the subject. Dismissing this notion of the 'essential self', Foucault replaced it by the notion of 'discourses', often quasi-scientific, which actually construct human subjects. In the *History of Sexuality* (1980), for example, Foucault argued that Victorian psychologists and sexologists constructed the dominant discourses of the hysterical woman, the masturbating schoolboy and the perverted homosexual. Such discourses actually change the way people behave as their submersion in the discourses frames their daily ways of thinking and acting. Catherine Belsey summarizes the postmodern feminist position on this:

> Subjectivity is discursively produced and is constrained by the range of subject positions defined by the discourses in which the concrete individual participates. In this sense existing discourses determine not only what can be said and understood, but the nature of subjectivity itself, *what it is possible to be.*
> (1985: 5–6, quoted in Kemp and Squires 1997: 237; my italics)

This does not imply that women didn't lose their tempers and adolescents didn't indulge in solitary sexual practices before the nineteenth century! Foucault's argument is that these practices are transformed by discourses into things seen as central to specific identities. The 'paedophile' may be a father, a good football player, a baker, a Christian; but these identities may be submerged by a discursively constructed identity which becomes, in Howard Becker's term, a 'master [*sic*] identity' (1963).

Foucault's influence was not just theoretical, as the quotation from Barrett shows. His exciting and innovative substantive studies drew attention to issues that were of great concern to feminists and opened up new avenues for exploring gender differences. In particular, his studies of the body, and the way it is controlled and made 'docile' through various disciplinary regimes (ranging from prison sentences to diet and exercise), were seen to be highly relevant to gender analysis and were drawn on by feminists such as Sandra Bartky and Susan Bordo to investigate the processes by which bodies were gendered.

The growing trend to consider gender as something inherently discursive as opposed to material, to approach gender analysis in terms of 'words' rather than things, as Barrett (1992) put it, was reinforced by the psychoanalytic work of Jacques Lacan, which incorporated a Derridean approach to language. Feminist literary theorists had had a longstanding interest in psychoanalysis; indeed, Rosemarie Tong, in her study *Feminist Thought* (1989), presents psychoanalytic feminism as a separate strand of work. Particularly influential were the theories of Juliet Mitchell; in *Feminism and Psychoanalysis* (1985) Mitchell put together her own version of a dual systems approach, using Marxism to explain the material inequalities between women and men, alongside ideas from psychoanalytic theory to explain difference in sexuality and emotions (what Connell referred to as the structures of 'cathexis') which she saw as the core of patriarchy. However, many feminists had difficulties with the work of Freud, as it seemed to present the feminine psyche as inherently inferior to male. Because the man had a penis, women were negatively defined in terms of a lack, suffering in Freud's view from 'penis envy'. The young boy's fear of castration, which prevented him from realizing his basic desire to have sex with his mother, placed the possession of the phallus as the core of adult masculine identity.

Lacan's contribution was to transpose Freud's ideas of the power of the penis to a symbolic level. Language is phallocentric, portraying men and masculinity as the norm and embodying what Lacan called 'the Law of the Father'. Through entering, as she inevitably must as she learns to speak, into phallocentric discourse, the young girl learns to accept herself as inferior and lacking. Once again, we see how discourses construct gendered identities: in this case, the idea of the man as active, the woman as subordinate and passive in her sexuality. This comes very close, of course, to the ideas of the radical feminists such as Daly and Spender whom we discussed in chapter 2. They similarly stress the exclusionary nature of language which has been shaped by men and renders the world of women invisible.

While Lacan builds on Freud's ideas, his shift from physicality to language is less deterministic. While we cannot feasibly dispose of male and female genitalia if humanity is to survive, we might aspire to alter discourse. In the meantime, Lacan offers a depressing, if powerful, view of gender dynamics. Unlike the penis, the phallus does not actually exist, in the sense that it is a symbol of patriarchal authority; for both sexes, it is something missing, aspired to, the source of what Lacan and his followers call 'desire', the perpetual yearning for something which will give us the sense of completeness. But this is experienced differently for men and for women (see Andermahr et al. 2000). Women feel a lack, which can only be assuaged (though this is an illusion) through a heterosexual union. But men experience a loss (as expressed through the Oedipus complex), which they counter by continual attempts to assert and reassert their masculine superiority. This explains the negative and aggressive aspects of what Connell called 'hegemonic masculinity' (see chapter 2). As Cranny-Francis et al. put it, 'voyeurism, sadism and fetishism are the little boy's responses to the fear of castration' (2003: 164); these are stages on the road to a resolution of the Oedipus complex and thus to a happy and secure adult male (and heterosexual) identity. However, as studies of contemporary male sexuality show, many get stuck en route; witness the massive burgeoning of fetishistic and voyeuristic entertainment aimed at men: pornography, lap-dancing clubs, manga comics. For women, Freudians and Lacanians see narcissism, hysteria and masochism as equivalent phases (Cranny-Francis et al. 2003), which women are likely to go through. Such forms of behaviour fit well with the stereotypical 'emphasized feminine' personality: passivity, dependency, coquetry and obsession with appearance. They also illuminate some of the problems around sexuality faced by women, for example the difficulty women find in getting out of relationships with violent and abusive men. There seems little hope in the Lacanian universe of happy equal sexual relations between a woman and a man. Indeed, a problem I find with all versions of psychoanalysis is that they seem to focus only on the dangers, not the pleasures, of sexuality and gender relations. Strangely, postmodern feminists who criticized their modernist predecessors for this very reason, arguing that they tended only to portray women as 'victims' and men as 'oppressors' and ignored the complexities of power, do not seem to find this difficulty with the psychoanalytic approach. Other issues are the apparently negative view of homosexuality (as a distorted form of adult sexuality) and indeed of all types of behaviour seen as feminine within the psychoanalytic paradigm. The ideal person appears to be the independent male heterosexual. However, feminists often take insights from psychoanalysis to combine with more sociological approaches, and it offers a powerful way to analyse what goes wrong between the sexes.

Postmodern and post-structural approaches to gender

It will be noted that the social theorists discussed above are all men and, apart from Lacan, none was explicitly concerned with inequalities between the sexes or the analysis of gender. As with the modernist feminist usage of Marxism, postmodern feminists drew on some of the ideas discussed above and appropriated them for their own use.

What, then, was the distinctive postmodern and post-structural approach to gender? First of all, postmodern feminists saw gender as socially constructed. Thus, gender was not a fixed or stable category. This principle was explored in a rich and influential text by Denise Riley, *Am I that Name* (1988). In this book she explored how the meaning of being a woman had altered historically over time. There is no universal version of femaleness and femininity. Moreover, individual consciousness of our gender is highly unstable and not a consistent base of identity. We are not perpetually thinking of ourselves as being women (or men). The sense of being a gendered entity is triggered in certain circumstances, for example when a man pays a compliment on one's appearance, when one is attracted to somebody ('you make me feel like a natural woman'), when one is enjoying a 'girl's night out', or, adversely, when one is pestered by somebody in the street (hissing, catcalling, bottom-pinching, etc.) or made to feel inferior by sexist stereotyping (women can't . . . park cars, make tough decisions; women lose their heads and panic, burst into tears when things get tough . . .).

In *Fractured Identities* (1996), I reworked this as the difference between *passive identity* (a potential which is always there but which like a 'sleeping' VDU screen only springs into life when some button is pressed) and the *active identity* which springs from negative or positive interactions which forefront our gender. Such a consciousness may then lead on to a *politicized identity*, when gender becomes a basis for political attachment, either generally as a feminist or by being involved in any of the array of groups that are active on behalf of women, from Women's Aid to the Women's Institute. Where my thinking is different from Riley's, perhaps, is that while I see gender identities as intermittent, variable and fluctuating, they are, for me, underpinned by a substratum of gender relations, which is always in operation.

It is not entirely clear whether Riley and the post-structuralists see any kind of substratum of this kind because of their unease with the idea of materiality. For many post-structuralists, gender is a discursive phenomenon; thus the objects of study must be the range of competing discourses and counter-discourses (of which feminism is itself one) of femininity and masculinity. The questions here become, 'How do we talk of gender?' and 'How does that in turn affect how we experience ourselves as women and men?'. Thus, gendered subjectivities and identities become central topics.

Some readers may at this point pose the question: 'If identities and subjectivities are fluid creations of changing discourses, how come for many people gender relations have the appearance of fixity and stability?' The answer offered by Judith Butler, the most influential post-structural feminist, is that it is through performativity – that is, the fact that we constantly play out gender, we 'do gender' through the clothes we wear, the words we use, the activities we carry out, the way we relate to our friends and relations. By countless repetitions of these everyday acts, we convince ourselves that our gendered selves are stable.

A characteristic move by postmodernists, which arises from this view of gender as unfixed and variable, is to criticize modernist approaches to gender as being 'essentialist', founded on the notion of a common identity as women. For postmodernists, essentialism became the cardinal sin and a reason for rejecting a lot of previous feminist work. This in turn has led to a stress on difference and specificity, which we may see as a second key feature of the postmodern feminist take on gender. It follows Lyotard's dictum that we need to look at very specific contexts to explore 'local narratives'. Researchers influenced by postmodernism and post-structuralism have thus tended to look at particular groups of women (women from different ethnic minority groups, lesbian women, disabled women, for example) and explore their differentiated experiences of gender relations. An important result of the 'postmodern turn', therefore, has been to expand the knowledge of how gender is experienced and to gain a deeper and more detailed understanding of different shades of relations, not only between men and women, but among women themselves.

While there are many different forms of gendered identities, experiences and meanings that could be explored, including, for example, class differences, the two prevailing aspects which have preoccupied feminists following the postmodern turn have been ethnicity and sexual identity. This is partly because of the key role of self-designated 'Black' feminists in deconstructing white feminist orthodoxy by declaring that their own experiences were simply at odds with those seen as typical in the 1970s feminist accounts. For example, modernist feminists such as Firestone or Barrett (before her conversion to postmodernism) had mounted a strongly critical attack on the nuclear family, which was seen as a major basis for patriarchal oppression of women. However, minority ethnic women in both Britain and America pointed out that the 'nuclear' model (the tight privatized couple with one or two children) was not necessarily their own family experience. Minority families tend to be larger, more integrated with kin, have non-nuclear unit family members cohabiting with them (uncles, sisters, grandparents, cousins). In the case of African-American and British-Caribbean families, the mother rather than the father is often the pivotal authority figure, and one-parent families are very common. Not only did minority women live in different types of family, they also often experienced their families as supportive not oppressive, as they acted as islands of safety in the white racist world surrounding them. The larger, looser family structures were also the basis for very strong women's networks, which helped women to deal with the trials and discriminations they often faced in their lives. It was here that Caribbean, Pakistani and Indian women experienced 'solidarity' and 'sisterhood', not in political linkage with white middle-class women.

This is a good example of the need not to take commonalities of gender for granted and to explore through careful studies the very different ways in which relations between women and men, between women and women and between men and men are managed in different social contexts. Indeed, this sensitivity to difference can be seen as the great contribution of postmodern feminism. However, at the same time, if this exploration of 'difference' is sited too much at the level of individuals and identities, there is a danger of neglecting the broader dimensions of gender and the patterns of gender disadvantage which spread across the different social groupings. For example, *all* women, of every class, ethnicity, age, nationality and religion, are vulnerable to rape and domestic violence. In all countries, ethnic groups and classes, the bulk of domestic work in the home is carried out by women (rarely less than 70 per cent). This is not to decry the importance of understanding 'difference' and in particular the way that certain groups of women are constructed as 'the other' (Muslim women, with their resolute attachment to veils and burkas, for example). It is to suggest that a balance is needed between focus on specificity and identity and a consideration of patterned regularities and common tendencies.

This is one aspect where many feminists exercise some caution over complete espousal of the postmodern stance. Another is in consideration of the political implications of deconstructing a common identity. Nancy Hartsock (1990) makes the point that no sooner had women discovered a common bond of experience and identity as a basis for a struggle to achieve equality with men, than post-structuralists declared such a movement invalid because it was based on false modernist assumptions. Kate Soper, in a spirited critique of postmodernism, argues that feminist theory has 'pulled the rug from under' feminism as politics: 'theoretically the logic of difference tends to subvert the concept of a feminine political community of women' (1990, quoted in Kemp and Squires 1997: 289). Soper suggests that postmodernism leads to political conservatism in that the deconstruction of categories leads inexorably to the splitting of women into ever tinier and more distinct groups, and eventually to a kind of 'hyper-individualism' which is prevalent in neo-liberal thinking: 'everybody's different' is the popular version of this. Thus postmodernism, by its very theoretical logic, must lead away from the radical perspectives of feminism and Marxism towards, at the best, a liberal pluralism, at the worst a nihilistic individualism: 'anything goes'; every woman for herself.

Judith Butler, performance and the deconstruction of gender

However, the feminists of postmodernity would deny that their position is conservative. Judith Butler, for example, declares that deconstruction holds the potential for a new type of radical politics that is based particularly on a gay and lesbian challenge to 'heteronormativity' (the assumption that it is 'natural' to be heterosexual and the definition of those who transgress as 'Other', 'unnatural'):

> If a stable notion of gender no longer proves to be the foundational premise of feminist politics, perhaps a new sort of feminist politics is now desirable to contest the reifications of gender and identity, one that will take the variable construction of identity as both a methodological and normative prerequisite. (1990: 5)

Butler is without doubt the most renowned and influential feminist writing within the post-structural perspective. Her two key texts *Gender Troubles* (1990) and *Bodies that Matter* (1993) have become canonical. As we have seen, Butler took a distinctive approach to gender, arguing that it was a construction based on the repetition of everyday acts and regulatory practices which reaffirm sexual difference and create a sense of coherence. Thus, she argues, gender is:

> [A]n identity tenuously constituted in time, instituted in an exterior space through a stylised repetition of acts. The effect of gender is produced by and, hence, must be understood as the mundane way in which bodily gestures, movements and styles of various kinds constitute the illusion of an abiding gendered self. (1990: 140)

This definition makes clear the everyday nature of the processes of gendering and, importantly, the active way in which gender is constructed: 'Gender is always a doing, though not a doing by a subject who might be said to pre-exist the deed' (ibid.: 25). Butler uses the term 'performativity' to describe this process to emphasize that it is not a single performance but a routinized repetition which creates the illusion of a stable self: 'gender is a performance that produces the illusion of an inner sex or essence or psychic gender core' (1991: 28).

For Butler, the notion of gender is not a given attribute but must include 'the very apparatus of production whereby the sexes themselves are established' (1990: 7). This production of gender is accomplished through culture and discourse, particularly through what Butler calls the 'heterosexual matrix', a set of precepts and practices through which our notions of ourselves, our bodies and our sexuality are made intelligible to us within a predominantly heterosexual world. Thus, as stated in chapter 1, Butler does not accept Oakley's distinction between sex and gender as valid. Sex *is* gender, because these are created concurrently.

It is here that Butler's vision of radical change is developed, because she sees non-heterosexuals – lesbians, bisexuals, transvestites, transsexuals – as occupying a 'third space' outside the binaries, which is the basis for the 'transgression' and potential rupture of oppressive rules of gender. As Monique Wittig (1981: 53) puts it: 'lesbian is the only concept I know of which is beyond the categories of sex (man or woman)'. That is because, in Wittig's view, a lesbian escapes from the condition of being a woman, which is servitude to men. So, for Butler and Wittig, non-heterosexual women and men are placed to challenge the norms of gendering and expose them as constructed rather than natural. Butler presents wearing drag and cross-dressing as subversive acts, a counter-performance that questions the naturalness of the heterosexual matrix.

It is pointed out by critics that simply adopting a non-heterosexual identity is not equivalent to challenging ideas of femininity and masculinity. For example, in some lesbian couples, one woman will play the masculine role, 'butch', and the other the 'feminine'. Transvestite and transsexual men are notorious for adopting conservative feminine styles of dressing and bodily presentation (perms, pearls and high heels). To be transsexual often means rejecting an identity in one half of the binary, as a man, and repositioning oneself firmly as a woman; the physical alteration of genital characteristics is an important part of this process. Cranny-Francis et al., drawing on the work of Sandy Stone (1991), advocate the notion of post-transsexualism, which rejects any kind of sexual binarism, instead calling for adoption of sexual ambiguity.

Butler's work exemplifies the best of the new feminism and illustrates a different way to approach the analysis of gender. She takes a view of gender as socially constructed, culturally and discursively produced. She uses the techniques of Derridean deconstruction to criticize essentialist views of women and emphasizes differences among women; in her case, the notion of difference is explored predominantly through sexuality, as she sees in gay and lesbian activities the potential for radical exposure of the constructed nature of gender. Such views are similar to those of other post-structural and postmodern feminists, such as Spelman, Riley and Wittig. Where Butler goes beyond the others is to provide an answer as to why gender appears so stable, inflexible and constraining. She achieves this through the notion of performativity; this also brings the body as a material entity firmly into the picture without falling into an essentialist view of body as destiny.

Yet I find a limitation in the way Butler's work rests so firmly on sexuality and bodily being as the core of gender, and neglects other aspects of the 'doing' of gender, such as the division of labour at work and in the home. Nor does her approach tackle the issues of male power and domination. It is, after all, only men who can rape, while, on the other hand, the ability to make decisions and to hold positions of authority, so largely monopolized by men, is not inscribed on male and female bodies. Butler's account dwells at the level of individuals, neglecting the ways in which social institutions are gendered.

In conclusion, feminism in the era of postmodernity has raised new issues and set new challenges for the study of gender. The vignette that follows this chapter is a reflection on differentiated identities, one key theme, and other issues will be covered in the next three chapters, which deal with the gendering of social life. However, in reality most feminist researchers use a mix of ideas from modernist and postmodernist frameworks in their study of concrete problems of gender. I believe this is a necessity, not only to gain a full understanding of gender relations, but also if the radical quest for gender justice and equality, which was the original motivation for the academic study of gender, is to be maintained.

As Pat Waugh concludes:

> If feminism can learn from Postmodernism, it has finally to resist its arguments or at least to attempt to combine them with a modified adherence to . . . an anchorage in the discourses of Enlightened modernity. Even if feminists have come to recognise in their own articulations some of the radical perspectivism and thoroughgoing epistemological doubt of the postmodern, feminism cannot sustain itself as an emancipatory movement unless it acknowledges its foundation in the discourses of modernity. (1992: 120)

'SISTERS UNDER THEIR SKINS'? IDENTITIES IN A GLOBAL AGE

Raphael Mokades, who runs a recruitment agency for minority ethnic graduates, wrote in the *Guardian* newspaper in 2005 about his identity. He described himself as neither black nor white but 'a subtle shade of beige'. Mokades, who is Jewish, told how at school and university white people saw him as brown or black, black people as white. This is a common experience for people who could be categorized as 'mixed race' and an excellent example of how difficult people find it to move outside binary frameworks.

Later in life, Mokades noticed a change in responses (an interesting sign of attitudes to ethnicity in a more acknowledged climate of multiculturalism):

> They all thought I was one of them. The black people thought I was black – light-skinned, certainly but black. Muslims assumed I was Muslim. Indians had me down as an Indian. Arabs thought I was an Arab. Greeks – well, check the surname.

Mokades speaks of his inability to identify with any 'minority ethnic community'. And this, he states, is common among his friends, who include: 'A woman who is half-Zimbabwean, half-English; another half-Filipino, half-German Brit; a guy who is half-Dutch, half-Nigerian:

and so on. All of us have complex identities.' Mokades and his friends see themselves in terms of what sociologists have termed 'hyphenated' or 'hybrid' identities. In the great cities of a globalizing world, where intermarriage between those of differing ethnic backgrounds is increasingly common, hybrid identities are multiplying.

However, we should not see this as a new phenomenon. Rudyard Kipling's great historical book, *Puck of Pook's Hill*, written in 1906, points out how Britain was constituted from waves of invaders – Anglo-Saxons, Romans, Vikings, Normans – mingling with the original Celtic tribes: like most others, Britain is a mongrel nation. The persistent movement of people around the world in search of new territories, wealth and fortune, new jobs and freedom from oppression has ensured a constant intermingling of tribal and ethnic groups which makes nonsense of any dogmas of racial purity. However, new patterns of migration and the ease of travel in the modern world have raised such mingling to new levels in the global metropolis. And in discussing hybridity, we have so far touched only on ethnicity.

To elaborate on the complexity and multifaceted nature of contemporary processes of social identification, I need do no more than consider the ins and outs of my own identity. 'Am I that name?', asked Denise Riley. To which my own answer is an emphatic 'yes'. I identify strongly as a woman, having moved, as I described earlier, from a passive to an active and thence politicized identity. Doing a degree and PhD in sociology at a time when feminism was a vibrant movement, I was involved in rallies, demonstrations, meetings, workshops and consciousness-raising groups, and I became committed to the quest for gender justice. But of course I am not just a woman, and at different times in my life that gendered identity has taken different forms. As a young woman who did not have children I espoused an identity as voluntarily childless, partly as a form of defence, a way to counter the sense of exclusion from the 'mothers' club'. In a world which still wants to define women in terms of fertility and maternity, childlessness can be a burden, especially when, as happened to me, it becomes involuntary. Although

unable to have children, I subsequently adopted an identity as surrogate mother to some of my partner's children;
pinned to my study wall is a Mothers' Day card inscribed
'To our Second Mum', which I prize hugely. Like many
other childless women, I also took on for myself a strong
identity as Aunt, having the pleasure of watching my
niece and nephews change and mature, while myself
being free from the terrible responsibility and anxieties
of parenthood. More recently, I had to come to terms
with the identity of 'Older Woman', grappling with the
social invisibility that comes with that role, the loss of
potential maternity, the ageing skin, the stiffening limbs
and the withering of youthful sexual appeal. How difficult not to fall into depression and self-pity as one walks
among the young women with their bared midriffs, their
alluring cleavages, their jaunty mini-skirts and furry ankle
boots, their glossy-coloured long hair and youthful glow!
Luckily it is possible to 'age disgracefully', wearing purple
clothes and red hats; thus, I and many of my contempo-
raries have attempted to reclaim and transform that stigmatized identity, to become feisty old hags or 'grey tigers'.
The postmodern notions of transgression and subversion,
and the homosexual strategy of 'queering', appropriating
and revelling in terms that were intended to wound and
stigmatize, show us that we do not have to conform passively to the labels that society seeks to categorize us
with. Like Mary Daly, we can celebrate the notions of
'hags' and 'witches'; we can demonstrate our freedom
and humanity by confounding stereotypes.

Contemporary fractured identities involve gender
intersecting with class, ethnicity, nationality, religion and
other potential or activated forms of identity which
emerge from our multiple positioning in the nexus of
social relations and dynamics. Some identities are never
activated. As an adult, I have no religious identification.
Sometimes, there can be an active process of disidentification or misidentification. In my case, like many people
who are English, I had little sense of 'Englishness'. My
family name was Martindale, which is also the name of
a location in the Lake District. There was some belief that
the family might have originated from there and, as a

result, as a teenager I liked to see myself as a Celt. This seemed much more romantic than the boring English affiliation. Also I have one Jewish grandparent, and although the lineage was tenuous (Jewish identity is allocated through the maternal side) I, like Sylvia Plath, always saw myself as 'a bit of a Jew'. Because I have dark curly hair and quite a large nose, I have often been identified by others as Jewish. Such misidentifications and disidentifications arise easily in the context of ethnic and national miscegenation and mixing.

Class is an area where misidentifications and disidentifications are common. Though by virtue of living in a class-divided society (as is acknowledged by the majority of British people) we are all placed in a specific location, the complexity and volatility of class relations makes it quite difficult for individuals to discern that location. Class also differs from gender and ethnicity as a form of social positioning in that its physical markers are less clear than those of gender and ethnicity. Clothing, accent and deportment may offer clues, but class is less easily 'read' by others than gender or ethnicity except in more extreme cases where a class cultural style is deliberately flaunted ('chavs', 'toffs' or 'Essex girls'). Beverly Skeggs's well-known study of young working-class girls on care courses in Lancashire (1997) revealed the opposite case. This particular class grouping was keen to distance itself from 'the poor' and to emphasize its respectability, a case, Skeggs suggests, of class disidentification. In my own research, I have, by contrast, interviewed some men and women who took the 'working class and proud of it' stance: a factory worker who refused promotion as she wanted to be 'just one of the girls on the line', a bank employee who described his background as ''the British working man – salt of the earth'. I found disidentification among people in jobs and circumstances that would be described by sociologists as middle class but whose working-class origins made them uneasy with that label.

I have dwelt on these issues at length to show how complex and differentiated processes of social identification have become. It is this that lies behind the postmodern theories of fragmentation and fluidity, as posited, for example, in the work of sociologists such as Beck and Bauman, who argue that old identities of class, ethnicity, and so forth are breaking down in the face of consumerist individualism. It is also the rationale for the postmodern feminist deconstruction of women which was discussed in chapter 3. However, this discussion relates to personal sources of social identification; that is how we see ourselves as *individuals* located in relation to the rest of society. In truth, personal identities have always been multiple, though the complexity and mobility of contemporary living does offer a more dense nexus of possible identifications. However, the formation of collective and politicized identities is different. This depends on lobbying, on political mobilization, on public activities which highlight the issues pertaining to a particular identity. Political identification with such a cause, be it the Labour movement, Islamic or Christian fundamentalism or second-wave feminism, involves individuals putting one element of their multiple positioning to the fore for the purposes of that particular campaign. So, in the case of the women's suffrage movement, middle-class and working-class women came together to demonstrate for voting rights; so too did white students join with African-American people in the US civil rights campaign.

It is important to stress this because of the problems that broke out in the 1980s in the British feminist movement as a result of the accusations of ethnocentrism from feminists who self-identified as black. Although many of the criticisms were valid and the attempt to allow a voice to women from different points in the nexus of multiple positionings and to foreground their different specific issues was admirable, this led to a fragmenting of the movement and its break-down into competing identity groups. This was a political epoch of difference and division. A black activist interviewed by Julia Sudbury described the events from her perspective:

It unravelled around race primarily, it unravelled around difference, it unravelled around the inability of women to negotiate difference among us and there were some white women who felt... that WE had ruined THEIR Women's Liberation Movement. They would still complain that we caused trouble by raising issues of class and race, these unpleasant disruptive things which weren't really feminist. (Sudbury 1998: 204)

Yet there can be unity within division, solidarity across fragments. As researchers have noted (Briskin and McDermott 1993; Phillips 1991; Yuval-Davis 1993), sensitivity to one form of injustice, such as gender, tends to bring sympathy for victims of other forms of disadvantage. This is the basis of 'rainbow alliances' or 'coalitions' which have formed in the Americas and in Europe in various contexts (Young 1990; Yuval-Davis 1993). Young defines a rainbow coalition as follows:

Each of the constituent groups affirms the presence of the others, as well as the specificity of their experience and perspective on social issues.... Ideally a rainbow coalition . . . supports the claims of each of the oppressed groups or political movements constituting it, and arrives at a political program not by voicing some 'principles of unity' that hide difference, but rather by allowing each constituency to analyse economic and social issues from the perspective of its experience. This implies that each group maintains significant autonomy. (1990: 188–9)

This is harder to achieve than to prescribe! Nevertheless, feminist political scientists continue to call for dialogue between the various disadvantaged groups as a way to formulate a common political agenda for social justice. In this kind of scenario, people can negotiate the various political frameworks available to fit with their own sense of multiple positioning, as can be seen in this account from a mixed-heritage woman, Patricia, talking about her union activism:

I belong to the women's self-organized group (SOG), but I do also belong to the Black members' SOG, yeah? So in classic union terms, it could be said that I'm joined to Black, to Black rather than women, yeah. Nevertheless, you know with women's international day and various things like that, I would go to some of those things, but I'm not so actively involved. . . . In some of the arenas I'm in I'm saying not enough attention is being given to disability.

Patricia was one of a number of women interviewed for an ESRC-funded study of black women within trade unions (Bradley et al. 2003). We asked the women whether they identified more as a black person or a woman. The answers were varied, reflecting personal experiences along with the context in which the women were employed and the activities of their union. Broadly, we found that women working in heavily male-dominated jobs tended to stress their identity as women and to report sexism. Where the union had worked hard to incorporate women and women were in the majority as employees, ethnicity came to the fore. This is exemplified in the following comments, from Marsha, a post office engineer, and Linda, a social services worker:

> I think for me it's the gender aspect because, I mean, I'm involved in the race issues as well, but I think there is a difference in the way black women are treated than black men are treated, in terms of the discrimination that people suffer from, and I think we all know that, and we all understand that double discrimination. . . . We have had problems and we still do have some of those problems where our ethnic minorities committee was very much male dominated. . . . If you just deal with the racism, it's not going to stop black women getting harassed because of their gender. Sometimes obviously it's difficult to tell if a white person is harassing a black woman, is it because she is black or is it because she is a woman? I think that if it's a white man harassing a black woman, I would say firstly it's because she's a woman and secondly because of her race. (Marsha)
>
> For me the sort of black issues comes out um, first. Talking to my white colleagues who are women, um, and because they are white women they see the gender issue as the main priority. When I talk to my manager, she's a woman, a white woman, and I'll talk about race issues and then she'll talk about gender issues, and somehow, I don't

think she actually makes the connection between you know, black and woman, and black women. . . . I say I'm a black woman, so can you imagine that it's sort of twofold for me, and then you have got black disabled people, and it's even worse for them. And as for black gay and lesbian people, forget it, because they could be stoned by their own community out there because of their sexuality. It's like I have got to deal with the race bit before the women bit comes into it. . . . You'll get the white team managers, women who are white team managers, how many black women team managers have we got? One I think. So you sort of see where, we were okay at a certain level, and then the white women sort of move on that bit further than us as black people. They are always just ahead of us. (Linda)

One of the case-study unions, UNISON, has made great play of its catering for various minorities through its self-organized groups: there are SOGS for women, black workers, gay and lesbian workers and disabled workers:

We have a black workers' group, we have a women's group here as well, which I am kind of like a member of. And, it's really good, it's a good forum for women too, coz it's different issues. Because there are black issues and there are women's issues as well, and I think the union has all these groups, and I think it's excellent, it, you know, it's support for one another, and it's also good to know that you are not the only one experiencing things that you are experiencing. (Nadia)

The difficulties of pulling the groups and their interests together has not yet been solved by UNISON, but the interviews showed that individual women were able to negotiate their way round the SOGs to get their issues to the fore. This indicates the tensions between identity-based politics and a general politics of justice and equality. However, perhaps the most striking thing is the way the SOG structure fails to confront class and class divisions.

Indeed, I have left writing about my own class identity to the end of this section, because I found it much harder to write about than the other aspects of my own multiple identifications. This is significant. In the interviewing work I have done I have found that people, young and old, find it difficult to talk about their own class and are not always willing to do so. This reflects a strong sense of unease that many British people have about the whole issue of class divisions (or 'distinctions' as we prefer to call them). This is because class identities are often stigmatized, causing a sense of shame. Class is a hidden secret. We all know it exists, but prefer not to think about it. Thus, many working-class people I have asked about their class position prefer to describe themselves as 'just ordinary people'. As mentioned before, middle-class people, especially those who have been upwardly mobile, are often reluctant to admit to being part of a more privileged group ('I suppose in terms of my job I have to say I'm middle class') or express themselves as having 'been lucky' at being born in a nice neighbourhood and going to a good school. Increasingly, we see our gender and our ethnicity as things to be promoted, celebrated. It is not so with class.

My own immediate family was highly educated but slightly impoverished middle class. My father, who had met my mother when they were both students at Cambridge University, had an interesting but ill-paid job in the voluntary sector. I grew up in a semi in a mixed inner-city area, and the kids I played with in my street were working class. When I won a scholarship to the leading girls' school in the city, I experienced a sense of being different, in that my parents could not afford the riding lessons or skiing holidays that many of my class mates, most of whom lived in the posher parts of town, enjoyed. My parents quarrelled frequently about money, leading me to cry myself silently to sleep. Looking back, though it is not how I would have experienced it then, they were slightly bohemian. Many of their friends were musicians, writers and painters; my mother used to wear vividly coloured dresses and dangly ear-rings; a slightly moth-eaten rabbit-fur coat was succeeded by one in shocking pink mohair which made me cringe when she wore it to school speech day. She also caused me agonies by stripping off completely in the communal changing rooms at the swimming pool, while everybody else, including myself, was performing polite contortions under towels. However, I joined with her in sitting down through the National Anthem in theatres and cinemas as a mark of republicanism. My parents voted Labour and had been members of the Communist Party when they were students: in the mock elections we had at school, the Conservatives had a resounding triumph.

In my teens, family money filtered down to us and we moved to a grander house and started to enjoy a more luxurious lifestyle. However, the childhood sense of not quite fitting in anywhere persisted in me and caused me to maintain a strong left-wing allegiance. All three of my long-term partners came from working-class backgrounds and each had been the first person in their family to go to university (an important source of upward mobility for bright boys from the working classes in the post-war decades).

My own experience of class, then, has been tinged with a degree of hybridity which features in people's class positions as in their ethnicity (Bradley and Hebson 2000). Cross-class marriages, post-war upward mobility, shifts in the occupational structure: all have contributed to the fact that people's class trajectories are more varied than was the case before the First World War.

So, are Judy O'Grady and the Colonel's Lady, to quote Rudyard Kipling again, really 'sisters under their skins'? Yes and no. As we shall see in the next three chapters, there are many things that the majority of, if not all, women have in common, whatever their class, ethnic, national or religious background. These include subjection to various forms of male authority, at home or in the workplace; responsibility for domestic work; pressure to be mothers; the threat of male violence; a constrained access to public spaces. Yet so strong may be the perceived (and actual) differences of class, ethnicity, religion or nationality, that women do not feel connected by these commonalities: these intersecting identities are experienced as more important. Anne Phillips sums up the effects of 'divided loyalties: the lack of fit between the oppressions of gender and those of class or race; the risk that what we want for the one cuts across what we want for the others':

> Class matters, not because it gets in the way of us feeling the same, but because of the choices it suggests between the goals that we pursue. . . . It is hard to avoid the notion of priority, for it is difficult to engage with all issues at once. If you talk about one thing, you drown out another. . . . Implicitly or explicitly you are making your choices, revealing what you find most important. And if this has been pointedly raised by the oppressions of race, it is equally relevant to questions of class. (Phillips 1987: 142–3)

Thus the notion of a shared sisterhood, a common gender identity, can only be a political one, not a structural one. But, as I have argued, gender is a politically framed concept. Difference is not a block to a movement for gender justice or universal women's rights. The Colonel's Lady and Judy O'Grady can hold hands in this struggle as they did in the fight for votes for women.

4
Gendered Worlds: Production

> Theorizing gender exclusively at the level of the subject risks
> letting social relations disappear from the realm of sexuality
> and gender, allowing gender to be seen as located primarily in
> the individual. This is one of the problems with psychoanalytic
> approaches. Gender is not only the psychic ordering of bio-
> logical difference, it is the social ordering of that difference.
> (Marshall 1994: 112)

In chapter 3 I took a similar line to Barbara Marshall, extending her criticism of psychoanalysis to Butler's post-structuralism. It is important, as Marshall argues in her book
Engendering Modernity, that we do not lose the sociological
input into the study of gender, which has tended to be superseded in the postmodern moment by philosophy, psychoanalysis and cultural and literary studies. Thus, the next three
chapters in this book deal with the 'social ordering' of gender
difference referred to by Marshall. As I argued in chapter 1,
this process of 'gendering' occurs at three levels: the macro-
level of the social totality, the meso- or institutional level and
the level of individual interaction (the micro-level). Within
social science, the study of these three levels is characteristically carried out in different ways. We approach the macro-
level through the construction of theoretical models, or map
it using statistical evidence; the meso-level is often tackled
through case studies; while interviews or observations are
used to address micro-sociological issues. In these chapters,

then, I will draw eclectically on these various forms of evidence to explore how gendering occurs.

We have emphasized that gender affects every aspect of our lives. In this short book I can only cover some aspects. I have made a choice to order my discussion round the notion of three key 'spheres' of social life: production, reproduction and consumption. These three terms are particularly associated with the social theory of Karl Marx. They are part of the vocabulary developed by Marx to delineate his view of societies as systemic entities made up of interlocking elements. The notion of production was at the core of Marx's world-view, as demonstrated in the key terms: mode of production, forces (technologies and raw materials) of production and relations (social arrangements) of production. Each type of society (social stage) has its distinctive mode of production by means of which goods and services necessary for the survival of society are developed. But it is also through the mode of production that profit is accumulated by the owning classes, who exploit the labour of workers to do so: this surplus is the basis of further expansion of society. Thus, for Marx, production was at the base of social development (as opposed to the 'noisy' sphere of exchange of money and goods), and all other aspects of society were formed around it. The term thus loosely corresponds to our contemporary notions of work, employment and the labour market.

Reproduction is closely linked to production, though it is a more imprecise term. Marx used it to cover the processes by which the 'conditions of existence' of a mode of production are recreated. This includes the birth and rearing of new labourers (what we call 'human reproduction'), but also all the social activities needed to keep the system going (such as the socialization of children into their future social roles, education and training, the physical and emotional nurturing of labourers). Women were seen as holding the major responsibilities for reproduction which was primarily based in the household.

Finally, consumption is part of the process of exchange, the use of the goods and services produced by the mode of production. This in turn feeds into social reproduction. Marx's followers have developed this idea more fully in line with the idea of the 'consumer society' which was developed in the post-war period. The Marxist take on the consumer society is that it serves as a kind of inducement to buy the consent of labourers to their own exploitation in the relations of production. The purchase of consumer goods is also seen popularly as a compensation for hard or unpleasant work. More recently, though, post-Marxist thinkers have highlighted consumption as a site of creativity and identity, as we shall see in chapter 6.

It is something of a dilemma whether to start with production or reproduction. On the one hand, employment and work relationships have been central to classical social theories, such as those of Marx, Weber, Durkheim and Parsons, and are still the starting point for many influential contemporary theories of social development, such as the notions of post-industrialism, globalization, the 'knowledge economy', neo-liberalism and regulation. Moreover, there is general agreement that the 'world of work' is highly gendered. As we saw in chapter 2, Sylvia Walby argues that the twentieth century has seen a switch from private patriarchy rooted in the family to a system of public patriarchy which is manifested primarily in employment and in the state. On the other hand, women have long been identified with the private sphere and responsibilities for care of the home and of children and, as we also saw in chapter 2, radical feminists took the family and men's control of sexuality to be the heart of patriarchal power; moreover, these early preoccupations have been reconfigured more recently in the postmodern interest in bodies and in the 'heterosexual matrix' discerned by Butler.

I have chosen to start with production, largely because I have made the point that gender must be understood in relation to change, and I see the economy as being the driver of change at the macro-level. This is not, however, to suggest that production is more important than the sphere of reproduction. 'Home is where the heart is', and in terms of individual motivation private events may outweigh the public dimensions. Employment and family relationships are both extremely important locations of the social ordering of gender. Moreover, the spheres of reproduction and production are intimately connected and co-dependent, as this and the next chapter will show. Indeed, in opposition to Walby's theory of the switch to public patriarchy, I shall argue that it is the pattern of gender relations in the family which continues above all to generate gender inequalities in the workplace.

Structures of inequality: the sexual division of labour

All contemporary societies display a clear sexual division of labour, although the precise form may vary between countries. For example, in India women work as labourers on construction sites, which is virtually unheard of in Britain, and there were greater numbers of women engineers in the countries of the Soviet bloc than in West European societies. In *Men's Work, Women's Work* (1989), I explored the history of the sexual division of labour, noting how in all but the simplest sorts of society men and women performed different production activities. The current sexual division of labour, which is remarkably similar in all the advanced industrialized societies, evolved with industrialization and became consolidated in the last half of the nineteenth century, an era when the idea of 'separate spheres' for men and women was particularly powerful. Readers interested in the history of the sexual division of labour are referred to that book.

In the twenty-first century work remains divided into 'men's work', 'women's work' and gender-neutral work (Hakim 2000). Although the latter is on the increase in western societies, patterns of segregation remain strong. This is unsurprising, since segregation does not only take a horizontal form (in which women and men are found in different types of job, occupation and industry) but has a vertical dimension: that is, within any industry, occupation or job, women tend to be in the lower echelons with men clustered nearer the top of the employment pyramid. Most CEOs and directors are men, while most junior office workers are women. Even where men and women appear to be doing the same thing, there are often subtle differentiations in what tasks they carry out, as they occupy what Rosemary Crompton (1997) calls 'gendered niches'. Such gendered niches reflect continued beliefs that women are more suited for some activities, men for others. Not only are men disproportionately found in top posts, but the gendered niches they occupy tend to be paid more highly than the female niche positions. For example, in management women often are employed in human resources, staff development and training, while better-paid financial managers and operations managers are men.

This is a crucial aspect of the gendering of work, as it maintains an enduring gender pay gap between men and women. Although this gap is less than in the past (throughout the nineteenth century women tended to earn between one half and two-thirds of men's wages), it is still considerable. In 2004 the average hourly earnings for full-time women were 18 per cent lower and for part-time women 40 per cent lower than those of full-time men (EOC 2004). There are strong cumulative effects of lower earnings over a lifetime. The current pensions gap between men and women is estimated at 43 per cent. The gender gap is also strong among younger employees, even though women are now better qualified than men in these age groups. Among teenagers in their first jobs, young women earn 16 per cent less. This means that men retain their economic advantage over women in the labour market, with knock-on consequences in the family, as we shall discuss later. If one person must give up work to mind the children, it makes economic sense for it to be the lower-paid partner.

My own profession, university lecturer, provides an excellent example of such processes. On the face of it, lecturing is a gender-neutral occupation. However, characteristically men and women are clustered in different subjects. There are few female lecturers in engineering, mathematics or the 'harder' sciences, such as physics. Within the social sciences, men dominate in economics. Women tend to be found in arts departments and in the 'softer' sciences and social sciences, such as biology and sociology. They predominate in the vocational areas of education, social work and nursing studies. Women are much more likely to be in the insecure fixed-term contract posts and to remain in them longer before getting a permanent post. Surveys within universities have demonstrated that, on average, women take longer to get promoted. In terms of vertical segregation, only 13 per cent of professors are women: and only a handful of women reach the topmost managerial position of Vice-Chancellor, although it was considered a breakthrough when Professor Alison Richard became the first female VC at Cambridge University in 2003. Put these facts together and you arrive at a situation where women earn less than men on average and thus also end up with lower pensions. This pattern is typical of other occupations. An Equal Opportunities Commission (EOC) survey in 2006 concluded that 'women were routinely missing out on senior jobs, starting on lower salaries and taking longer to get promoted' (*Guardian*, 27 January 2006). The same report also highlighted that out of 870 organizations surveyed 16 per cent were in breach of EO legislation, in that pay differences between men and women were only explicable in terms of their gender.

The strength of gender segregation is reflected in the statistics of the British labour market. Women make up 46 per cent of the labour force. However, 44 per cent of women and only 10 of men work part time. We have seen how sharply that affects earnings. Moreover, while women are working in greater numbers in the labour market than at any time since industrialization, in many sectors horizontal occupational segregation remains strong. For example, in 2003, 92 per cent of taxi drivers were men, as were 88 per cent of security guards, 86 per cent of software professionals, 84 per cent of ICT managers, 78 per cent of police constables and sergeants, 75 per cent of marketing and sales managers and 61 per cent of medical practitioners. Meanwhile women comprised 96 per cent of receptionists, 89 per cent of nurses and of hairdressers, 88 per cent of care assistants, 86 per cent of primary and nursery teachers, 83 per cent of general office clerical assistants, 82 per cent of cashiers and checkout operators, 79 per cent of cleaners and domestics and 73 per cent of waiting staff and of sales assistants (ONS 2004). Women are clustered within a smaller number of occupational sectors than men, disproportionately in public-sector jobs and low-level private services (Purcell 2000). Only in a few areas (chiefly the professions, management and the expanding financial services sector) are proportions more equal; and in these areas vertical segregation is high. In manual jobs, occupational segregation has hardly declined.

However, some things are changing. The *Guardian*, in its useful feature *Graphic of the Week*, drew a contrast between the position of women in 1975 and in 2006, which reveals how far things have changed over the past three decades (*Guardian*, 14 January 2006). In 1975 there were 9.1 million women in employment, in 2006 there were 12.5 million. In 1975, 47 per cent of mothers were working, but only 25 per cent of mothers with pre-school children; by 2006 the figures had increased to 66 per cent and 52 per cent, respectively. While in 1975 only 15 per cent of mothers had returned to work eight months after giving birth, in 2006 this had increased to 70 per cent. It is clear from these figures that not only have women increased their workforce participation, but that it has become the norm for mothers to return to work. Although this may be financially driven, since most people believe that two salaries are necessary to achieve a decent or desirable standard of living for a family, there is a sense in which mothers' employment is about more than that – about keeping the seat warm for future career take-off, about staying in touch with the world of employment, not being sucked entirely into domesticity. For, amazingly, according to a survey carried out for British Gas in August 2003, families gain very little in immediate financial terms by mothers working. The 500 mothers surveyed earned an average per month of £864 after tax, but spent an average of £808 (90 per cent) of their wages on childcare and domestic help costs (*Guardian*, 28 August 2003).

The *Guardian* graphic tells us about the changes in the quantity of women's involvement in the world of production, but not about the quality of that involvement. As work remains segregated, women still work in jobs which are rated inferior and less rewarded. As we have seen, the gender pay gap remains, but it has diminished for full-time working women who in 1975 earned 29 per cent less than full-time men; in 2006 the pay gap had lessened to 17.1 per cent. In 1975 only 1.8 per cent of managers were women; in 2006 this had risen to 33.1 per cent. In 1975 there were virtually no female directors (0.6 per cent); by 2006 the figure was 14.4 per cent, which is still not particularly impressive. One might say that women have come a long way in 30 years, but there is still a long way to go.

Discourses of gender: breadwinning, suitable work and heteronormativity

In *Celebrity Big Brother* in 2006 Dennis Rodman, a black American basketball star, berated Faria Alam, a British woman of Asian ancestry, about her behaviour. He told her that women should stay at home, taking care of cooking and cleaning. The role of men was to do 'this and that' and to 'bring home the dollars'. Although Rodman might have been winding Alam up as part of a tactic to establish himself as dominant male in the Big Brother House, his statement was a clear summary of the male breadwinner ideology or discourse, which still holds strong even in the twenty-first century.

Over the past two centuries this discourse has been a major underpinning of the sexual division of labour at home and in employment. It holds that the duty of a mature adult man is to maintain his wife and children financially. Because this role is demanding and exhausting, it requires support from a wife who takes full responsibility for domestic work and childcare. This discourse was developed in the early industrial epoch, when work moved outside the home. It became a rallying call for British trade unions, which fought to acquire a breadwinner or 'family' wage sufficient for a man to cater for his family needs. If a man could not earn a family wage, then his wife (and/or other family members) had also to 'go out to work' to supplement his earnings. Otherwise a wife should stay at home. This supplementary employment should preferably be part time to allow the wife some time to tend the home, and thus it would receive only what Janet Siltanen (1996) has named a 'component' wage. This is a wage which is insufficient to support the total subsistence needs of an individual. In a more derogatory version, this becomes 'pin money', the idea that women only work to attain luxuries for the family and for little personal items (silk stockings, cosmetics and jewellery). These ideas have been used to justify the practice of paying women less than men.

Some argue that the ideology of the male breadwinner has become outmoded as a result of economic restructuring and changing gender norms (Crompton 1999). Social policy experts have traced how in Britain a 'strong male breadwinner' regime is being replaced with a 'modified male breadwinner' regime, where the norm is for the man to work full time and the woman part time (Lewis 1992; Rubery et al. 1996). This has led in Britain to the statistical prevalence of dual-earning families. Things vary around Europe. Yeandle's analysis of data suggests that a dual-earning model is becoming accepted in the Scandinavian countries and France (Yeandle 1999): by contrast, according to sociologist Norman Schneider, 'the classical family picture is still very much alive in Germany. Women are expected to look after the children while men go out and work' (Harding 2006). Rosemary Crompton (1999) believes that the male breadwinner is on the decline in Britain. Yet evidence suggests that, if we dig below the surface, traditional attitudes and behaviour persist.

With colleagues, I carried out a survey of young adult men and women in Bristol, which was funded by the ESRC (Fenton et al. 2002). We asked them if they believed the idea of the male breadwinner still existed; the majority said 'no'. Indeed, many promoted the counter-discourse of personal equality, stating that partners should share tasks and responsibilities. But when we asked about their preferred arrangement for a couple with children, 27 per cent chose the man working and the woman at home, and another 38 per cent felt the wife should work part time. Only 8 per cent believed in both partners working full time. This was confirmed by the actual practice of married correspondents with children: 150 women had stopped work altogether compared to 9 men; 22 women believed they had missed out on promotion compared to 1 man. Of the men, 56 per cent said their working patterns had been unchanged following the arrival of the child, compared to around 9 per cent of the women (Bradley and Dermott 2006). Women continue to sacrifice their careers to childcare. Most married women said they did the bulk of the housework. Despite discourses of equality, the male breadwinner tradition is deeply embedded. There is a vicious circle of conformity: gendered economic inequalities impel couples to choose the higher-earning man to be the main breadwinner, which leads women to stay at home, which helps perpetuate the pay gap. Women are caught by interlocking structures and discourse.

Two other discourses support the sexual division of labour and the gendering of jobs and occupations. These are a discourse of masculinity, femininity and 'fit work', and a discourse of heteronormativity at work. The former evolved after industrialization in parallel with the breadwinner discourse. It stated that certain types of work were suitable for men and others for women. To step across the boundary line of gender segregation would be to risk impairing one's masculinity or femininity. Heavy, physical, outdoor and dirty work was typically assigned to men on the grounds that women were not physically strong or robust enough for it, so that they risked illness, injury or bodily impairment. Other jobs, in a prudish Victorian era, were seen as unsuitable for women because they would bring them into contact with unrespectable and sexual matters (for example, this affected medicine and the law). Though some of these taboos are being weakened, there is still debate as to whether, for example, it is suitable for women to be in the police or armed forces, where they will encounter violent criminals and engage in hand-to-hand combat. Only men are deemed suitable as killers. Gender-traditionalist Inspector Morse was shocked when he found his new pathologist was a woman! Conversely, men are seen as unfitted for repetitious and fiddly or sedentary work, such as unskilled assembly work, on the grounds that they have not the patience or finesse to carry out the tasks. It is assumed (there is no scientific evidence) that men have a lower boredom threshold than women. A more contemporary example is the unease about men working in childcare and childminding, given concerns about abuse and paedophilia.

This last example points to the troubling presence of sexuality and sexual urges in the workplace. Paradoxically, the modern theorizations of bureaucracy and organizations portray the sphere of production as an impersonal, de-sexed space; yet this is far from the case, a fact recognized in the countless soaps which deal with hospitals, hotels and legal practices and all the heady romantic dramas within them. Work is an important site of the discourse of heteronormativity, where heterosexual relations are initiated and celebrated. Surveys indicate that nearly a third of people have met their partners at work, and up to 70 per cent of people have had a relationship with a co-worker. This is not surprising given how much of our daily time is spent at work. In a privatized world, many older people move from work to home with limited engagement in other parts of the public realm. Many companies like to have family members working together and encourage marriage between employees, which is seen as likely to increase loyalty to the company.

This is part of the informal relationships of the workplace, but heteronormativity is also built into the formal structures of employment, and, it can be argued, increasingly so, as a number of studies have shown (Adkins 1995; Halford et al. 1997; Hearn and Parkin 1987). There has been a considerable expansion across the globe of all kinds of sex work: prostitution, telephone sex, lap-dancing clubs, glamour photography and a whole array of pornographic production activities. Glamour and the hint of sexual availability are also important in many other sectors of the economy: the entertainment industry, hospitality and catering, fashion and beauty, leisure and health. In all these areas, young women and men, but particularly the former, are employed for their appearance, required to dress and present themselves in specific ways. Lisa Adkins's study (1995) shows how important appearance is for women in hotel work, where receptionists, bar staff and waitresses are there to provide 'eye candy' for male customers.

Arlie Hochschild's renowned book on airline hostessing, *The Managed Heart* (1983), developed the now popular idea of 'emotional labour', describing forms of work where part of a job is the handling of emotion and feelings, presenting a particular version of the self in order to satisfy the client or customer. At core, emotional labour is about 'keeping the customer happy'. Such labour can be draining, since it involves the acting out of emotions which may be very different from those one is actually feeling. Emotion work has been strongly associated with women because of its link with caring and nurturing, the archetypal qualities of the mother; and increasingly much of it is also highly sexualized. One could see the work of a prostitute as the ultimate in emotional labour, performing the actions of pleasure and satisfaction to please a man, without feeling them oneself.

In their discussion of the gendering of work, Halford et al. (1997) suggest that the underplay of heterosexual relations in organizations helps make work tolerable to employees. They believe that in some sectors of the economy what they call 'constructive heterosexuality' has replaced discourses which feature family symbolism, or the paternalism which was typical of Victorian firms. Flirting and joshing between the sexes are common features of factories and offices and can add an element of pleasure to dull or routinized work. As Halford et al. put it:

> Sexualised discourses play a large role in working interactions, and the organisations themselves are tolerant of such cultures and indeed even acquiesce or support them. This marks a major break from the past. . . . Such cultures are organised around constituting the workplace as arena of constructive heterosexuality in which mixed-sex work teams 'pull together'. (1997: 267)

At the same time, the discourse of heteronormativity helps to maintain boundaries between men and women at work by emphasizing the difference and otherness of each sex. Sexualized jobs are also usually gender-specific, thus reinforcing discourses of gender-suitable work.

This is well illustrated in the account offered by Yuko Ogasawara of Japan's 'Office Ladies', or OLs as they are colloquially called. Indicatively, the very naming of clerical workers in Japan is gender-differentiated: office ladies and salaried men. The OLs are meant to bring feminine charm and decorativeness into the office situation. Their relation with their male superiors is nicely summed up by the fact that on Valentine's Day they are meant to give *giri choco* (obligation chocolates) to their bosses. Ogasawara describes the differences in men and women's roles:

> Structurally, female clerical workers are discriminated against in the bank. Clerical women are called 'girls' while the men are never referred to as 'boys'. They perform many routine jobs such as filing, and typing, and more menial tasks such as wiping desks, cleaning ashtrays and pouring tea for their bosses, male colleagues or visitors. They are frequently spoken of as being 'office wives', who look after the needs of dependent men. Furthermore, while men are evaluated individually for their work performance, most women in the bank are

automatically given grade C on a scale of A to D. This is because the purposes of evaluation are different. For men, evaluations are made primarily to help the management decide whom to promote. Since the company does not intend to promote clerical women, serious evaluations are considered to do more harm than good by disrupting harmonious relations. (2004: 245)

In this account we can see the more traditional form of the discourse, emphasizing family links. The strongly patriarchal values of heterosexuality and marriage have been transferred into the workplace, so that the office ladies are expected to wait on men. Since they are seen as 'wives' rather than workers, the expectation is that their husbands are the bread-winners and there is thus no need for them to seek promotion. The tasks allotted them are seen as suitable for them because of their domestic nature: cleaning and tidying, forms of house-keeping for their male superiors. In this way the division of labour in the workplace is naturalized, based on the 'distinct nature' of men and women as demonstrated in the marriage partnership. In an interesting twist, Ogasawara states that women are satisfied with this obvious discrimination because of the high demands that Japanese companies place on their male workers, in terms of extraordinarily long working hours and commitment to the company. Women are happy to be dependent on male breadwinners because of the extra freedom afforded them. As Kimoko Kimoto, in a study of Japanese retail organizations, also observed: 'Women, in exchange for their boredom-inducing jobs, gain abundant free time. Their leisure activities, such as skiing, scuba diving and foreign travel are extremely lively and colourful' (2005: 86). Thus marriage becomes the great goal for Japanese young women who do not want to end up as drudges like their male colleagues.

Gendering in the workplace

The Japanese case is a rather extreme illustration of how the gendering of jobs confirms the traditional gender order. But even where there is more room for change and challenge, statistical evidence confirms that gender segregation is strong. How are these gendered structures and discourses maintained in the normal practices of working life? Studies show that the process of gendering occurs at both the interactive and institutional level.

Individuals learn very early on what work is suitable for either sex. Studies of schoolchildren, such as those of Davies (1989) and Skelton (1989), show that quite young children have well-developed ideas of what jobs are suitable for women and men. They gather these from observing the adults around them, and from the images presented to them in books and on television. They see that their teachers are mainly female, and that the driver of the bus that takes them to school is a man. They are likely to observe their mothers cooking and cleaning while their father mows the lawn and puts up the shelves. Toys and games remain relentlessly gendered. Quickly, children come to identify caring tasks with women, machines and technology with men. This is before they begin to visualize themselves in the world of work. When they actually start to make choices about their future careers, they do so in adolescence, which, as we have seen, is a time when gender stereotyping and peer pressure are particularly strong. Boys, in particular, do not want to make job choices which might compromise their fragile masculinity.

These pressures and influences from friendship groups, families and media push young women and men into gender-traditional choices, as is seen in the take-up of NVQs, apprenticeships or placements on youth employment schemes; girls choose hairdressing and childcare, boys choose mechanical maintenance and building crafts. The reasons why were researched by Fuller et al. (2005). They found no major opposition to non-gender traditional choices among young people, but pointed to a more subtle process of steering. Young people lacked information about the range of opportunities on offer, while schools and the government's Connexions service were putting little energy into challenging gender stereotyping. However, the researchers stated that the strongest influences on occupational choice were family and friends, and they noted that most of these young people moved in social worlds in which traditional patterns of behaviour were little challenged (ibid.; see also Kingston 2005). Interestingly, studies show that where people break out of such choices it is often because of unconventional family relations; being brought up in a one-parent family, for example, may demonstrate to children that a mother or father can take on both sexes' roles. Devine's (1992) study of engineering showed that girls who chose to do engineering degrees had often been very close to their fathers and been encouraged by them.

Once choices have been made, new employees enter into highly gendered workplaces. They will find themselves absorbed into the existing patterns of behaviour which are hard to resist. McDowell's study of City of London financial institutions, *Capital Culture* (1997), highlights the part played by bodies and dress in the gendering of work. The body that is seen as normal in these companies is a male one, in the conventional pinstriped suit and tie. Women's bodies, with their colourful clothing and accoutrements, stand out as different, as intruders in the office sphere. They bring with them connotations of menstruation, fertility, pregnancy, which are out of place in a workplace. Feminine embodiment threatens to disrupt the rationality and impersonal order of the economic sphere. McDowell points out how women have to face daily choices of what to wear, quite different from male uniformity. This involves a fine balance: to wear dowdy clothes or adopt a male pinstripe suit is to compromise your femininity. It is expected that women will wear skirts to demonstrate their sex, but the skirts must not be too short or the clothing too provocative or their credibility as serious workers will be undermined.

Equally intimidating can be a situation where women are compelled into dress conventions derived for men. An example was reported by the British Association for Women in Policing which noted that women police officers were being forced to wear clothing (trousers, shirts and protective gear) designed and shaped for men. The heavy clothing was chafing the women's skin, causing burns and rashes. Their bra straps were showing through the flimsy shirt material. In one police district, women were being issued with underwear (long johns) with a fly-front fastening (*Observer*, 22 January 2006). The message offered is clear: male bodies are the norm and your bodies literally do not fit, are out of place. Women's physical discomfort symbolically mirrors the mental discomfort many women in the police service have reported. Dress codes thus disproportionately affect women and are an important way in which both men and other women 'police' women. The general stress on women's body and clothing, with their potential for being 'out of control' (look at all the fuss about fatness in 'celebrity' magazines like *Hello* and *Heat*) once again confirms women's difference, and their secondary status in a 'man's world'.

Of course, gendering involves both men and women. The studies in the useful collection edited by Collinson and Hearn, *Men as Managers, Managers as Men* (1996), explore the ways in which masculinities are bound up with the performance of certain types of work. For men in traditional manual work – 'hands', as the Victorians termed it – strength and craft skills were a source of masculine pride (Hollway 1996). As the content of jobs changed, aspects to do with brain and intellect became the markers of successful men: being in positions of authority, having command of technical expertise and specialist knowledge. A successful manager may display his status via the possession of a secretary or PA, his own 'office wife'. There is increasing likelihood, however, that women will compete in these areas, but men have been adept at developing practices that shore up their position and keep women out. We should note here that such processes may not be without pain. As in the case of the Japanese salarymen, being a breadwinner is not necessarily easy.

In a classic early study, *Men and Women of the Corporation* (1977), Kantner pointed to the importance of male homosociality at work as a way of keeping women in their place. Various kinds of male bonding continue to facilitate the marginalization of women colleagues: discussion of sport, socializing in pubs, weekend golfing trips, visits with clients to lap-dancing clubs are commonly reported. Research on women in professional and managerial work highlights the way in which older men in powerful positions sponsor and mentor young men, helping them to get promoted earlier than women. While women have begun to retaliate by setting up their own networks and mentoring schemes, they are disadvantaged by not holding the most powerful decision-making positions. Lower down the occupational hierarchy, male bonding often takes the form of sex talk and low-level sexual harassment (Williams et al. 2004). Indeed, sexual harassment is a potent weapon in the gendering of jobs. It reminds women of their traditional 'place' in society, to serve and pleasure men; it intimidates and undermines some women and stops them realizing their potential; others cope by becoming 'one of the boys', but in doing so may set themselves apart from their female co-workers. Just as with the sexualization of jobs, sexual harassment emphasizes the difference between men and women and helps maintain gendered boundaries between jobs.

Another key issue is time. We have noted the pressures on Japanese men, compelled to work overtime, take work home on their free days and socialize in sake and karaoke bars with their male workmates (Kimoto 2005). While in western society overtime is generally not compulsory, the spread of the 'long hours' culture of voluntary overworking provides the basis for feats of heroic masculine endurance which women, with their greater domestic responsibilities, often find it hard to match (Casey 1995; Cockburn 1991; Wacjman 1998). Indeed, the time parameters of work are increasingly a mode of gender differentiation. Women are much more likely than men to have non-standard forms of work contract with reduced or variable hours. Purcell states that 'in the UK women constitute well over half the flexible workforce (however it is defined) and the overwhelming majority of employees in non-standard employment' (2000: 134). The concentration of women in these jobs re-emphasizes their status as secondary workers.

Technology and knowledge are also at the core of gendering. Men have long used their control and mastery of various types of technology to justify higher wages. Technology has been, and remains, highly gendered. Men are identified with complex machine tools, with scientific innovation and with expert computer knowledge. Cockburn's series of classic studies of the gendering of jobs and technologies (Cockburn 1983; 1985; 1991) showed how important technological 'mastery' was in maintaining male dominance in workplaces. She provides a memorable account of how male printers felt emasculated when metal-based printing technology was replaced by computer publishing. The men were reduced to sitting helplessly by their VDUs while computer technicians serviced them, making them feel 'just like women'. In the popular radio programme, *The Archers*, it is revealed that, after his wife's death, one of the male characters, Mike Tucker, does not know how to operate a washing-machine, and manages to shrink his daughter's knitwear when he does try to use it. This example shows, of course, that there is nothing inherent about technical knowledge or mastery. It has to be learned, by either sex. Nonetheless, domestic machinery is commonly identified as female, while in the industrial context women often operate complex machinery, but rarely repair or maintain it.

Korvajarvi (2004) notes how, in Finland, the early call centres, which dealt with processing orders and customer service issues, were staffed by women; but in the newer ones, focused on 'cold calling' to sell products or on offering technical advice, men had come to predominate. This is an interesting example of how technologies change gender as the jobs involving them evolve: typewriters started out by being operated by men, but then became the preserve of female secretarial workers. In contrast, the first computer operators were women, and computers were for a long time presented as 'gender-neutral' machines; however, recently there has been a decline in the number of women taking degrees in computer studies. Once again, this is a technology in which women are commonly operators, but where designers, programmers, trouble-shooters and repairers are largely male.

Conclusion: gendered work

In a well-known and influential article, Joan Acker (1990) set out a model for the studying of gendering. She spoke of four sets of processes involved in the gendering of organizations. First is the construction of divisions between women and men. We have discussed this in terms of the sexual division of labour and the association of particular jobs with women or men (sex-typing). Second, the construction of symbols and imagery, which express, justify and maintain such divisions. Here we have described three dominant discourses which underpin the division of labour. We have also noted the imagery of work and workers, which presents men and male bodies as the workplace norm. Acker's third set are the processes of interaction in the workplace, which help keep men in dominant positions, such as the sexual interplay, harassment and male bonding procedures explored above. Finally, there are the internal mental processes by which women and men locate themselves as individuals and employees, for example in terms of their choice of occupations, and which lead them to identify and act in gender-appropriate ways. All these processes produce the gender order of organizations and help to reproduce them.

Acker's analysis, then, proves a fruitful way to categorize the processes of gender, and we shall apply her framework to our consideration of reproduction and consumption in subsequent chapters. First, though, we will look at the interface between employment and domestic labour.

HAVING IT ALL: FAMILY AND EMPLOYMENT IN WOMEN'S LIVES

The birth of a child will affect a woman's internal land-scape like an earthquake, followed by a flood, followed by a volcanic eruption. For a man it will be more along the lines of a heavy shower. (Maushart 2002)

During the period in which I was researching and writing this book I became amazed at the constant outpouring of newspaper stories and articles dealing with women, childbirth, working mothers and parenting strategies. 'Woman, 62, gives birth to 12th child'; 'Pregnancy job barrier in 1 in 4 firms'; 'Stuck on the "mummy track" – why having a baby means lower pay and prospects'; 'Childcare rises to 25 per cent of income'; '£165,000 – the cost of bringing up a child'; 'Fathers fear childcare mars career'; 'New dads want to be with baby'; 'Fathers play greater role in childcare'; 'Fatherhood ruined my marriage – twice'; 'Hardworking supermums beat 1950s counterparts'; 'It's not shameful to want others to help us care for our children'; 'Germany agonises over 30 per cent childless women'; 'More men needed in caring careers'; 'If not nursery, what?': these are some of the headlines that flag up the persistent issues of concern. As a society, we in Britain seem obsessively focused on parenthood; this is also an issue in Europe and America.

I do not think it an exaggeration to say that choices made following the arrival of the first (and second) child are the most crucial current gender issue in the societies of the developed world. (What concerns Third World women most is rather different and will be discussed in subsequent chapters.) How do we care for our children and at the same time allow women to develop their potential and have careers if they wish to? How do we make work family-friendly? These questions are asked interminably and yet we don't seem to find the answers. In this vignette I want to focus on this dilemma, which links together inexorably the issues of the gendering of production and the gendering of reproduction, the themes of the two surrounding chapters.

For my generation of women, the 'baby-boomers', the objectives seemed clear: we demanded the right to work, which had so often been denied to our mothers and grandmothers. We wanted state and employers to help us combine family lives and careers. The Scandinavian solution – the provision of good universal state nursery and pre-school facilities – seemed the best policy option, but other policies such as employer-provided nurseries, childcare tax credits or flexible working hours offered some help. One of the original demands of the British Women's Liberation Movement, as formulated at the Ruskin conferences in the early 1970s, was for 'free 24-hour childcare'. But if the state and employers proved less than adequate in offering help, then we would do it ourselves. 'Juggling.' 'Having it all.' These were the key terms in the 1980s and 1990s. There was a boom in the demand for servants (nannies, au pairs, domestic helpers) from middle-class professional women determined to develop their careers (Gregson and Lowe 1994). In the next chapter I refer to the relaunch of *She* magazine in 1990 with a brief to appeal to 'independent' working mothers. In the editorial about the relaunch, the editor described the common situations of herself and her creative director, Nadia Marks:

Nadia, who postponed motherhood for the first ten years of her married life, has given birth to two sons. I've been in and out of marriage, have edited *Cosmopolitan* and now live with the father of my handsome, perfect, brilliant, etc. son, Thomas, aged 21 months. . . . . The reason for telling you these intimate details is to put across the point that Nadia and I, in common with most of *She*'s staff and contributors, are nothing if not jugglers. And I believe we can make *She* even more relevant as the magazine for women of the 90s who juggle their lives. (Quoted in Woodward 1997: 268)

Juggling was certainly a theme of the 1980s and 1990s. When we studied the lives of the trade union activists discussed previously, we were amazed at the extraordinary multiple burdens they took on: most were mothers; all had jobs, as well as working voluntarily for their trade union (Bradley et al. 2005). But many of them had other political and community commitments as well. Here are two of them talking. The first, Shahnaz, is married with two children, is a teacher, and is very active in her union. The second, Anita, is a widow, also with two children.

So I've developed a portfolio of research, contribution to programmes, expertise in a couple of areas like social policy and management. I've also got involved in lots of extra-curricular activities outside. For example, I'm a magistrate and I get time from college to do that. . . . And I'm a deputy chair for a housing association worth in excess of 40 million. Deputy chair for that. Not an exec director, deputy chair. I'm a governor of a secondary school. I'm the women's officer for our constituency. I'm interested in politics and I stood as a local candidate in 2000. So I do lots of things and all that helps me to keep myself alive, energized, motivated and current. (Shahnaz)

I am a full-time mum, I work, I am a taxi driver, I am a banker, I am everything at the moment that's how I feel, plus I am a first aider, plus I am a union rep, so at the end of the day when I go home I am absolutely whacked. But my job does not stop there. I have to carry on and cook and clean and spend time with the kids and that, but sometimes it would be nice if I had somebody to offload on. (Anita)

Shahnaz, Anita and the many women in similar situations to whom we spoke were, in essence, living their lives in the public sphere *as men would do* but on top of that still retaining the main responsibility for running the household, albeit with help. How do these women manage? Many mentioned supportive husbands, mothers, relatives and neighbours; quite a number had extended family networks to call upon, but the notion of juggling and good organization was also a prevailing theme.

> My husband takes the children to school and my father will pick them up. And they're at home because my parents are at home. Like tonight, my husband's not coming back 'til about 9.30. And then I'm at a union meeting tomorrow. I go back home tomorrow night, I'm at a regional meeting on Saturday. My in-laws are coming Saturday afternoon and staying 'til Sunday. You know, and in-between I've got marking to do. [Laughs] I just manage it. It's hard. I think we work a lot harder than our mothers did. Because they knew exactly what they were doing and we're trying to be superwomen. (Shahnaz)

> It's all about priority making. It might sound bad but if I have an exam to take during the week I generally put work aside 'til I've done it. Then I concentrate on work again. (Neera)

> I don't know! I'm just extremely organised. . . . I have a big board in the kitchen, on the kitchen wall. Everything is plastered on there highlighted and then keyed so I can organize them. (Bella)

> It's very much a case of juggling. Because some nights we have to sit down with our diaries and say, right you do this, you do that. We spend a lot of time trying to juggle, slot things in. (Shelley)

Using these tactics, the women in our study combined their threefold roles as mothers, workers and union representatives with evening classes, studying for degrees, working for a range of voluntary organizations (supporting the homeless, working with young children, Women's Aid, housing associations), serving as councillors, giving advice on equality issues.

Unsurprisingly, Shahnaz spoke of a possible burn-out. Lives with multiple burdens may be exciting and fulfilling, but can come with costs. Among this incredibly active generation of women, determined to take advantage of the new opportunities in employment, but still wanting children, there are many I know personally who have just stopped: suffered ill-health, taken early retirement, 'downsized' to a less demanding job, taken up art or writing and generally quit the rat-race when it all became too much for them. Coward (1992), studying successful career women, and Marshall (1995), researching women managers, both spoke to women who found the strain of combining high-flying jobs with looking after young children overwhelming and decided to focus on motherhood.

The stories of the black activists are instructive in highlighting issues of difference and specificity. These women were enabled to carry out their array of commitments partly because in the Caribbean, Africa and Asia, parenting is not viewed so exclusively as the responsibility of the nuclear family unit. Extended family and kin are regularly involved in parenting (especially grandmothers) and neighbours and community may also be drawn upon. Children are viewed as an asset for the family and community rather than as a private responsibility. Those who do not have jobs care for the children of those who do. It is quite common for children of British-Caribbean parents to be sent home to their islands for periods, to be brought up by relatives and subjected to discipline in the home and at school, which is seen to be too lax in British society. No stigma is attached to these practices of what we might call extended family parenting (which, incidentally, were also quite common in previous centuries in Britain). This pattern of behaviour is also common among African-American communities, where it is sometimes referred to as 'out-mothering'. Thus women are not made to feel guilty at being apart from their children (although they may be sad about it). The other major difference is that young African-Caribbean women, and some from less affluent Asian backgrounds, often choose to have children earlier and then develop their careers subsequently, as compared to young white women in the UK who currently tend to delay their first child until a stage where their career is 'established' and they can afford a house of their own.

The retreat back to the home, as described by Coward, therefore particularly affects white women, who lack the tradition of extended family parenting. Without such support networks, white women must find other solutions; this generally means sending children to nurseries, or employing nannies and child-minders. Apart from the expense and often complex arrangements of ferrying children between locations, women agonize about how this may affect their child's development. Most of the women who talked to Coward reported deep feelings of guilt, as did women in other studies (Brannen and Moss 1991).

What about the new generation of young people? How are they responding to these dilemmas? This generation has no sense of 'coming out of the kitchen'. They do not share with my generation the sense of freedom and entitlement that comes from having escaped from a gender regime of domesticity (Walby 1997). They have grown up in a world where all adults are pressured towards paid employment, and many have seen their mothers struggling with multiple burdens. This may act as an inspiration, since many young adults regard their mothers as their key role models. It may also serve as a deterrent or warning. Another factor is that this generation has grown up in what I have called a 'climate of equality' (Bradley 1999a) in which there is a strong attachment to the idea that we are all equal as individuals.

In 2003, we interviewed Gillon for the Bristol Young Adults' Study. Gillon is a young man from a working-class background who has had an unsettled work history, holding a number of jobs, largely in retail. When we first talked to him he was unsure of his future and was working in a charity shop but anticipating leaving. At a second interview three years later, things had dramatically changed. Gillon had married his girlfriend, started a degree and was living at home with his parents. Both he and his wife were doing vocational courses which would lead to steady careers. When asked about the future, Gillon said they would like children. He believed in equality and felt he and his wife should share childcare and housework. He saw no problems in this, nor did he anticipate that having children would have a negative effect on either of their careers.

Gillon's optimism may appear naive, but is quite typical of young people I have worked with. They have ideals of sharing but quite unrealistic ideas of the impact that having a baby will have on them. This is where the earthquake, flood and volcanic eruption described by Maushart take effect!

We can contrast Gillon's hopes with what actually happens when a young couple have a baby. The mother faces a number of choices: carry on working and hand over her child to another carer, thus missing out on the experience of looking after her baby; give up working and jeopardize her career; ask her partner to become a 'househusband', thereby jeopardizing his career; work part time and spend the rest of the time looking after the baby. If we set out the dilemma in this fashion, it is not surprising that the latter was the most popular choice among the young Bristol women we interviewed. However, in choosing the part-time option, the woman places herself as a secondary worker. Although her career is not necessarily abandoned, it will be retarded.

These young women did not simply want to 'go back to the kitchen'. Most of them wanted some kind of job or career in the future. On the other hand, they took maternity very seriously and wished to enjoy their baby. In a way, they still wanted to 'have it all', but *sequentially rather than concurrently.* They did not want work to overwhelm their lives and had a strong commitment to ideas of 'work–life balance'. Katrina exemplifies the thinking of many we interviewed in terms of sequential planning. She had three children and was currently study-ing to be a social worker:

> My family are my first priority and my studies come second and the work has to fit in. My family will always come first regardless and eventually work will take the priority

of where my studies come now, and I suppose it's just
another case of juggling.

But:

> This isn't where it ends. This is just where it begins. . . . I've
> decided to go for the degree because the social work
> qualification is changing and in a couple of years every-
> one will need a degree. . . . And eventually, after I've
> been in social work for a number of years, and I hope I
> do well, and my children are older, I hope to do a degree
> in child psychology . . . later in life that will be the career
> that I turn to.

Unfortunately, prevailing work cultures and social
security policies make it hard to combine full-time work
with being a mother. Especially in professional and
service careers, the 'long hours' culture is unfriendly to
mothers. Employees are supposed to show their commitment to the organization, and thus their suitability for
promotion, by working voluntarily beyond allotted
hours. Meetings are held at breakfast time and in the
evening (Casey 1995). There are requirements for mobility, for attending training courses at weekends and
lengthy 'away-days'. All of these pose nightmares for
childcare; they are often little resisted by men and single
women who use these opportunities to further their
own career advancement.

Lack of high-quality universal nursery provision means
that only wealthy women can find the alternative childcare they feel comfortable and confident with. The supply
of non-employed grannies to look after children is drying
up as older women choose to stay in the labour market
and retire later. This pushes working-class women to stay
at home. If they work part time, the money they earn is
often insufficient to cover transport and childcare provision, providing a disincentive to working. Similarly, lone
mothers often find the costs of being employed in low-
paid work are such that it makes economic sense to
remain on benefit.

Besides all this, there is the emotional aspect of caring and motherhood, which proved so important to many of the women we interviewed. Ironically, a number of them spoke of the pressure they were under to develop careers and the guilt they felt about *not working*.

> The guilt I can feel just being at home is quite tremendous. And we have an image of how we should be career women, do the housework and be a mother. But if I really talk to people who have children, they all love just to stay at home while the husband goes out to work. (Romy, full-time mother)

This new type of pressure and guilt is reflected in a rueful comment from Linda: 'From the point of view of women being able to stay at home, that's not so easy anymore as it used to be before all this equality.' Damned if you do and damned if you don't!

The pressure of changes in the gendering of production and reproduction falls heavily on this generation of women. Discourses of gender create for them subject positions of *both* 'the good mother' *and* 'the career woman'. They read about juggling, 'having it all', have seen their mothers doing it and feel it is required of them. But the prospect daunts many, along with the concern about its effects on children and feelings of 'missing out' on 'enjoying one's baby'. Arlie Hochschild, in *The Time Bind* (1997), studied American mothers who chose to prioritize their careers and leave children in all-day nurseries. One of the most poignant images in Hochschild's book is the 'Waving Window' in the nursery, where the carers hold the children up in the early morning to wave goodbye as the mothers rush off for their nine o'clock start.

Jayne typified those women whose feelings ebbed and flowed as they tried to achieve this impossible balance. She swung between career ambitions and her wish for more children:

> When you have children things do change and I think that my generation, where we were brought up to believe

that we could do it, we could have it all, we could have everything and I think that's rubbish actually and I've really come full circle on that. And I think that you *can have it all*, but there's a big cost.

In the second series of the TV show *Desperate Housewives*, Lynette, the most ordinary and likeable of the main characters, swaps her life as an exhausted, harassed mother of three rowdy out-of-control young boys in a role reversal with her husband. He becomes the full-time carer, while she returns to work full time in an advertising agency. As the demands to work late for excessive hours become increasingly pressing, she is desperate to see more of her boys. When the chance comes up to have a nursery at work, which will mean her youngest can be accessible at the agency, she needs a certain number of women to sign up and turns to her boss's wife, a full-time mother in pretty pink clothing. For her pains, she gets berated by this smug woman: 'How can you leave your children?' 'Why did you have children if you didn't want to look after them?' Lynette fights back: 'I am a successful career woman *and* a good mother.' 'Well,' replies the other, 'that may do for you, but I want to be a *great* mother!' Lynette's defeated expression sums up perfectly the psychic suffering of women caught up in this frontline battle over gender roles.

5
Gendered Worlds: Reproduction

In our exploration of the world of work we have noticed how, despite the persistence of gender segregation, there is a degree of fluidity, the potential for change. As we turn to consider the realm of reproduction, we come face to face with the two great imponderables which are so frequently used to explain gender difference and inequality: child-bearing and rearing; and male and female sexuality. We have just explored the strong link made by young women with the maternal role. While relations of production are clearly man-made, here we encounter the strongest presentations of gender difference as natural. People from socio-biologists, to psychologists, to doctors, to first-year male undergraduate students have utilized these 'facts of life' to explain to me the inevitability of women's commitment to mothering and men's subsequent dominance of the public sphere.

The feminist position runs counter to this in arguing that reproduction, like all other human activities, is a social not a purely biological act. We do not copulate like other mammals, as anyone will know who has watched a David Attenborough special! Though, self-evidently, biological functions are involved in procreation and motherhood, they are overlain by multiple layers of social and cultural practice. While bodies are involved, how we think about our bodies, deploy them and even experience bodily sensations is a product of social learning and persistent social interaction.

In theorizing reproduction, feminists of the second wave were highly influenced by the Marxist approach, utilizing Engels's definition in *The Origins of the Family*. Engels stated that reproduction was of 'a twofold character', involving the production of survival needs, 'food, clothing and shelter', and the production of human beings, 'the propagation of the species' (1972: 26). This connected to two major themes of second-wave feminism: the exploration of domestic labour (popularly childcare and housework) and of maternity and motherhood. Significantly, two of Ann Oakley's first empirical investigations were into these areas, to which little previous academic attention had been given (Oakley 1974; 1980).

Sexuality was also an important focus of second-wave attention, as it has been for postmodern feminism. It might be possible to argue that, as society has increasingly separated out sexual activity from procreation, it is no longer a crucial part of the reproductive sphere. Yet, even if, by the end of the twentieth century, sexual activity had become primarily recreational, intercourse and sexual organs are still involved in the making of babies. Moreover, sexual impulse and desires are central to the formation of couples, families and, thence, households. Therefore in this chapter I deal with domestic labour, motherhood and sexuality as three crucial and related aspects of gendering.

The domestic division of labour

Just as segregation endures in the workplace, so it does within the household. As discussed in chapter 4, it remains the case that many mothers take time out of paid employment to look after children. Cases of role reversal, with the male partner staying at home, are rare, usually something like 1–2 per cent of couples. Where it happens, it is often because the father is unemployed or because the woman earns substantially more than he does. There is an increasing body of lone-parent fathers, but they are vastly outnumbered by lone-parent mothers. Despite the growing discourse of 'parenting', the looking after of young children is far from evenly shared, with the father tending to 'help out', while the mother shoulders most of the burden. In the main, mothers are voluntarily taking on the bulk of the work; but, as has been shown in earlier chapters, in doing so they are forgoing the chance of attaining equality with men in the labour market.

Linked to this is the continued disparity in the distribution of other household tasks between men and women. Early chroniclers of women's increased labour market participation in the post-war period assumed that this would (sooner or later) be matched by men taking a greater share of domestic labour (Klein 1965; Young and Willmott 1973). However, this shift has proved to be limited. Despite widespread views among young people that household tasks ought to be shared equally, research studies show that in the majority of cases women carry out the bulk of housework; characteristically, women report performing around 70 per cent of household tasks (Sullivan 2000; Warde and Hetherington 1993). Baxter's cross-national study (1998) found that in dual-earner families in Australia, Canada, the USA and Norway, men reported doing only 25 per cent of total housework. Anderson et al. (1994) found that the amount of time a full-time housewife with children spent on housework had remained fairly stable over the twentieth century, at 60–70 hours per week. Men's share has risen slightly over the same time-span, but is still only on average 5–10 hours per week even where the woman is in employment. We still have housewives, desperate or not, while the househusband remains an exotic phenomenon.

Men are also picky in what they do, choosing to leave the more mundane activities to women. For example, with children, they tend to be involved with playing, bedtime story-reading and excursions, rather than routine maintenance tasks such as washing clothes and feeding. Sullivan (1997) studied time diaries from 408 couples in six locations in Britain and found that men's domestic tasks were still mainly gardening and DIY, and the women's were cooking and cleaning. Valentine reports on a survey, funded by a supermarket, of 43,000 respondents, which found that in 75 per cent of households women did the bulk of cooking; working-class households were more likely to display a traditional division of tasks than middle-class households (Valentine 1999). Moreover, while men may help with cooking or cleaning, the responsibility for planning and coordinating the household routine continues to fall on women. They are the household managers. Warde and Hetherington conclude from their study of 300 households in Greater Manchester that there was a 'continuing and pervasive conventional division of labour between women and men' (1993: 43). We can sum it up: women 'do the housework'; men 'help'.

Because of the stress in Marx's work on productive labour, Marxist feminist writers devoted much attention to the analysis of domestic labour, in what is referred to as the 'domestic labour debate' (Gittins 1993; Malos 1980; Murgatroyd 1981). There was disagreement as to whether housework should be seen as 'productive' in the technical Marxian sense; that is, did it contribute to the creation of surplus value? Some argued that by providing services to male labourers (cooking, washing and cleaning), which otherwise would have had to be provided commercially, housewives were directly contributing to capital accumulation by keeping down the level of wages, thus allowing capitalists more profit. Others argued that the contribution was an indirect one, though none the less vital. By nurturing and caring for both the current and upcoming generations of wage-earners (husbands and children), housewives were providing for the reproduction of the conditions of capitalism. Such arguments lay behind the campaign of some second-wave feminists that women should be paid 'Wages for Housework' in recognition of how crucial their work was for the economy. Other feminists, however, rejected this idea, arguing that paying women to stay at home would only perpetuate their exclusion from the public sphere and thus their continued social marginalization.

Although these debates have fallen out of sight, the role of domestic labour in perpetuating gender inequality remains crucial. A very interesting recent attempt to integrate the analyses of wage labour and domestic labour has come from Miriam Glucksmann with her concept of the 'total social organisation of labour' (1995; 2005). Glucksmann suggests that we should reconceptualize work and labour, acknowledging the way that work in the private and public spheres, paid and unpaid labour, market and non-market activities are interrelated. She describes this approach as 'a relational approach focusing on modes of linkages and connections, intersections, configurations, patterns, networks' (2005: 21).

Thus, Glucksmann brings together the analysis of production and reproduction (and to some extent consumption). For example, she points out that the conditions of men's full-time employment in wage labour are shaped by their ability to depend on the unpaid labour of women at home; and that married women enter the labour market under constraints that do not operate on men (that is, the woman's work must be compatible with domestic responsibilities), while men's labour power is unconstrained (they can work overtime, compulsory or voluntary, as needed) and thus is more highly valued and rewarded. This is a useful reworking of Marxian concepts, which helps us to understand how domestic and waged labour are interconnected, and the gender inequalities that result.

The differentiation of sexuality: unequal rules and heteronormativity

It might seem odd to talk of structures of sexuality, since we view sexual behaviour as such an individual and personal matter. But in fact sexual behaviour is just as much socially and culturally learned as are family and work practices. It is also highly variable, as work on tribal societies has shown. In many pre-modern societies, sexuality is tightly controlled and rule-bound. Cultural anthropologists explain this as the requirements of inheritance: the father needs to know that his heir is in fact his own child, not that of another man. This led to the strict surveillance of women's sexuality, especially among wealthy and aristocratic groups (to whom, as the history of the English kings and queens attests, inheritance matters very greatly). This is one of the origins of the 'double standard' by which men have been allowed sexual freedom and to have many partners, while women are pressured to be monogamous and to confine sex to marriage.

These rules have been reinforced by the world religions such as Catholicism and Islam which, while theoretically recommending fidelity and chastity for both sexes, are in fact prepared to overlook male promiscuity, while condemning and punishing non-monogamous women. Islam and some versions of Christianity allow polygamy for men, but not

women. Women caught having sex outside marriage are ostracized and outcast, in some societies even being seen as legitimate prey for rape and murder. In England in the first half of
the twentieth century women who had illegitimate children
were sometimes incarcerated for years in mental hospitals.
Those who did not suffer this fate were often ostracized, as
one woman remembers, describing her pregnancy in 1944:

> Being an unmarried mother was considered a terrible sin in
> those days. I was terrified and would lie awake fretting and
> wondering what would happen when people eventually found
> out. Back then, most unmarried pregnant girls, including a
> friend of mine, were sent away to live in homes until their
> child was born, then forced to give it up for adoption. (Joyce
> Wild, writing in the *Daily Mail*, 2 February 2006)

Joyce Wild concealed her pregnancy from everyone until she
actually went into labour. Luckily, her mother, though furious,
allowed her to keep the child, perhaps because the absent
father was a young soldier away at the front. Joyce's story
also illustrates one major and deep-seated difference between
women and men: men never have to 'lie awake' terrified as
to whether they may be pregnant and what to do if they are.
Thus there is often an element of fear and risk attached to
sex for women that is not experienced by men, and which
leads them to treat sexual intercourse more lightly.

In short, there was one set of rules for men, one for women,
often legitimated by naturalistic explanations about men's
and women's sexual drives. As the well-known piece of dog-
gerel has it:

> Hogamus, higamus
> Men are polygamous
> Higamus, hogamus
> Women monogamous!

Although the scientific evidence for the view that men are
programmed to spread their seed about and impregnate as
many women as possible, while women seek to trap one man
in order to ensure protection for their offspring, is highly
dubious, this view prevails strongly in many quarters, has

been historically enacted via the double standard and is particularly strongly entrenched in the media coverage of celebrity culture, which acts so powerfully on many young people's ideas today. Thus, for example, Brad Pitt and Tom Cruise are portrayed as 'love rats' for leaving Jennifer Aniston and Nicole Kidman, respectively, to weep alone. From another generation, Jack Nicholson summed it up: 'A woman has a sexual experience and she has to wait to see what happens. A man has one; he has to look for someone else. It's not a question of morality. His glands are all designed to overcome his morality so that we don't end the species.'[1]

While these kinds of view seem in many ways deeply old-fashioned and out of touch with contemporary sexual mores, within the discourse of heteronormativity a dominant mode of portraying heterosexual relations as unequal and different, in terms of the predatory male and the ensnaring and sometimes betrayed woman, remains quite deeply embedded. Popular culture is often involved with this. We can leave out of account the misogyny of gangsta rap, with its derogatory vision of how to treat women ('hos' and 'bitches'), but soft rockers James set out a common bifurcated vision in their song *Dumb Jam*:

> He's only human, only male
> Bound to stray, bound to betrayal
> The moon is rising, it's a physical thing
> Nothing can hold him, not even a ring.
>
> She's only human, only female
> Bound to victim, bound to betrayal
> The moon is rising, it's a physical thing
> She's only acting on the rite of spring!

While the actuality of individuals' sexual relations must expose the crudity of these stereotypes, there is a danger that the major counter-move is to reinvent women as predators not prey – a development which will be discussed in the next chapter – rather than seeking to normalize egalitarianism and freedom in sexuality and sexual relations, the feminist ideal

---

[1] From *OK* magazine, quoted in the *Guardian*, 25 July 1996.

promulgated by writers such as Vance (1992) and Segal (1994). In the meantime, other aspects of sexual culture and morality continue to differentiate women and men. For example, while it is seen as perfectly acceptable for men to date younger women, there is still some social stigma surrounding older women who acquire younger partners, derogatorily labelled as 'toy boys'. When, after the death of my long-term partner, I joined a dating agency and expressed the view that, as I was pretty active and youthful for my chronological age, I would like to meet some men a little younger than myself, I was told this was impossible; younger men required partners of child-bearing age. Thus it appears legitimate for older men to 'trade their wife in for a younger model'. Here again, we see double standards; as Arber and Ginn point out in *Gender and Later Life* (1991), the close link between women and mothering means that a woman who has lost her fertility is seen to have lost her value, to be 'on the shelf'; while masculine value is defined by power and money, which tends to accumulate, not diminish, over the life-course.

Another aspect of heteronormativity is the pressure it puts on both sexes to conform as active heterosexuals. Alternative modes of sexuality, homosexuality, bisexuality and even voluntary chastity, are seen as deviant, if not sinful. The oppression of gays and lesbians remains a major issue in many societies around the world. In North America and Europe the Gay Rights Movement has brought a degree of freedom and acceptance for gay, lesbian and bisexual people to express their sexuality. There has been slow progress in this direction, with, for example, the recent granting of civil contractual rights to gay and lesbian couples in Britain. However, some elements of what radical second-wave feminists such as Adrienne Rich (1980) and Sheila Jeffreys (1990) referred to as 'compulsory homosexuality' remain. It is still difficult for gays and lesbians to 'come out' in particular contexts, such as the workplace. At school, young gays and lesbians are more vulnerable to bullying than other young people. It is estimated that one in three is bullied. Moreover, bullying appears to have increased: interviews with schoolchildren in 1984 and 2003 revealed a 10 per cent increase in physical attacks and a 29 per cent increase in verbal abuse; some of these young people are driven to self-harming or suicide attempts (Shabi 2005). Lesbian couples have had difficulty in adopting children or gaining access to in vitro fertilization. Attacks and even murders of gay and lesbian people are still common, both in less cosmopolitan societies and in urban metropoles such as London. Accusations of lesbianism are still a common way for heterosexual men to express their anger against women, particularly if their sexual advances are rejected.

In the feminist context, Rich (1980) spoke of the lesbian continuum, in an early critique of binary categories. Attacking the idea that people were either straight or gay, she suggested that we may be drawn in various ways towards our own sex as well as the other; but 'women-directed' impulses to hug and kiss other women, for example, may be suppressed as unnatural. In the postmodernist moment, feminist radicals made great play of 'polymorphous perversity'. Women like Madonna paraded their ambiguous sexuality with displays of intimacy with both sexes. But this strategy of transgression and 'queering', though it has no doubt helped to promote a more questioning and liberal approach to sexuality in some quarters, has as yet made little impact on the vast cultural apparatus that continues to promote heteronormativity, including most of the world churches.

Discourses of difference: mothering, caring and heteronormativity

We discussed in the last chapter the breadwinner discourse which underpins the sexual division of labour both in the workplace and in the household. This is supplemented by a powerful discourse of motherhood, which has taken different forms in different epochs, but the core of which is usually similar and contains the following key propositions: all women are designed to be mothers; women who do not become mothers will be unhappy and unfulfilled; those who do become mothers are compelled, either by biological instinct or by moral pressure, to put the well-being of their child(ren) before anything else. This is what Oakley calls the 'motherhood as destiny' approach. It follows that, since motherhood is women's key function, they must expect to make sacrifices and alter their behaviour to cope with its demands.

A powerful critique of one version of the motherhood discourse was provided by Elisabeth Badinter in *The Myth of Motherhood* (1981). Badinter surveyed French history to expose the fallacy of the view that mothering is a natural or instinctive practice. Rather, she argued, it was socially learned and socially variable. She pointed to various types of contemporary and historical evidence in support of her argument. Infanticide, child abuse and maternal depression show that not all women want children or find mothering easy. In previous centuries, child-rearing practices were widely practised that we would now see as cruel: for example, the use of swaddling clothes which bound children tightly, thereby restricting their mobility, and doping children with opium were common practices among the poorer classes in France (as they were in England). Meanwhile, rich women in the eighteenth century spent as little time as possible looking after their children, entrusting them to nurses and servants. Society women believed that breastfeeding would adversely affect their figures, so it was common to send babies to be cared for by wet-nurses, often peasant women living in the country. There were even baby farms where unwanted children were looked after en masse. Badinter argues that the contemporary idea of motherhood and the 'maternal instinct' only emerged in the late Victorian epoch, the period when the notion of 'separate spheres' was particularly dominant. It was backed by religious ideology which promoted the idea of motherhood as sacrifice and required women to give up their own desires and freedoms for the sake of their children.

A new version of this is described by David Cheal, drawing on the work of Sharon Hays (1996) on 'intensive mothering'. Cheal defines this as 'a self-sacrificing commitment made by a mother to focus most of her time and energy upon managing every aspect of the child's relationship with its environment' (2002: 104). The objective is to ensure that the child has the best possible 'start in life'. Cheal describes this as an international ideology which is especially strong in America and Japan. It reflects the fact that modern versions of motherhood emphasize the emotional and psychological aspects of caring, not just the physical welfare of children. Mothers are required to make a persistent show of their affection and also to provide constant stimulation to their young children. Later, they will help them with their schoolwork and ferry them to after-school classes and activities. This type of mothering is described by Cheal as 'emotionally absorbing, expert-guided, labour-intensive and financially expensive' (2002: 104). Unsurprisingly, its main proponents are the wealthier middle classes.

The birth of such ideologies of total motherhood coincided historically with campaigns against married women working, which was seen as injurious to good housekeeping and the well-being of husbands. Victorian reformers such as Lord Shaftesbury fulminated that if wives worked, men would be driven to drink and children would become delinquents. This proposition, which held women responsible for morality and civilized behaviour, became a favourite theme and contributed to an accompanying discourse of domesticity, which again emphasized that women are 'naturally' drawn to domestic concerns and to caring and nurturing activities. Thus the dependent housewife became a social ideal which persisted through the late nineteenth and early twentieth centuries. Many organizations and occupations (including teaching and the civil service) operated a marriage bar, whereby women were expected to quit their jobs on marriage, or at least when their first child arrived.

Although the cult of motherhood as a full-time occupation began to decline in the 1950s, as women's labour market participation rose, the Victorian ideals remain quite deeply embedded in many areas of society. In Catholic countries, such as Italy and Greece, the cult of the mother persists. What Esping-Andersen (1990) labelled conservative welfare regimes have also given sanction to full-time motherhood, with Germany being a prime example. In the more secularized countries, such as England, occasional panics about working mothers continue to break out from time to time. Post-war 'juvenile delinquency' was linked to 'latchkey' children hanging about in the street after school until their mothers got home from work. Recently, working mothers have been implicated in the problems of 'failing boys' and their falling behind girls in examination performance. Even more recently, reports have stated that pre-school-age children who spend time in nurseries may suffer developmental and psychological damage.

There is strong support for these ideas in the right-wing press, and there is no doubt that they cause anxiety and guilt among parents. What Berger and Berger called the 'war over the family' (1983) continues. The popular TV series *Wife Swap* frequently pitted working mothers against full-time carers, resulting in furious exchanges. The full-time carers considered the working mothers to be selfish and neglectful; the working mothers felt that the full-time carers were lazy and dependent, with fathers who did no work around the house being a particular target of criticism.

Brannen and Moss (1991) and Woodward (1997) have explored new evolving ideologies of 'working motherhood' and 'independent motherhood'. These can be seen as 'counter-discourses', which propose, for example, that 'quality time' with children is as effective as full-time motherhood and that a working mother, as well as helping her children have a better standard of living (food, clothes and holidays), can provide them with more stimulating company. In a genera-tion, dual-earning couples have become the norm, and a new discourse of 'part-time motherhood' may help to release women from the pressure to stay at home. We have noted Walby's argument (1997) that the current form of the gender regime frees women from the fate of domesticity. Kathryn Woodward takes this further by pointing to the emergence of a new model of motherhood exemplified in the relaunch of *She* magazine in 1990 under a new editor, Linda Kelsey – which I touched on in the vignette that precedes this chapter. The editorial from the magazine was accompanied by a picture of Kelsey and the creative editor, Nadia Marks, with their three young children. The image was of dynamic working mothers without a man in attendance; the message was 'having it all', the mission to produce a magazine 'that celebrates self and motherhood under one umbrella' (quoted in Woodward 1997: 268).

We have discussed already the guilt that many women feel on leaving small children at home. Interestingly, Kelsey resigned from *She* in 1995, which was interpreted as a dem-onstration of the strains of trying to 'have it all'. We saw that young women in Bristol held full-time motherhood as an ideal, even if it was in practice unrealizable. The desire to stay at home was not something forced, and many who had returned to work straight after their maternity leave spoke of the regret they felt at being deprived of time with their babies. All this suggests that the discourse of domesticity and caring remains compelling.

Badinter, in *The Myth of Motherhood* (1981), made it clear that she was not mounting an attack on motherhood as such, but on the ideas of 'total motherhood' and the maternal instinct. She argued that the role of fathers was commonly ignored and suggested there was no reason why they should not be involved in the care of small children. Indeed, governments in Europe have tried quite hard to promote the idea of shared parenting through their social policies. However, in the UK this new policy discourse seems to have had limited effect on actual parenting practice. Esther Dermott has researched the new forms of fatherhood (2005) and found that the young fathers she studied held strongly to an ideal of 'involved fatherhood'. However, this involvement operated at the levels of emotion and intimacy rather than practical responsibilities. In the couples Dermott studied, the committed and involved fathers still spent much less time with their children than did the mothers.

It can be argued, indeed, that the renowned 'genderquake' which we are said to be undergoing has had little impact overall on the discourses of masculinity. Women's family roles and behaviour are changing, but male identities lag behind. This is clear in the discourses around female and male sexuality. The old Victorian view of women as sexually passive, whose impulses must be awakened through romantic love and skilful male initiation, is becoming a thing of the past. 'Essex girls', 'ladettes' and tabloid 'It' girls are allowed to be as sexually passionate and voracious as men. This has been a major change since the 1950s; Carol Vance (1992) and Lynn Segal (1994) were among those feminists, often labelled 'sex radicals', who proclaimed women's rights to sexual freedom, pleasure and experimentation. Vance's work was especially influential; she stated that sexuality for women was a source of both 'pleasures' and 'dangers'. The goal must be to find safe spaces (literal and metaphorical) where women could enjoy the pleasures of sex without the fear of the dangers. However, as Segal states in *Slow Motion* (1990), change has been less noticeable among men. The discourse of men as naturally driven sexual predators, the male 'seething volcano of sex' rhetoric, has not been displaced. As she rightly notes, this is oppressive for men as well as women. Performance anxiety and fear of impotence are common among men.

Meanwhile, the idea of young men as sexually rampant still helps to legitimize the sexual double standard; and this is considerably worse in non-European societies such as Latin America and sub-Saharan Africa, where women, too, buy into the view that men are inevitably promiscuous and unfaithful. The massive commercial global development of the sex industry, mainly if not entirely targeted at men, affirms the privilege given to men's sexual needs and the view that they cannot be satisfied by a single partner. Perhaps the extreme version of the discourse of uncontrollable male sexuality is found in strict Islamic societies, such as Saudi Arabia. The view is that men cannot help themselves from pursuing women and that women are temptresses even if they do not intend to be. Thus temptation must be allayed by the complete veiling of women in the company of any men who are non-family members. This discourse appears to be accepted by the vast majority of both men and women, and the latter willingly adopt head-to-toe black clothing as protection from male abuse and lusts. The end result of this is that Saudi men have no opportunity to learn how to interact in a non-sexual way with women and so the system of sexual apartheid persists (Whitaker 2006).

Micro-processes of gendering: mothers, fathers and families

We saw in the last chapter that learning about the sexual division of labour begins early. It is even more true in the home, where the mother's centrality is an early lesson in gender for most children. Young women interviewed by myself, colleagues and students in Bristol repeatedly spoke of their admiration for their mothers and how they acted as role models. Women learn their view of mothering from observing their mothers. As Chodorow noted in *The Reproduction of Mothering* (1978), using the psychoanalytic perspective, young children's initial identification is with their mothers. While the link between mother and daughter tends to persist and strengthen throughout their lives, young boys, if they are to assume an adult masculine identity, will have at some time to disidentify with their mothers. This action of separation can have a profound and violent effect on the boy: it often takes the form of aggressive repudiation of girls and all things girlish.

We noted in previous chapters the strains that men have to put upon themselves to conform to the ideals of hegemonic masculinity and to take up the role of main breadwinner. This means suppressing parts of themselves which may run counter to these masculine imperatives. Stephen Whitehead outlines these psychological processes very well:

> Not all men are at ease with a masculinist corporate culture, and many seek to address the inherent tensions of attempting to manage contrasting ways of being by focusing on their paid work to the exclusion of all else, particularly relationships and family. And there is a comfort in this act, for so long as the man sustains his undivided attention on work he is avoiding looking into his life and values – and the costs his actions incur for him and others. Moreover, his sense of power and potency becomes reified in the workplace, whatever impotencies may exist for him outside it. He comes to live his life and exercise his being in what is ultimately an artificial, cultural-social configuration – the compartmentalization of the public and private. The singularity of this practice ... contributes to the mythology of men's heroic projects. A further effect is that men come to be associated with commitment, dedication, careerism, presenteeism and singularity of purpose. (2002: 128)

Whitehead's insights seem to me correct, and terribly sad. To survive in a competitive world, men are forced to do violence to themselves, splitting off the parts of them which threaten masculine ascendancy. Of course women and children suffer too in this process: we think of 'absent fathers', of lone mothers and their children struggling in poor housing on run-down estates, of marriages strained by the lack of time spent together, of the depression suffered by many mothers who have given up social life and jobs and feel trapped at home with young children. But the suffering of men is often overlooked when discussing gender inequality. This is noted by Caroline New in an essay on the oppression of men:

> Capitalist . . . economies accumulate value at the expense of the living bodies of men through the requirement to overwork in paid employment. . . . The acceptance of overwork has traditionally been supported by the 'man as provider' ideology, now less widespread, but also by the fear of unemployment. Overwork falls also on middle-class and upper-class men, although working-class men are assigned the dirtiest, most dangerous and exhausting jobs. Their bodies are treated as disposable. The masculine ideology of strength and endurance encourages men to accept and even take pride in these destructive effects, with serious implications for men's health. . . . Men are obliged, in certain circumstances, to kill and be killed in the service of the nation-state, and may be punished if they refuse. . . . Enormous numbers of men are killed, injured and traumatised by warfare. (2001: 741–2)

The dynamic of gender in the household is thus complex. While men tend to possess economic power through holding the main breadwinner role, their absence from the home leaves women in a dominant role as household managers and coordinators of the home. While it may be the man who is the ultimate disciplinarian, nevertheless children will often see the mother as the powerful one. Indeed, I have argued elsewhere (Bradley 1999a) that women *do* command power in the household through their control of domestic resources. While the sexual division of labour in the workplace is visibly unequal, the household is more likely to be viewed as a site of equality, the domestic division of labour as a rational sharing, a balance of power.

Research has found that young couples, in particular, hold egalitarian views about marriage and believe in the equal sharing of tasks (Bradley and Dermott 2006; Wetherell et al. 1987). Why, then, does the traditional domestic labour reproduce itself so quickly after marriage? Some of the issues are practical: young women tend to learn household skills such as cooking and ironing from their mothers, while men are less likely to do so. There may be a degree of 'learned helplessness' on the part of some men, which leads women to take the path of least resistance and do the jobs (for example, ironing or sewing) themselves. It is also the case that some women enjoy demonstrating domestic skills and use them as a way to assert power in a relationship. Women's magazines, of both traditional and modern types, are packed with recipes and menus and tips for household management. Subtle messages of media imagery may push women towards homemaking and men to the more technical jobs.

Research in the United States reported by Maushart (2002) showed that the birth of the first child had a dramatic effect on couples. As well as a switch to a 'more traditional' division of labour (Maushart pithily describes this as 'women going from doing most of it to doing almost all of it'), there is a massive rise in reported conflict, a decline in frequency of sex and a sense of diminished marital happiness and satisfaction, especially for women. She quotes researchers Carolyn and Philip Cowan, who observed that couples who previously shared the prevalent egalitarian view of marriage are astonished by the slide into traditionalism: 'they describe the change as if it were a mysterious virus they picked up when they were in the hospital having the baby'.

Of course, some women prefer domestic work to work in the labour market. Jools Oliver, wife of TV chef Jamie, told the Press: 'I was never really a career girl. I wanted the babies, the baking, the roses round the door' (Llewellyn Smith 2006). The *Sunday Telegraph*, from which this quotation was taken, proclaimed Jools Oliver as a role model for a new generation of young women. One such they interviewed was 'Jennifer', a Bristol social science graduate who was working as a receptionist in a health club, a poorly paid job 'that requires no qualifications except charm'. She told the reporter:

> My life isn't about work. It's about going out in the evening, meeting people, having fun. So I wanted a job that wasn't demanding at all. I'm just not interested in all the stress that comes with pursuing a career. (Ibid.)

Her priority was to find a rich husband, have children and perhaps later find 'a job that's fun'. Of course, it is easier to make this kind of choice if you have a wealthy husband like Jamie Oliver: not only does his wealth substitute for his wife's potential income, it also allows for a standard of living in which the experience of being a full-time mother and house-wife is very different from that of a single mother bringing up a child on a deprived housing estate.

However, it is the arrival of children which confirms women's domestic role, as Hunt (1980) found so long ago. When a baby comes, couples rethink the package of tasks they must cover between them. Since it is women who take mater-nity leave, who switch to part-time working, it seems rational that they take on more domestic tasks; so the drift to tradi-tional gendering begins. This is why the compulsory 'Daddy weeks' of Scandinavia (where men are compelled to stay and look after the baby while the mother is at work) seem such a good idea. Meanwhile, the association of women with domes-ticity is reasserted, and conservatives are happy to proclaim that women are voluntarily accepting that 'a woman's place is in the home'. The other side of the coin is that in some cultures and contexts a man's masculinity is seen as compro-mised if he takes on domestic tasks.

We have discussed the pressure on boys to conform at several places in this book. Here we consider its impact on sexuality. Very important things happen to the relations between girls and boys at adolescence. Obviously, there is the development of a dating culture, an interest in other boys and girls primarily as potential sexual partners. This culture is highly hierarchical in nature with a pecking order of 'fit' boys and girls. But studies of adolescents also show that it continues to enshrine a version of the double standard. Girls who gather a reputation for being 'easy', having sex with a number of boys, become labelled as 'sluts' and 'slags', while boys who are successful at 'pulling' women gain a positive repute as a 'stud' or a 'bit of a lad'. This was a finding from research carried out by Smith (1978) and Lees (1986). More recent research by Holland et al. (1998) found this still to be the case. Girls had to manage their behaviour carefully to avoid negative labelling, while boys were free to do as they liked. Holland et al. used the concept of the 'male-in-the-head' to portray the relations of power they saw at play here. Girls and young women allow their behaviour to be controlled by the definitions of boys and young men, reaffirming the greater importance and domination of men. Wood's interesting study of young men's talk (1984) shows how sexual bragging is a key part of adolescent male culture, with boys using sexual experience to boost their personal status. By contrast, their continued derogation of young women is a way of affirming their own superiority.

Some of this seems to carry over into adult male cultures in the workplace and within leisure. Although recently under attack, the practice of putting up pin-ups of naked women in male workspaces is well known. Increasingly, it seems, groups of male workmates indulge in male bonding via visits to lap-dancing or strip clubs. Passing comment on the attributes of women in the vicinity, and the fashion for sending 'stripo-grams' or 'kissograms', are further manifestations of aggressive male sexuality at work. These practices are the subject of increasing contention, as they may be outlawed through EO workplace policies, while others defend them as 'harmless fun'. But these kinds of workplace practice cannot be seen as trivial: once again, they serve as symbols of hegemonic male sexual discourse, illustrating the voraciousness of male sexual appetites, the availability of female bodies to men and the right of men to establish what is appropriate sexual behaviour for both sexes.

Conclusion: gendered households

In the kitchen of a friend there are two mugs: 'Marvellous Mother' and 'Fantastic Father'. The 'male' mug is large and sturdy. It is blue and carries a picture of a man in a bowler hat and suit driving down a street in what appears to be a souped-up pedal car. Marvellous Mother is smaller and slimmer, tapered in shape and pink. A 'typical' housewife with headscarf stands in a shiny well-equipped kitchen. The mugs are, no doubt, an example of 'postmodern irony', but they also seem to indicate the ambivalence of attitudes around the gendering of the household. Although we endorse equality in marriage we find it hard to realize.

Marvellous mums do the cooking and sacrifice careers (if they had them) to look after young children. Fantastic fathers go out to work, earn good incomes and play with their children. As we have seen (applying Acker's model again) the domestic division of labour persists in a highly gendered way. Imagery of house*wives* and *men* in business suits is widespread. Discourses of motherhood, female domesticity and male sexual fecklessness underpin current family and household relationships. Interactions in the family seem to push men and women into these gendered pathways. Girls and boys develop traditional ideas about gender, families and sex from a young age. Laddish male sexual cultures remain strong at school and in the workplace, an issue we shall explore more in the vignettes that follow.

It seems hard for women to escape what we might term 'compulsory motherhood', despite the sharp rise in single young people (12 per cent of households now consist of one person compared to 6 per cent in 1971) and more women stating that they have chosen to be childless. Against this, most young women still have ambitions to 'start a family' and have high expectations of the pleasures of bringing up children. Of the young women who were interviewed in Bristol who did not yet have children 89 per cent hoped to have them in the future (Bradley and Dermott 2006). Yet again, one is reminded of Firestone's sharp verdict that love lies at the core of gender inequalities (1971). Meanwhile, young men espouse more egalitarian ideals of marriage, and flounder about trying to be good fathers, but are also pressured by external cultures to take on the attitudes and practices of 'hegemonic masculinity'.

It seems, then, that Walby's view about women's escape from domesticity is overstated. True, it is easier nowadays to choose *not* to be a housewife or mother. But once the choice to have children is made, the old processes of gendering set in once again. Tony Chapman sums it up in his study of gender and domestic life:

> Cultural notions of masculinity and femininity run deep. Traditional ideas about marriage . . . continue to produce partnerships where men are older, earn more money and by definition have more say over many aspects of domestic life. And for

couples who want to have children conventional nuclear family forms remain a convenient option for many, because the traditional gender script helps women and men to decide who should do what. (2004: 206)

MEN AND ME: ARRANGEMENTS BETWEEN THE SEXES

In Charlotte Perkins Gilman's feminist Utopian novel, *Herland*, three young American men discover a society composed entirely of women. Terry is a dashing young Casanova, Jeff a sensitive man who idolizes women as the 'fair sex' and Van is a sociologist – who seeks an objective understanding of the strange society he has encountered. From a carefully cultivated genetic freak, there has evolved a race of women who give birth parthenogenetically. There is no longer any need for men amongst them. In this unisex society, women embody what we see as the attributes of both sexes – strength, scientific prowess, physicality alongside nurturing, kindness, dedication to beauty. The whole society is a collective dedication to Motherhood, but not motherhood as we know it and as described in previous chapters – the fierce and sometimes competitive commitment of a woman to her own children. Here, the love and commitment is given collectively to all society's children. There is no conception among the women of what we think of as a 'home' or a 'family'; there is no war, no conflict, no competition, no hierarchy to speak of; problems of resources are solved collectively to provide everybody with life's necessities, and a mixture of selective breeding and education have ensured that each woman has a superior and moral personality.

The thing that the young men find hard to grapple with at first (and Terry can never come to terms with) is the lack of the distinctively feminine and masculine, that bipolar world which I have described in earlier passages in this book. The women do not behave like women: they do not flirt, do not want to be looked after 'chivalrously' by men; they are independent, rational, don't understand the meaning of 'home'; they have no impulse to dance attendance on men qua men. Indeed, they have no concept, as Terry complains, of 'man', 'manliness' or masculine needs. They think of men only in terms of potential fatherhood. The outside world is, for them, an alternative model for bringing up children, one in which there are fathers instead of just mothers; the rest is outside their comprehension. They have no grasp of recreational as opposed to procreational sex (a difficulty Gilman struggles with in her narrative).

Gilman's attempt to portray a non-gendered world brings home to us the immense difficulty we face in thinking outside the bipolar box. We are so used to the idea of the sexes as Other, to masculinity and femininity as opposing 'sides', that the idea of the loss of gender is disturbing. Out of the Otherness, after all, comes the play of passion, tenderness, affection, desire, erotic possession that is our dominant contemporary mode of heterosexuality. Thus a big problem for heterosexual feminists has always been how to handle their relationships with men. Kitzinger and Wilkinson (two lesbians) edited a collection of pieces by feminists about being heterosexual (1992). In one chapter, two young women, Rosalind Gill and Rebecca Walker, speak of the contradictions in their personal struggles to reconcile feminism and romanticism, their sexual fantasies of 'being swept off their feet' by 'the knight in shining armour' being at odds with the ideals they hold of equality and female independence. The apparent dismissal of romantic heterosex, alongside the critique of masculinity, is the reason that so many women, especially in the younger generation, have rejected feminism and fear its logic. Here, I believe, is the crunch that lies at the heart of contemporary gender relations. Is it possible to reconstruct our versions of femininity and masculinity in a way that brings freedom to both sexes? And can we retain gendered pleasures while avoiding inequality? The second-wave feminists were insistent that the personal is political; but can there be a political solution to personal desires? One can sympathize with the second-wave feminists who decided their own solution was to adopt lesbianism as a political identity, as a way to avoid 'sleeping with the enemy'; and understand why there has been such a growth in single living; or why young lone mothers choose to raise a child on their own rather than marry a young man who is not seen as responsible enough to be a father or breadwinner. How can the sexes better live together?

Personally, I have been lucky in that all three of the men with whom I have had long-term relationships were to some degree 'New Men'. They liked the company of women, were prepared to share housework and cooking, sympathized with feminist ideals, took pride in my career accomplishments, made no attempt to push me into a domestic role. Of course there are many men like them, and many women who share my fortunate experience. But in the course of my life I have encountered the other forms of masculine behaviour: a boyfriend who demonstrated his masculinity through a chain of conquests; another who smashed up my house when I ended our relationship; a man who expected his wife (in full-time employment) to do all the cleaning and cooking and criticized her food whenever he considered it wasn't up to scratch; a doctor who told me that the cure to my health problems was to stop working and have a baby; a boss who flaunted his masculine power by telling me off loudly in front of a class of students; men at work resentful of a woman being in a position of authority over them and furious at being told what to do by her.

In general, my own experiences, like those of most of my acquaintances, point to a distinction between men in the public sphere and men as private individuals. When men are in groups, the hegemonic aspects of their masculinity tend to be displayed, as they seek to maintain their place in the patriarchal pecking order: senior men over junior men, heterosexual men over gay men, men over women. Their habitual doing of gender pushes them into competitive behaviour: sporting rivalry, claiming the streets as their territory and climbing the ladder at work are all part of masculine display. Women learn to fit themselves round these forms of behaviour, often appearing as audiences or support services. Watch men in a swimming pool: they swim wildly, using the more showy strokes, creating waves and knocking into other swimmers, while women stick carefully to their own lanes, swimming neatly, aware of other users. Or men at the bar, crowding round it, leaning elbows on it, talking loudly, shouting across the pub to other men, while women queue politely trying to catch the bar staff's notice. Journalist John Harris describes a typically twenty-first-century form of this masculine behaviour: the 'boom-voiced' business cell-phone user, 'yelling all that stuff about "being kept in the loop" and "touching base" into his phone before the train enters yet another tunnel'. Harris quotes American post-structural academic Thomas de Zengotita, who analyses these actions as 'performative habitualities'. Zengotita describes the plugged-in cell-phoners as displaying in their posture and vocalization 'a sense of throbbing connectedness to Something Important' (Harris 2005). Note that, of course, women can 'do masculine' too!

But what of men in private? Here things are different. For those of us in the West, imbued by western thinking, the search for 'Mr' or 'Miss Right' remains at the core of our subjective life experience. Love is still to most of us the most important thing in our lives, whether we find love with the other sex or our own sex, with our children or our families more generally. So how do men measure up as lovers and friends?

Social scientists have been traditionally wary of dealing with emotions, but more recently have begun to move into this area. Anthony Giddens's work, *The Transformation of Intimacy* (1992), has been particularly influential. Giddens coined the term 'pure relationship' to describe a peculiarly late modern form of intimacy which was detached or 'disembedded' from external relationships, such as family or community choices, and freed from economic considerations. The relationship is valued for its emotional content alone, as individuals seek a perfect match in terms of emotional and sexual compatibility. Giddens also speaks of 'plastic sexuality', where contraception has allowed sex to be effectively uncoupled from procreation, and where there is room for experiment, fantasy fulfilment and quest for sensation. This contrasts with the nature of marriage and love in pre-industrial societies or in the developing world, where marriages are to a considerable extent economic arrangements, set up by families, sanctioned and approved by the community and surrounded by religious ceremony and rites. Now soulmates' columns in newspapers and Internet chatlines have replaced the village matchmaker and the dowry.

But although the 'pure relationship' may be the ideal of men and women alike, as evidenced by the obsessive reporting of who is dating who in the celebrity magazines discussed in the next chapter, there are gendered difficulties here too. Just as men have become specialists in violence, as we shall see later, so women have become the specialists in emotion. Functionalist sociologists linked this to the reproductive and nurturing role, thus suggesting its inevitability. The constructionist position would point to the way girls and young women are trained to read emotions and cater for emotional needs from a young age. Think of all those magazines for teenage girls which instruct them in how to get and please a boyfriend. As we have seen, service jobs for women often involve emotional labour, while sociologists studying marriage have argued that here, too, it is women who have to perform the 'emotion work', keeping partners happy, managing conflict, being sensitive to moods and needs (Duncombe and Marsden 1993; Mansfield and Collard 1988).

Both women and men themselves see men as having difficulty in noticing, interpreting or expressing emotions (Seidler 1992; Whitehead 2002). Phillip Beadle, a 'super-teacher' who has become famous for his success in working with difficult adolescent boys, as portrayed in the television programme *The Unteachables*, talks of them as suffering from some of the characteristics of autism, the inability to empathize with others' feelings or even identify them. He reports on a test to demonstrate this: women and men are paired off and have to mime different human emotions using only facial expressions, while their partner guesses the emotions. Beadle found (2005) that men perform poorly at this task. As we have seen, men are trained from an early age to 'master' (telling term) and suppress their emotions.

The mother–daughter relationship, as psychoanalysts have pointed out, involves a close identification, and is characteristically strong and binding. Daughters may quarrel with their mothers during adolescence, as they assert their rights to freedom and sexual maturity, but the closeness is commonly restored as the young woman settles into adulthood. While fathers and sons often develop a strong bond, this is usually through doing things together (playing football, watching sports or washing the car) and not through sharing or discussing emotions. If the boy does not take to 'boys' things' the relationship can be strained and traumatic. Even where it is close, it is often unvocalized. One of the most poignant of popular songs is *The Living Years* by Mike and the Mechanics, where the singer expresses affection for his dead father and laments 'Oh I wish I could have told you, in the living years'. Men can carry around with them a crippling weight of unexpressed emotions accumulated over the years; in the men's groups formed in the 1980s, many men for the first time shared their intimate feelings with others.

In an excellent discussion, within a broadly poststructural framework, Stephen Whitehead (2002) explores men's private selves in relation to trust, intimacy, friendship and emotions. His broad conclusion is that all these are hard for men because of the deep anxieties they feel around their manhood and their sexuality, and also because of their desire to control. These factors make it difficult for men to let go, which Whitehead sees as a prerequisite for the achievement of real trust and intimacy. The fear of losing control means that men, while perpetually striving for love and intimacy, often fail to achieve them. Studies of married couples have presented depressing findings. Mansfield and Collard's research among 60 newly married couples (1988) found that soon after marriage the women expressed disappointment with the relationship because the emotional intimacy they craved for had not materialized; they complained that men would not discuss their feelings. A similar study by Duncombe and Marsden (1993) revealed that men could only express their intimacy through sexual intercourse, while for women, romantic expression and displays of affection were seen as the precursors to sex. Men demonstrated their commitment to the marriage by working to support the family, which in turn affected their ability to have time or energy for displays of intimacy to their partners or children. The absent father is an iconic figure in much fiction and autobiography.

Friendship is also paradoxical for men. From adolescence onward (if not before) they tend to go around in groups or gangs, while girls are more likely to have one or two 'best friends'. Although male friendship groups may spend hours in each other's company, this is once again about *doing* rather than talking. Exchanges within the group may take a physical form of playful punching, slapping and a lot of jokey name-calling, 'good to see you, you old bastard', and so forth. Thus, even in situations of warmth and companionship, embodied masculinity remains on display. Moreover, where friendship groups are heterosexual, there is a wariness about a display of emotionality which could be misinterpreted. Gay men, by contrast, are able to express more overt emotionality in groups, which allow them safely to express their identities, find protection from homophobia and also provide them with sexual partners (Nardi 1999).

It is easy surveying this literature to blame men for all the problems. However, they themselves can be victims. Something of a sensation was caused by Norah Vincent, who spent a year in New York masquerading as a man. Vincent was a lesbian, who already affected quite a boyish style. She made herself a beard, cut her hair in male fashion, bound her breasts, built up her frame by weightlifting and wore a prosthetic penis. Disguised as

'Ned' she hung around with a group of men on bowling nights, and chatted up and dated women. While she enjoyed the company of men on the Boys' Nights Out, Vincent found the experience of relating to women hard. Being rejected for a date was humiliating, and she found the women's chatter about their emotional lives trivial and boring and was dismayed at what she saw as the subtlety and force of women's sexual power. By contrast, 'Typical male power feels by comparison like a blunt instrument, its salvos and field strategies laughably remedial next to the damage a woman can do with a single cutting word: no' (2005: 27). As a result, she felt she could envisage how the experience of rejection could be twisted into retaliation in the form of misogyny and rape.

Vincent's account seems to ignore that women, too, experience rejection. As a masquerader, she may not truly have experienced the real force of confident male sexuality. Nevertheless her narrative highlights difficulties which many men may experience. She concluded that being a man was hard and expressed herself 'proud, free and glad in every way to be a woman' (ibid.: 27).

Given the importance of the 'pursuit of love' in contemporary societies (Whitehead 2002: 160), it must be in the interests of both men and women to work together to improve the arrangements between the sexes and achieve greater emotional security. But this seems hard to accomplish. More than one in three marriages in the UK end in divorce, with women filing the divorce petitions in the majority of cases (Pilcher 1999). Whitehead is sceptical about our ability to achieve the 'pure relationship' except in a transient sense, given the difficulties between the sexes: men's fears around emotionality and commitment, their difficulty in picking up 'emotional clues' and women's dissatisfaction with men's emotional unresponsiveness. Given the trends, Whitehead suggests that 'Friendships will come to provide the most constancy for individuals and, thus, possibilities for social change, particularly in an age when increasing numbers of women and men are choosing singledom and not coupledom' (2002: 161).

6
Gendered Worlds: Consumption

In this chapter we turn to the gendering of consumption. Like production and reproduction, the term 'consumption' has Marxian connotations, though Marx himself never provided any elaborated theory of it. But it takes its place in the Marxian scheme as the set of processes by which goods and services produced in the sphere of production are purchased and utilized. It is thus vital to the realization of profit. In the capitalist mode of production, consumption assumes a particular importance, as production capacity goes so far beyond the mere satisfaction of basic needs (food, clothing and shelter for subsistence). As later commentators such as Thorsten Veblen (1925) and Vance Packard (1957) argued, capitalism depends on a highly sophisticated manufacture and manipulation of needs, desires and anxieties, which makes people continually dissatisfied with what they have and wanting more. The 'more' can be status goods, such as cars, designer clothes and shoes, jewellery or luxury holidays; it can be perceived needs, or 'must-haves' in the current jargon, such as mobile phones, microwave ovens, leisure club memberships and iPods, things we got along without before but which are now seen as necessities; it can be things which we see as defining us as individuals (interior decorations, house-plants, CDs of our favourite music, collections of anything from antique teapots to Barbie dolls, new hairstyles, nail paintings); or things which we feel we need if we are going to cope adequately with life's demands (face creams, anti-wrinkle applicators, plastic surgery, botox injections, tamiflu stocks, vitamin pills, yoga sessions). Thus has developed the great edifice of contemporary consumer society.

While we are all consumers, the processes of consumption have been clearly gendered, if in different ways in different times and places. In capitalist industrial societies there has been a particular link between housewifery and consumption: while the man is out at the office or factory all day, it is the wife who holds the main responsibility for purchasing and consuming. Thus women have often been the key targets of advertising and marketing techniques. As the consumer market has grown more complex and sophisticated, men too have been targeted as consumers of particular goods and services, but these processes of 'niche marketing' remain highly sex-specific. As active consumers, too, women and men's activities and preferences are very different, especially if we turn to commercial leisure, now one of the major sources of capitalist profit. Leisure is discussed along with consumption in this chapter, since there is a school of thought which states that our identities are now more structured by what we do in our spare time than by our roles in the production system (Bauman 1992; 1998; Bocock 1993). Leisure, commercial and non-commercial, is also a major source of gender differentiation.

As we mentioned in chapter 5, Glucksmann's notion of the 'total social organisation of labour' (TSOL) can be expanded to include consumption. Glucksmann also draws upon the more orthodox Marxist terminology of production, exchange, distribution and consumption, a linked cycle of economic processes, which she suggests can be used as a 'lens' through which to view labour (2005: 26). She stresses overlap in the cycle. The boundaries between work and leisure are not always clear, while consumption itself involves a fair amount of work: housework, for example, includes shopping and cooking which are key consumption areas. Glucksmann thus proposes a new category of 'consumption work':

> Routine practices such as shopping, driving, grooming, and appreciating cultural goods, for example, may variously be interpreted as work, consumption and leisure. Buying and using goods and services commonly demands labour to be

undertaken in addition to whatever gratification, pleasure, fantasy or desire are also involved. (2005: 33)

Glucksmann points out that this 'consumption work' involves the use of skills, which may be similar to those used in production – for example, the configuration of a new computer, the assembly of flat-pack furniture or applying make-up for a party. Cooking is a good example of a form of skilled labour that straddles the spheres of production, reproduction and consumption: cooking as a job, cooking for family, cooking for a dinner party. Lury makes a similar point about linkage in relation to shopping:

> Shopping may be seen as an instance of consumption in relation to the cycle of commodity production (that is, production of goods for exchange in the market), but as a moment of production in relation to household or domestic production (for exchange in the family). What this dual location of shopping illustrates is the importance of looking at cycles or circuits of production and consumption. (1996: 123)

Shifts in the location of work (the increase of homeworking, the running of small enterprises from home, the birth of the 'mobile office') are also helping to blur the boundaries between production, reproduction and consumption, where the home may be the site of all three. Conversely, an interesting piece of research by Pettinger (2005) highlights the way that workplaces can be the site of consumption practices: especially for single people, employment can be a base for socializing, forming friendships and sexual partnerships. Pettinger's study of retail workers shows how their shared ideas about consumption (fashion, beauty, joint evenings) helped to bind them as a work team and was a key part of the attraction of the job. Pettinger studied small organizations; but as a kind of counterpart to the long hours' culture, some large corporations also provide more formal on-site consumption facilities, such as cafés, restaurants, gymnasiums, games rooms and sports facilities – even shops. The computer, with its Internet links, its music player stores and CD/DVD inputs next door to its office and word-processing programs, EXCEL, SAGE and other data storage and manipulation packages, is a potent and ubiquitous symbol of the fusion of production and consumption, work and entertainment. Leisure and consumption activities (playing in a band, making jewellery, hairdressing, artwork, painting and decorating, gardening) can also develop into wage-earning activities. But the ways in which these connections and linkages occur is highly gendered, as this chapter will show.

Gendered divisions of leisure and consumption

Consumption is a broad term. I use it here in its economic sense to mean the acquisition and usage of goods and services, which under the capitalist economic system take the form of commodities; that is, they are produced *first and foremost* to make a profit by means of exchange in the market, rather than because of their use value (though of course they may be useful too). However, as cultural studies theorists have pointed out, consumption is also a cultural process, in the sense that both the commodities and their usage become imbued with meaning for consumers (Featherstone 1991; Hollows 2000). This symbolic and meaningful nature of consumption has made it increasingly powerful in the formation of individual identities; these meanings and identities are deeply shaped by gender and class.

Perhaps the key issue in the gendering of modern consumption patterns was the historical switch from market selling to shopping. In tribal societies, where production was tightly geared to subsistence and surplus products were strictly limited, consumption was a hierarchical matter and lay chiefly in the hands of leaders and chiefs, who were normally men. The potlatch feasts of the Native American Indians and the *kula* exchange system observed by Malinowski (1922) in the Trobriand Islands (the ritual giving of coveted goods such as shells) are good examples of male-instituted consumption practices. In feudal and pre-modern societies, consumption was facilitated mainly by trade and through markets or bazaars. Gender roles varied in different societies, as they do in contemporary societies in which markets still predominate.

For example, in Africa today women play a major part in markets as both sellers and purchasers; in Islamic societies market stallholders are usually men, and women may or may not be involved in purchasing, depending on the strictness of rules of gender segregation. In craft production systems in pre-industrial Europe, the makers were usually also responsible for selling, and most 'craftsmen' were indeed men, but women might help on stalls and were themselves producers in certain areas, such as dairy produce, ale or embroidery and lace. So gender roles had a degree of fluidity within a producer household and were quite complex.

The big change in consumption is seen to have occurred in the mid-nineteenth century, with the emergence of the department store (Chaney 1983; Hollows 2000). This development consolidated the role of women as consumers in industrial societies. Since middle-class women had been largely pushed out of their productive roles by this juncture, they had the time, inclination and resources to become expert shoppers. Thus shopping became identified as a female activity, highly linked to the housewife role. This subsequently became the case in working-class families as well, and in the first half of the twentieth century in Britain shopping became mainly women's business. According to Lury (1996), women are responsible for implementing 80 per cent of consumption decisions; shopping now takes up the equivalent of a full day a week as compared to two hours in the 1920s, since the range of goods on offer and the types of retail outlet have expanded greatly. The task of consumption and housework has been elaborated over the century. Maintaining the house has moved beyond keeping things clean and tidy and the simple provision of food to determining the style of the house, the presentation of food and of living space. As Lury explains, housework has become an aesthetic and emotional form of work as well as a care-taking one. The woman must present the home as an expression of her individuality and labour on the presentation of her appearance and that of her children. Finally, she must cater for their emotional needs and those of her partner.

Some argue that changes in the last few decades of the twentieth century drew men more into shopping. The emergence of the 'New Man' ideal in the 1980s involved attempts by advertisers such as Next and Levi Strauss to include men in the consumer market for fashion (Mort 1996; Nixon 1996). 'New Man' was presented as much more body- and appearance-conscious, so that trendy clothing and beauty products could be aimed at him. Magazines for men, such as *The Face* and *Arena*, produced stylized images of men's clothing and bodies comparable to those in the longstanding women's fashion magazines such as *Vogue* and *Elle* (Mort 1996). Men took to the catwalk in increasing numbers alongside female models at designer houses like Gaultier and Comme des Garçons (Nixon 1996). Mort interprets this as an attempt to create a distinctive market aimed at young men, and points out that the magazines and advertising companies involved specifically recruited young men to develop their campaigns. The end result, suggests Mort, was 'the portrayal of the world as a masculine playground' (1996: 82). This trend has continued into the 'laddish' culture of the 1990s and 2000s, exemplified by *Zoo, Nuts* and *Loaded*.

By the start of the twenty-first century, the days were receding when wives and mothers shopped for their menfolk's clothing at Marks and Spencer or knitted them baggy jumpers for Christmas! Manufacturers faced with heightened global competition were also moving towards the identification of specialist niche markets. Greater involvement of women in the labour market meant that they had less time to shop during the day, which led stores to change their opening hours and include more evening shifts and full weekends. This in turn meant men were more able to participate in shopping. Nixon (1996), developing Walter Benjamin's ideas about the development of spectacular consumption and the *flâneur*, the voyeuristic consumer of the modern city experience, argues that the commercialization around the idea of the New Man created a new mode of representation of masculinity. This drew young men more deeply into the spectacle of shopping.

However, the type of shopping done by men and women is still different. Women (sometimes accompanied by partners) continue to do more of the domestic-oriented shopping (for food and household goods). Though men buy their own clothes more than in the past, they tend to do so in specialist men's shops. Women are more likely to use department stores as well as boutiques and are responsible for buying young children's clothes. Men shop for their personal leisure consumption (CDs, electronics). But it is women who go on 'shopping expeditions', while men's shopping tends to be briefer, more focused and more pragmatic. When I was in New York recently on a weekday, I visited the famous Bloomingdales. In its restaurant 'The Blue Express' (shaped like a train carriage) I sat among the 'ladies who lunch': who are also the 'ladies who shop'. Thorsten Veblen coined the word 'conspicuous consumption' to describe the lavish display of wealth and expensive goods to affirm one's status or power. Conspicuous consumption is not new: as mentioned earlier, it was the habit of tribal chiefs and later on of monarchs and aristocrats ('the field of the cloth of gold') demonstrating their social dominance. Now women typically take the lead in consuming conspicuously as a mark of their success, through shopping: wives of the rich and famous, such as Victoria Beckham and Colleen McLoughlin, Imelda Marcos and Ivana Trump, or women famous in their own right, such as Kate Moss or Madonna.

Not only is shopping a gendered activity, shops are also gendered spaces. Contrast a fashion boutique with an electronics store. The latter is staffed by men, and spaces are hard-edged, organized to show the goods in a functional way. In the boutique the staff will be highly groomed young women, often wearing some of the shop's merchandise; goods are draped decoratively around in the manner of a boudoir, tempting people to look and finger the materials. The shop is colourful and highly 'dressed', angled to tempt women in to spend time and browse, in contrast to the electronics shops where most goods are prepackaged in boxes or transparent plastic bubbles so that they can be seen but not tried out. It has been noted that the boutiques are careful in the usage of mirrors, choosing ones that emphasize body length not width.

The gendering of staff in shops has a long history (Bradley 1989) and reflects the owners' perceptions of their customers' gender and needs. The assistant in the electronics shop needs to be technically knowledgeable and able to give advice about specifications and usage. The young women in the boutique are there to give the association with glamour and provide advice about colour, shape and fit, if a female friend or family member is not there. Such shops are unfriendly to men, who hover nervously outside changing rooms, longing to escape to the nearby disc store. Similarly, women may feel out of place in the modern DIY outlets, where salesmen experienced in the construction industry discuss tools and techniques with male customers, before picking the goods from the storage racks behind the counters.

Consumption is not confined to shopping, so let us turn to leisure, which is also gendered. From the nineteenth century onwards, married women with children have had less leisure than men, unless they belonged to the more affluent classes when they might literally become 'ladies of leisure'. This is because the housewife role has no clearly defined limits, unlike paid employment; habitually, when the man leaves his workplace his time is 'his own', to be spent watching television, going to the pub, watching sport or indulging in his hobbies. The wife, however, must see to the evening meal, put the children to bed, prepare everything for next day's departures. The rise of women's paid employment did not mean that they gained a similar leisure entitlement, because of the existence of the double burden – or the 'second shift', as Hochschild labelled it (1989).

Of course these domestic constraints on leisure do not affect single women to the same extent, but there is another type of constraint that is shared by almost all women: the restrictions they face in the use of public space. Men's leisure has characteristically involved the outdoors. Young men are visible presences on the street, often with strong territorial attachments. But for women, the street, particularly at night, is a dangerous and in many societies a forbidden place. It is significant that one term for prostitutes is 'streetwalkers', or that we talk of prostitution as 'going on the streets'. Historically, men have worked quite hard to keep women from public venues. In strict Islamic societies women cannot enter the public realm unless accompanied by a male relative. In the West, women's use of public space is limited by the fear of harassment or attack. Travelling alone opens women to abuse. It is still considered not quite normal for women to enter pubs if they are on their own, though a group of women may be more confident to do so. Newspaper stories of rape and murder play a potent part in keeping women in line. It is in this sense that second-wave feminists made the controversial statement that 'all men are rapists'. It is not that this is literally the case, but any man who is a stranger to a woman may potentially be an attacker.

Thus women voluntarily put limits on where and when they go out in a way that men rarely consider doing. This restriction is compounded by the fact that, until very recently, women were much less likely to have access to a car. In 1975 just over 40 per cent of women aged 30–49 held a driving licence compared to over 80 per cent of men in the age group. Since then the gap has diminished, but in every age group a higher proportion of men hold licences (Social Trends 36, 2005).

Rosemary Deem, in a classic study of women's leisure based on research carried out in Milton Keynes, summarized the constraints put on women's leisure as follows:

> For women, 'safe' out-of-home leisure spent alone or with female friends or relatives generally means going where there are other women, good transport and few or no men. Public or community leisure, then, is less available to women than to men. Additionally some of what appears to be women's out-of-home leisure may be nothing of the sort. When I was researching leisure-centre use in Milton Keynes, I found that many of the women ostensibly using such centres were not actually doing so – they were accompanying their children, who were the main users of the facilities. (1986: 7)

Finally, the actual leisure activities undertaken by men and women are different. Men's leisure tends to revolve round sport, with drinking (especially in pubs and clubs) as a popular sub-theme. In 2002, 40 per cent of men had taken part in an organized sports competition over the past year as compared to 14 per cent of women. Men comprise 75 per cent of members of British sporting organizations (the only area in which women dominate is gymnastics) (Social Trends 36, 2005). The importance of sport in many men's lives cannot be underestimated: it is a source of emotional attachment, belonging and identity; it is the site of bonding with other men; and engaging in sport, whether as player or as spectator, is, as we saw earlier, an important way in which men assert and display their masculinity. Moreover, the popularity and media preoccupation with men's sports (football, boxing, rugby) as opposed to women's sports (hockey, netball) acts as a symbolic representation of men's social dominance: what men do is exciting, important and of central interest.

Talbot (1979), surveying data on women's leisure back in the 1970s, noted that women were involved in a narrower range of activities than men. In fact, women's leisure tends to revolve around interaction rather than activities. Chatting with friends is a key 'female pleasure'. Teenage women develop their own 'bedroom culture' (McRobbie 1991) with their best friends, sharing gossip and secrets, trying out make-up, clothes and hairstyles. Only a minority join the boys in the street or on the playing field. For a brief period, as part of a heterosexual couple, young women and men may share in leisure (films, clubbing, shopping) until the family circumstances compel women into accepting less personal free time. Among older women, the most popular activities are the indoor ones: reading, watching TV, knitting and sewing. Even the sports most popular with women (yoga, swimming and dancing) are indoor ones. At its most extreme, as has been reported of various working-class communities, men and women can occupy two virtually separate leisure worlds (Kerr 1958).

Gendered bodies

At the symbolic level, this difference between women and men's leisure and consumption patterns is exemplified in the imagery associated with their bodies. The ideal male body is that of a sportsman, hard, well built and muscular: witness the extreme popularity among young men of gym routines and weightlifting to develop the famed six-pack of taut abdominal muscles. Women's bodies, by contrast, are sexualized, displayed scantily clad, and the ideal is of thinness taken sometimes to positively unhealthy extremes. The constant glamorization of women's bodies and their prevalence across all forms of media as 'objects of desire' puts considerable pressure on women and has been a major theme in feminist research (Bartky 1990; Bordo 1993; Grosz 1994; Martin 1987). The presentation of women's bodies to male observers and the implication that the purpose of female physicality is to please men has been viewed as a key aspect of male social domination.

Surveys repeatedly show that the majority of women in America and Britain are unhappy with their bodies and appearance. Studies show that between a half and three-quarters of women have dieted because of dissatisfaction with their weight (Frost 2001; Pilcher 1999). Frost describes this as 'body-hatred', a set of negative emotions that tends to emerge with puberty. Roberts (2004) reports on a survey of 3,000 women in 10 countries carried out by the cosmetic company Dove, which ran an advertising campaign to promote the idea that beauty can take diverse forms. The survey found that half the women felt 'disgusted' by their own bodies. As Emily Martin (1987) has powerfully argued, the consumerist objectification of women's bodies results in women becoming alienated from their own bodies: they, too, see them as objects, external to their 'selves', indeed dismal and unruly objects which need to be disciplined and beaten into shape. These negative feelings have resulted in the ter-rible rise of eating disorders, anorexia and bulimia, in young girls and women (and some young men) (Bordo 1993). Roberts (2004) points out that preoccupation with their bodies can lead women to feel isolated and helpless because of negative self-images. This echoes the arguments of Naomi Wolf in *The Beauty Myth* (1990) that competitive rivalry among women undermines the impulse for collective action to secure gender equality. Misery is blamed on the self, its inability to resist the temptations of food, its weakness in sticking to regimes, and attention is drawn away from the social arrangements which act to disadvantage and demoral-ize women.

All this is reflected in the obsession with dieting and with the range of beauty products and services designed to alter bodies and improve appearance. Women's bodies are the targets of major commercial enterprise, with persistent adver-tising for shampoos, hair dyes, cosmetics, 'because you're worth it!'. All these play on women's anxieties about their appearance and self-image, especially young women. The targets of advertising are broadening in their scope: 63 per cent of 7–9-year-old girls wear lipstick (Bowcott 2004) and a barrage of products are designed to cater for older women's concern about their 'wrinkles'.

Perhaps the most startling phenomenon is the rise of plastic surgery. What used to be a rare procedure, undertaken mainly by actresses whose livelihoods depended on their beauty or people with major deformities or injuries, has now become a mass commodity, with pages of advertisements in women's magazines offering an increasing range of options. Plastic surgery offers the lure of perfection. *Grazia* magazine interviewed 1,000 women across the UK and found that 11 per cent had undergone cosmetic surgery (nose jobs, line removals, botox injections, breast extensions) and 54 per cent intended to have it in the future (*Guardian*, 12 July 2005). In the United States the number of breast augmentations per year rose from 32,607 in 1992 to 264,041 in 2004, an increase of more than 700 per cent (Levy 2005). Women are even being tempted to have genital surgery to construct a perfect vagina and improve their sexual performance and desirability. Thus women's dissatisfaction with their bodies is perpetually provoked and exploited for profit.

Susie Orbach argues that this kind of body hatred is now being exported from western societies to the developing world. She provides some examples: three years after television was introduced to Fiji, an epidemic of bulimia broke out among young girls, affecting 12 per cent of teenagers; in Iran, 35,000 women have had their noses reshaped (Orbach 2005). Plastic surgery is also booming in Japan, while the *Times* of India reported on how women were responding to mid-life crises, marked by 'empty nest' syndrome, straying husbands and declining fertility in a country preoccupied by having children, by turning to 'toy boys, botox kitty parties, shopping fiestas'. The paper reports a boom in anti-ageing clinics, fitness trainers and in gym attendance among older women, and cites the case of a 42-year-old lawyer, Namita Mehra, who used her wealth for a facelift: 'I want to feel young again. Why should only men at 40 have affairs and great sex? I just went out, got myself a new face after the plastic surgeon worked on my face for hours. Soon I had these young boys vying for my attention' (Walia 2005).

Discourses of consumerism: housewifery, slenderness and celebrity

Namita Mehra's tale encapsulates the major thrust of the discourse of consumerism, which arguably holds most of the capitalist world in its thrall. The discourse targets us all, women and men, and its message is relentless: spend, spend, spend is the way to happiness. Cheer up your drab life by purchasing the latest trendy products, the 'must-have' handbag or iPod nano. Faced with the dissatisfactions of growing older, the wealthy Indian woman can buy herself back into self-satisfaction. No wonder we speak ironically of 'retail therapy'.

The key driver of the consumer discourse has been America. The spread of American culture and way of life throughout the world, what George Ritzer (1993) calls the 'McDonaldization of society', and the long reach of the global corporations have ensured that we are all of us, wherever we may reside, increasingly bombarded by advertisements, sellers, cold-callers pressurizing us to spend. The Internet has extended the global reach of consumption and brought with it new modes of purchasing and selling (e-Bay, Amazon, online travel). The credit card industry fuels consumerism, trapping increasing numbers of people in debt. Orbach (2005) links consumerism to globalization: 'What binds people together in the global village is an ability to identify with and recognise one another speedily through consumerism and specifically through the brands, clothes, food and music we wear, eat or listen to'. This kind of shared consumerism can leap over barriers of ethnicity, nationality and politics, pulling the world's divided peoples together in shared aspirations for status goods. Similarly, Marxists argue that the ideology of consumerism, which posits us all as greedy striving individuals, overrides distinctions of class and gender generated in the spheres of production and reproduction. Consumption induces a false consciousness of equality.

While all this applies equally to both sexes, Orbach emphasizes the special place of the objectified female body in the imagery of consumerism. Scantily clad women are used to advertise and tempt men and women into consuming: 'In this global market place, a woman's body shape has itself become a brand, her brand, her membership and entitlement to occupy space'.

The turning of useful goods and services into consumable commodities has become increasingly linked to the commodification of female (and sometimes male) bodies. This can be seen in the massive burgeoning of all forms of pornography, the prevalence of prostitution, the rise of telephone sex chat-lines and upmarket strip clubs such as Spearmint Rhino, and the global organization of all aspects of the sex industry through illegal trafficking of women, especially from deprived parts of Africa and the former Soviet bloc.

One specific strand of the consumerist discourse concerns the role of the housewife, mentioned earlier. This was closely related to the discourses of the male breadwinner and of domesticity discussed in the previous two chapters. It is worth considering the historical evolution of this discourse, as explored by historians (Clark 1982; Hall 1980). The idea developed in pre-industrial England and was a powerful one. Housewifery was a set of skills, and the housewife a woman in command of her household, often directing the labour of servants. Such a woman would commend herself as a marriage partner for a successful man. However, as we saw earlier, the coming of industrialization led to the splitting up of public and private, work and home, production and consumption (Hamilton 1978). Thus a shift occurred from the housewife-as-producer to the housewife-as-consumer.

Veblen (1925) highlighted the role of middle-class women of the 'leisure class' in this process. Their function became primarily one of signifying and maintaining their husband's status (Edwards 2000). Theirs was the responsibility for maintaining and styling their house and possessions as markers of the man's standing. As the male-dominated trade unions developed the campaign for the family wage, it became a sign of prosperity and success for working-class men, too, to keep their wives out of employment. Thus evolved the cult of the 'dependent' but decorative housewife in the early twentieth century. The evolution of the housewife role was temporarily disrupted by both the world wars, when the economic needs of the state drew women into jobs to replace men away at the front and into the 'war effort'. However, the strength of the housewife discourse was consolidated in the 1930s by the implementation of a marriage bar in many occupations, such as teaching and the civil service.

Temporary affluence after the Second World War led to a more voluntary withdrawal of married women from the labour market, and arguably the cult of the housewife reached its apogee in the 1950s and 1960s. Women married earlier and dedicated themselves to homemaking; but ironically this led to malaise and dissatisfaction, 'the disease without a name' identified by Betty Friedan (1963). Her path-breaking book *The Feminine Mystique* holds a significant place in the narrative of the American feminist movement.

Following Friedan, second-wave feminists tended to view domestic labour as an oppressive burden and demanded that women should be liberated from it. There is considerable dispute over this. Levitas (1998) points out how nineteenth-century socialists and feminists took the same view that housework was trivializing and demeaned the status of women. A characteristic solution was to suggest that it should be collectivized, so that the burden of work was removed from individual households and women. Since this failed to happen, the view of consumption as trivial, frivolous and soft-centred, compared to the serious masculine world of production, persisted. The link between consumption and women thus established femininity as trivial and impulsive. As Hollows points out, the figure of the consumer-housewife 'enslaved by her desire for goods' (2000: 115) has been contrasted to that of the rational, efficient, active masculine figure. The housewife as portrayed in *The Feminine Mystique* is impulsive, irrational, childish, dependent and easily manipulated. Friedan cites an advertiser's view of the female consumer: 'American housewives can be given the sense of identity, purpose, creativity, the self-realisation, even the sexual joy they lack by the buying of things' (Friedan, quoted in Lury 1996: 129).

More recently, there have been attempts to rehabilitate the figure of the consumer-housewife. In a study of Victorian homemaking, Branca (1975) presents the full-time housewife as a pioneer of modernity, working alongside the male entrepreneur to construct the brave new world of consumer capitalism. The emphasis here is on the new kind of skills and technologies that the woman had to master as house-wifery was reconstructed. The role of the creative consumer has also been celebrated by postmodernists, who have called for the re-evaluation of 'female pleasures'. Although this approach may risk romanticizing housewifery and consumption, there is a germ of truth here. Levitas (1998) points out that at the core of domestic labour there are caring and nurturing tasks that are absolutely essential to social and individual well-being. She calls for these skills to be acknowledged: indeed, the re-evaluation of whatever is seen as 'women's work' is becoming a central objective for contemporary feminism.

Two other discursive frameworks of more recent origin may be briefly mentioned here, which target younger cohorts of women. The first is the discourse of slenderness, which has become presented as the paradigmatic condition of feminine beauty. Fashion models have become increasingly skinny and childlike, with Kate Moss, once a prime purveyor of the style nicknamed 'heroin chic', portrayed as the most important icon of the fashion scene. The obsession with size and weight legitimizes the massive commercial apparatus of the slimming and exercise industry. Ironically, it has been noted that it is women themselves who police the cult of slenderness: women criticizing other women's clothing and figures; women's magazine editors who commission endless articles on diet and exercise; and the catty commentators of celebrity magazines such as *Heat* and *Hello* who take delight in pictures of female stars wearing unbecoming clothes, having 'bad hair days' or showing glimpses of cellulite.

The idea of celebrity is one that appears also to have taken hold of a younger generation and provides an interesting take on desirable gender roles. Male celebrities are footballers, pop stars and 'hunks' from Hollywood; female celebrities are models and society girls, soap stars and actresses. The perfect – read slender – body is a prerequisite for female celebrity, and the stream of occasions when celebrities are on display (Oscars and BAFTAs, fashion weeks in London, Paris and New York, film premieres and musical galas and festivals) feature a predictable parade of revealing haute couture gowns, cleavages and flashes of thighs or midriff. The message to young women is remorseless: sexiness and beauty are the keys to success. Although body image is perhaps also increasingly an element of male celebrity, the array of prized attributes is greater. George Clooney may set a million female hearts beating, but he is also a skilled actor, director and scriptwriter, as well as, increasingly, a political activist and social critic. Pamela Anderson, Jordan and Jodie Marsh are famous simply for their physical attributes – natural and enhanced – and their nebulously constructed 'personalities'. But the lack of real cultural or creative talent is precisely what gives the discourse of celebrity such a bite. As Andy Warhol said, we can all aspire to be famous for five minutes. The extraordinary example of Chantelle, the non-celebrity who won *Celebrity Big Brother*, explains the lure of consumerist celebrity: capitalism says to us what Chantelle's mother famously cried out to her: 'Live the Dream!'

Consuming at the micro-level: households and cultures

Consumption appears to be an area where individual choice is paramount, but, as we have seen, choices are gendered. What are the interactive processes which help structure these choices? As with productive and reproductive work, consumption work is partly learned in the household. Class is important here: consumption patterns are shaped by income, but also by cultural norms. Thus high-earning socio-economic groups – employers, managers and professionals – are more likely to be active consumers of social, cultural and sporting events. 'Elite' modes of consumption – art, classical music, opera, fine wines and gourmet food – are tastes first learned in the family. A gender element may be introduced here: young men and women are likely to adopt many consumption practices from their parents. For example, men help their sons practise sporting skills, while mothers often assist in grooming their daughters to acquire socially desired attributes of appearance in their particular milieu. Mothers take daughters shopping for clothes and pass on to them the techniques of housewifery. Conventional practices of socialization are key here, too: toys and games remain highly gender-specific, with boys channelled towards vehicles, construction toys and juvenile versions of adult sports, while girls receive dolls and doll's houses, cuddly animals, jewellery kits and princess outfits. It is hard for individual parents to resist these trends to gendering, since they are so culturally widespread, and are reinforced constantly in presentations of gender in the media, as well as in the marketing of toys.

However, as consumption practices are also highly age-specific, peer groups and cultures play a key role. Historically, youth cultures have been male-dominated, with young men setting the cultural styles (skinheads, mods and rockers, punks, goths) and women playing a supporting role as hangers on (Hebdige 1979; Brake 1980). As already mentioned, male subcultures tended to be centred on the street, while young women's activities were quieter, based on homes and shopping. The tighter control exercised by parents on girls may have channelled them into home pursuits. But recently there has been a shift, with women playing a more conspicuous part in the public arena, in a way which might be seen to challenge male control of public space.

Ariel Levy has described one version of this in her bestselling book *Female Chauvinist Pigs* (2005). She describes the development among young American women of a highly explicit sexual 'raunch culture', in which young women use their bodies deliberately to titillate men. The exemplar she uses is a TV programme called *Girls Go Wild*, in which young women are egged on to flash their breasts, buttocks and pubic areas to male spectators and viewers. Similarly, young girls at high school compete to display as much of their bodies as possible in cropped tops and micro-skirts, eager to be the 'hottest' and 'flirtiest' among their classmates. Young women interviewed by Levy cited porn stars, pole dancers and strippers as their heroines and role models. All this is vindicated as a demonstration of women's freedom to enjoy their own sexuality and to have fun; sexual display is seen as a form of empowerment for women. But Levy argues that the ultimate goal of all this freedom and power is simply to please men and cater to their sexual fantasies. What is the real freedom in learning to strip or pole dance? As Levy puts it:

While Janet Jackson introduced Americans to her right nipple at the notorious 2004 Super Bowl half-time show, Justin Timberlake's wardrobe managed not to malfunction. Not one male Olympian has found it necessary to show us his penis in the pages of a magazine. Proving that you are hot, worthy of lust, and – necessarily – that you seek to provoke lust remains women's work. (2005: 33)

Paris Hilton, whom Levy sees as the embodiment of raunch culture, described herself as 'sexy not sexual' (ibid.: 30). Oddly enough, being 'hot' (which Levy defines as being 'fuckable and saleable': ibid.: 31) is not equivalent to sexual satisfaction. Yvonne Roberts (2005) reports on an American survey of 18–29-year-old young women which found that 27 per cent got little pleasure from sex, seeing it as a 'necessary ordeal'. Similarly, the 'hot' young women interviewed by Levy seemed apathetic about sex itself, experiencing it mainly as something to confirm their desirability to men, and something that men wanted. Interestingly, the American research suggested that sexual enjoyment is at its height among the over-50s – an age at which the quest to be 'hot' has normally been abandoned as futile and people are more interested in affection and sensation than appearance.

Natasha Walter (2006) has taken up the crusade against what she describes as 'cultural sexism' (the spread of pornography and the kind of sexual display and interplay by women featured on 'reality TV' programmes) in the British context. She claims that young women she has talked to were deeply depressed by 'our Nuts-and-Loaded culture which suggests that their only chance of fulfilment and empowerment is through pandering to the so-called ironic fantasies of chortling men'. Like Levy, Walter is critical of postmodern feminists who have advocated sexual liberalism and the enjoyment of 'female pleasures' as part of a refocused movement of gender liberation. Too much focus on the body and sexuality has led young women to believe that sexual freedom is the be-all and end-all of gender equality.

Levy, Walter and their supporters are possibly offering an exaggerated account of the spread of raunch and porn culture. On a recent visit to an American university campus, I noted how sensibly and decorously the young women students were dressed compared to some of those at my own British university. There are plenty of young women, especially those from minority ethnic backgrounds, who are offended by blatant sexual display and steer clear of it. Young Muslim women explicitly choose to veil themselves, as they deplore the thought of becoming sex objects. There are many ways of 'doing gender' as a young woman, and raunch is only one of them.

Elsewhere (Bradley 1999a), I have argued that sexual power is one form of resource women can use in their struggles for equality. This has always been the case and can be a significant source of power for individual women. Selling sex has, throughout history, been a subsistence strategy available to women, however much we might deplore the fact that this can be a necessary or profitable option. We should welcome any resource which enables women to escape from poverty and total dependency. However, the use of sexual power results in gains for individuals not for the body of women, and the gains are too often at the expense of other women.

I have dwelt at length on 'raunch culture', despite believing that it is not a majority phenomenon, because it seems to me indicative of what may happen when strict boundaries established by gender roles and rules are challenged: women take on practices and behaviours defined as 'masculine' and not the other way round. Our own British brand of raunchy young women were nicknamed 'ladettes' by the media, while Levy's interviewees spoke of being 'one of the boys' and distancing themselves from 'girly girls'. Levy also discusses a new group of lesbians who call themselves 'bois'; their ideal is to 'play' at sex and flirtation, to have fun, avoiding long-term serious commitments, thus mimicking the behaviour of young gay and heterosexual 'boys'.

We can see this in another British consumption trend among young women: their participation in 'binge culture', bouts of heavy public drinking. While young men have long been in the habit of drinking themselves silly and cavorting in the streets after receiving their pay packets, the involvement of young women, including many from middle-class families, in these practices has provoked a new moral panic. Coverage has featured pictures of provocatively dressed young women staggering about and vomiting in city centres. This trend is backed by statistics: between 1988 and 2002 the proportion of women in the 16–24 age group exceeding the recommended maximum weekly drinking level rose from 15 to 33 per cent (<www.statistics.gov.uk>). During the same period, the proportion of young women binge drinkers (defined as drinking large amounts of alcohol on a single occasion) rose from 24 to 28 per cent, while among young men it fell from 39 to 35 per cent. These figures were the highest in Europe apart from the Netherlands and Ireland.

Young women do seem to be taking on more aspects of stereotypically male behaviour. The World Health Organization (WHO) found recently that British adolescents were among the most violent in the world, with nearly a third of girls (29 per cent) and two-thirds of boys (59 per cent) reporting that they had been involved in a fight in the past year. While this again can be interpreted as young women gaining the freedom to express themselves in a way that their brothers have long had, freedom does not seem to have brought happiness. Surveys by *Bliss* magazine and by the Institute of Psychiatry and King's College London revealed increasing levels of emotional distress among teenage girls. They felt pressured both at home and at school, were adversely affected by family break-ups, felt immense pressure to look good and reported using drink and drugs to offset their unhappiness (Ward 2005). Gender troubles, it seems, are not resolved by 'acting like a man'. Perhaps what we really need is for more young men to adopt the quieter aspects of feminine behaviour.

Conclusions: gendered consumers

While consumption is portrayed to us as the realm of freedom, independence, choice and fulfilment, this is, to a degree, illusory. Consumption choices are shaped and constrained by class and gender, as this chapter has shown. The identification of women with consumption has only contributed to their secondary social status.

I have shown that patterns of consumption are, as TSOL theory suggests, highly linked to relations of production and reproduction; women's marginalization as producers and prime responsibility for reproductive labour has informed the differentiated patterns of consumption and leisure outlined in this chapter. These patterns are supported not only by the general discourse of consumerism, but also by the gender-specific discourses of housewifery, slenderness and celebrity. These discourses frame the way women make their consumer choices and are implicated in the way contemporary femininities are construed. Interactions in the home and among peer friendship groups steer young men and women towards consumption and leisure activities that are seen as gender-appropriate. Cultural norms about beauty and sexual desirability are deeply internalized by young women and men.

But we have noted that a significant group of younger women are resisting traditional pressures and developing cultural and consumption styles that imitate those of young men. This development can be viewed positively as a breaking down of taboos that constrained young women's behaviour, or negatively as a mistaken view that sexual permissiveness equates to gender equality. Whatever the interpretation, it is a useful illustration of the fact that movements towards gender neutrality characteristically involve women becoming 'more like a man' and not men becoming more like women.

There can be no doubt that for many women their consumer and leisure identities are an important form of 'female pleasure' which they would be reluctant to give up: fashion and beauty, shopping and going out on the spree with girl-friends may help to compensate for lowly paid employment or provide an escape from the daily routine of housework. But can gender equality be achieved by equality in consumption? The Conclusion will address political problems of inequality and exclusion caused by the gendering of production and reproduction. It is true that some very wealthy, very talented or very beautiful women can buy themselves out of these problems. But this is not possible for the majority. Middle-class Victorian women took to feminism as a way to get themselves out of the 'gilded cage'. It seems that we are all too willing to step back into it!

IT DOESN'T HAVE TO BE THIS WAY: GENDERED UTOPIAS

On the evening of 1 January 2006, university student Katharine Horton took a stroll down Lamai Beach at Koh Samui in Thailand to make a call to her mother on her mobile phone. There she was attacked by two young local fishermen who had swum ashore from their boat after an evening spent drinking and watching pornographic videos. She was hit on the head, raped and her body dumped in the sea, where it was discovered the next morning.

I have used Katharine Horton's story to initiate a discussion of what sociologist Jeff Hearn has called 'the violences of men' (1998) because it illustrates so well many of the key gender issues related to violence against women. It exemplifies the danger that women confront, consciously and unconsciously, when they venture out into the public sphere, especially in an unfamiliar context. This constricts women's use of public leisure as discussed in chapter 6; it confines many single women, especially older ones, within their homes. Moreover, the threat of rape or sexual assault is used both as a mechanism of social control, to keep women 'in their place', and is also a reason for women to become dependent on male protectors, partners or relatives. In many societies adult women can only enter public space in the company of such a protector.

In the many discussions of violence against women, the role of pornography has been a major bone of contention. Radical second-wave feminist Robin Morgan famously declared that 'pornography is the theory, rape is the practice' (1980: 128). The view that pornography, in presenting women as eagerly available for men's pleasure, did not only demean women but also incited men to violence was held by many radical feminists. Two of them, Andrea Dworkin and Catharine MacKinnon, initiated a failed attempt to get an Ordinance making pornography illegal accepted in the American cities of Minneapolis and Indianapolis (Bryson 1999; Levy 2005). Against this, liberals and sex radicals argued that censorship was an infringement of individual rights and that pornography had positive functions and educational value. The involvement of young women in the flourishing industry of pornography, as producers, employees and consumers, was highlighted, and the idea of a direct link between pornography and sexual violence was challenged. The ensuing intellectual divide between the Campaign Against Pornography and Feminists Against Censorship had the same corrosive effect on the American feminist movement that the debate over ethnicity had in Britain. However, the Horton case confirms my own view that there is a causal link, albeit not a simple direct one, between the consumption of pornography and the prevalence in a sophisticated globalized world of high levels of sexual violence against women.

Katharine Horton's tragic death also is emblematic to me of the limits of gender equality in the lives of young women. This new generation have been described as post-feminist, and indeed in my contacts with them many have said that they see gender discrimination as a thing of the past. They think equality has been achieved. This gives young women the confidence to demand their shares of social pleasures, in the belief that the world is their oyster, there to be enjoyed. But, as women like Horton find when they step out into that world on their own, things are darker and more complex.

Lest I seem to be making too much out of a single example, it is worth considering what we know of the prevalence of violence against women. Accurate statistics are difficult to obtain, because the stigma and fear which surround sexual and domestic violence lead to much of it going unreported. Thus statistics are often estimates, on the basis of self-report surveys and official crime reporting. According to the British Crime Survey estimates, 47,000 women are raped every year. Only 20 per cent of reported rapes go to trial, and of these only a fifth or so result in a conviction. Experts estimate that one in four women experience domestic violence over a lifetime (Women's Aid 2005). The 2004 British Crime Survey reported an estimated 12.9 million incidents over the course of a year against women, plus 2.5 million against men (Walby and Allen 2004). These figures seem even more horrendous when expressed in another way: as Stanko (2000) estimates, in the UK an act of male domestic violence towards a woman occurs every 30 seconds.

We must note that men suffer domestic violence as well; nevertheless the vast majority of cases are by male perpetrators (including attacks on other men). A report for the ESRC, which was based on monitoring calls made to the police on one day in 2000, found that 81 per cent were from women attacked by men, 8 per cent men attacked by women, 4 per cent women attacked by women and 7 per cent men attacked by men (Stanko 2000). More than 100 women in Britain are killed by their partners every year. Over the course of 2004/5, 19,836 women and 24,347 children were accommodated in refuges in England, a steadily increasing figure (Williamson 2006). According to the 2004 British Crime Survey, 50 per cent of all adult women have experienced domestic violence, sexual assault or stalking. Abuse in milder forms such as sexual harassment or pestering is also extremely common. For example, two Nepalese studies conducted in 1997 and 2001 found that 48 and 47 per cent, respectively, of women had experienced harassment in the workplace, with the problem most marked in the garment and carpet industries (Sharma 2005). These occurrences frame women's experience of gender.

Of course women are not the only victims of male violence: other men and children are very frequent victims. But 90 per cent of violent crime in Britain is committed by men. What is worrying is that this aspect of male behaviour may be accepted as inevitable and even justified. A survey carried out by Amnesty International found that one-fifth of respondents believed a woman who wore revealing clothes was partly responsible if she was raped (Bindel 2005). Another survey sponsored by the NSPCC and carried out by teenage magazine *Sugar* found that 43 per cent of respondents (teenage girls aged 13–19) believed it was acceptable for a boyfriend to get aggressive if a girl misbehaved. One in six had been hit by their boyfriends, 4 per cent on a regular basis, and a third of respondents had experienced aggression within the home (Carvel and Morris 2005).

If we turn to the international picture, things are much worse. Many countries have hardly begun to tackle the problem of domestic and sexual violence. In Japan, domestic violence was not made a criminal offence until 2001; in 2005, reports of abuse rose by 17 per cent, as the taboo on discussing it was lifted (*Guardian*, 10 March 2006). While it is even more difficult to estimate the extent of violence in most Third World countries, given limited reporting facilities and the isolation of rural areas, the charity Women at Risk estimates that globally domestic violence is the biggest killer of women aged 19–44, rather than war, disease or hunger. In Guatemala, which has the highest level of reported femicide in Central America, some 2,000 women have been killed over the past three years alone (Mazariegos Garcia 2005). Moreover, in many countries, those reputedly in charge of law and order are some of the worst abusers. There have been many cases of rape by policemen and soldiers in Pakistan and India. During my two visits to Delhi there were daily reports of rapes in the city, which, despite being the prosperous and modernizing capital of a buoyant economy, has become notorious for violence against women. The involvement of the soldiery, of course, becomes even more stark in wartime. Raping and slaughter of girls and women from the opposing side have become standard weapons of war in many parts of the world, as witnessed by the mass rapes in Rwanda and in Bosnia. According to Amnesty International, at least 40,000 women and girls have been raped over the last six years in the Congo. Torture is also common around the world, and against women it often involves sexual abuse. For women in the Third World generally, male violence ranks with poverty as the central concern in their lives.

This picture of violence in the developing world is also a reflection of the lower valuation put on women in many of these societies, which leads women as well as men to abuse their own sex. An acute example is the abortion of millions of female foetuses in India, facilitated by the widespread use of ultrasound technology to identify the baby's sex. It is estimated that as many as 13 million girl children have been lost over the past two decades, leading to a severe gender imbalance in the sub-continent. In 1981 the ratio was 962 girls for every 1,000 boys aged up to 6. By 2001 it had fallen to 927. Where ultrasound is not available, it is known there are high levels of infanticide of girl babies. A report in the *Observer* noted the trend among British Indian women to go to Delhi for abortions of girl children, where they are cheaper and more readily available. Women interviewed by the paper reported family pressures to have a son, especially in relation to the continuance of family businesses. Interestingly, Dr Bedi, a clinician from Delhi who was also interviewed, ascribed this behaviour to an extension of consumer culture and the right to choice. However, it is also clear that this prioritization of male children is deeply embedded in the culture. Dr Bedi quoted a popular saying: *'ladka marey kambakth ka; ladki marey bhaagwan ki'* ('who loses a male child is a fool; who loses a girl is fortunate') (McDougall 2006). Feminists in Delhi have made the issue of the 'missing girls' a central plank of their campaigning.

The centrality of male violence in gender relations is stressed by Hearn in his study of men's violence to known women, based on extensive interviewing with 75 men:

> Violence is a means of enforcing power and control, but it is also power and control in itself. . . . Men's violence to

known women can be understood as standing at the centre of patriarchy or patriarchies, patriarchal relations and patriarchal institutions. It can be seen as in large part a development of dominant-submissive relations that exist in 'normal' family life. Men may resort to violence when men's power or privilege are challenged or under threat. . . . To argue for such a perspective on violence is not to say that all men are violent all the time or that it is only men who are violent. Rather it is men who dominate the business of violence and who specialize in violence. (1998: 36)

Hearn's position states that male violence is not an aberration or act of deviance, but is part of the structuration of relations of masculinity: male violence to known women is 'an inherently gendered way of men referring to themselves and to violence. Men's doing of violence to women simultaneously involves "being a man" and symbolically showing "being a man"' (ibid.: 37).

So does it have to be this way? It may seem odd to start a piece on alternatives and Utopias with a discussion of male violence, but this was a deliberate choice, as was the decision to leave discussion of this topic to near the end of this book. The link between hegemonic masculinities and aggression and violence, the prevalence of male violence against women and the use of the threat of violence to keep women in check and in thrall to men are key parameters of gender relations. While we may be prepared to join with postmodernists in wishing to celebrate the pleasures of gendered difference, and the positive aspects of masculinity and femininity, in the last instance we come up implacably against the destructive facets of gendering: the constraints placed on women's freedom and choice by their childbearing role and the suffering imposed on women by men's violences. These two aspects of gendering are the mainstays of gender inequality. Consequently, in seeking to find better ways of doing gender, it seems logical to confront these two factors. As private individuals, millions of women and men live together in peace, pleasure and happiness; but these individuals live in gendered worlds where gendered inequalities persist. How have feminists and those who have pursued the goal of equality in societies dealt with these seemingly intractable problems?

It is intriguing to look at the tradition of Utopian thinking to see what solutions have been posed to these dilemmas. Classic Utopias such as those of Thomas More (early sixteenth century) and William Morris (nineteenth century) portrayed peace and harmony as a sine qua non: the fair sharing of social resources and the curbing of greedy desires put an end to the perpetual competition and striving which the seventeenth-century philosopher Thomas Hobbes described as the 'war of all against all'. Victorian feminists saw women as having a 'civilizing' function, which might tame the brutal, more instinctive behaviour of males, and this is reflected in Gilman's *Herland*, which was discussed earlier. Here the males were all killed off in earlier warfare, and the surviving women were saved from extinction by the miraculous parthenogenesis. Thus Gilman solves the problem of male violence and the penalty for motherhood by getting rid of men!

Interestingly, the same stratagem is used in one of what Tom Moylan (1986) refers to as 'critical Utopias', post-war works of science fiction exploring the likelihood of socialism, feminism and environmentalism in possible future worlds. In her novel *The Female Man*, Joanna Russ also envisages men as absent from her feminist Utopia, Whileaway. In this society, each (female) child has two mothers, but lives in a 'family' of some 30 women. Moylan describes the character of Whileaway and its inhabitants in these terms:

> Whileaway is a woman's place that thrives on the pleasure principle in a post-scarcity, non-phallocratic, non-capitalist, ecologically sensitive, anarcho-communist society. Hard work, tidiness, privacy, community, freedom, creativity and a love of nature emerge as the primary values in a society that is purposely shapeless, without the linear order imposed by a central government or male abstractions. (1986: 71)

Many of these are common features of most Utopian fictions, but the absence of men is the feminist slant. Other commentators have listed a number of feminist Utopian fictions which envisage a single-sex society (Kumar 1991; Sargisson 1996). This mirrors the common device of a symbolic barrier or wall which separates the Utopian society from its mainstream or dystopian neighbours. Utopias are often islands, or on remote plateaux, as is Herland. Thus in Ursula Le Guin's well-known novel, *The Dispossessed*, the anarchist rebels were exiled to a moon to set up their own Utopia in opposition to the rival oppressive capitalist and Stalinist societies of the homeworld. The idea of separating women from the male oppressors is a fictional strategy which mirrors the separatist strand within second-wave feminism. Women must be apart from men (at least for a time) to achieve strength and autonomy; and men's absence at a stroke solves the issues of violence and the skew in social roles which appends to motherhood.

Is it possible to conceive of a good society for women which includes men? One well-known version is Marge Piercy's *Woman on the Edge of Time*. In her Utopia, Mattapoisett, men are present, but share the gentleness of women. In fact Mattapoisett's inhabitants are androgynous, so that when the heroine of the book, Connie, encounters her first Utopian woman, Luciente, she at first misidentifies her as a man because of her quiet strength. It is a feature of much Utopian writing, whether or not it is explicitly feminist, that living arrangements are flexible and communal, with children being brought up by the community, in a way parallel to the Caribbean system described earlier. This is the case in Mattapoisett too. But Piercy takes a more radical approach to the problem of motherhood by having the babies grown external to the womb in communal hatcheries. Children are assigned three 'co-mothers' (who may be men) with whom they will eventually bond, but women escape the physical constraints of pregnancy. Although they have strong relationships with the co-mothers (the triad being seen as a less possessive unit than the nuclear family dyad), the children are brought up in communal nurseries by expert carers. This scenario parallels the controversial arguments of Firestone in *The Dialectic of Sex* (1971). Firestone argued that gender equality would never disappear as long as women carried children in their wombs, and suggested that radical developments in science and reproductive technology might be the only answer.

The feminist Utopias we have considered draw on two established bodies of critical minority political thought – socialism and the radical brand of feminism. From socialism come the concepts of collectivism, equality, fair sharing of resources, be it in a scarcity or post-scarcity context, rejection of competition and fighting. From radical feminism come notions of separatism, androgyny, the end to exaggerated forms of femininity and masculinity, shared parenting and technology overriding biology. Since these ideas are from minority politics, it is not surprising that there is little sign of such arrangements coming into being. Nor would most people feel that a single-sex or androgynous world is a desirable end, given the pleasure taken by most in the company of both sexes: the experience of difference and of gendered pleasures.

However, as Moylan (1986) and Levitas (1990) make clear, the function of contemporary critical Utopianism is not to provide blueprints of ideal societies but to throw a critical light on existing social arrangements (in many Utopias the ideal society is contrasted with some version of Earth/Terra) and to promote forms of practice which seek to do things differently. Thus Utopias allow us to think how pleasant the world would be if women were free from the fear of assault and if motherhood brought only joys and not penalties. That in turn allows us to envisage ways of bringing this about. Thinking can lead to doing.

We have noted that Herland, Whileaway, Mattapoisett and their ilk are societies based on communal institutions and collectivist ethics. Is it possible to achieve greater gender equality within an increasingly individualistic society such as the UK? In terms of really existing societies the social democratic societies of Scandinavia have taken the greatest steps towards gender parity, with their extensive systems of state nursery care, quota systems for political representation and generally much more egalitarian policies of redistribution of wealth. Feminists in other European countries have long been looking enviously at their forms of social provision, even though it is acknowledged they are not yet paradises of equality: gender segregation remains strong in the workplace and there have been recent elections of right-wing governments determined to cut back on welfare provision.

Some of the policies, including some Scandinavian practices, which could help improve things in neo-liberal societies will be briefly discussed in the Conclusion. There are ways in which gradual improvements, such as have occurred since the 1960s, can be sustained. But in order to tackle the intransigent problems of male violence and the penalty of motherhood, more is needed than policies; we will need more radical changes in the way we think, act and feel.

We will need to cultivate a climate in which male violence of all kinds, unless legitimately channelled into sport or state protection, is considered socially unacceptable. We need more exemplars of non-violence; in particular, we need to teach young men that force is not an acceptable way to get the things they want. We should take every chance to expose the futility of violence, including terrorist acts and warfare, as a way to solve problems between individuals, groups or nations. We must stop turning a blind eye to assaults, ensure that women who experience violence are not stigmatized or shamed into silence. We must criticize the mode of thinking that blames the victims of violence even in part for the attack. Perhaps all secondary-level schools should have painted on their walls the old second-wave feminist slogan:

> However we dress and wherever we go
> Yes means yes and no means no!

We also need to rethink our attitudes to motherhood. At the moment, the contest between the proponents of full-time motherhood or working motherhood is fatally dividing women themselves, thus weakening them in the regard of men. Women must learn to respect the choices made by others and provide support for mothers whatever they decide. Felicity Huffman, the acclaimed actress who plays the struggling but sparky Lynette in *Desperate Housewives*, reflected in an interview for the *Guardian* in 2006 on how the character's problems echoed her own experience of being a mother:

> In the 1960s and 1970s we were fighting against the icon of the perfect wife. . . . In the new millennium, we're fighting against the icon of the perfect mother. In America, you're not allowed to talk about how it's driving you crazy, or how you don't like it or how if you have to give a bath one more time, you're going to pull your hair out. Because then you're considered a bad mom. There's a very established conversation or litany which is, 'Isn't motherhood the best?'

The 'icon of the perfect mother' is a version of the 'intensive mothering' discussed in chapter 5. Huffman describes her own experience of motherhood as challenging, exhausting and frustrating ('I feel like I go from one mistake to another'), while acknowledging that others may find the experience harmonious and fulfilling. The point here is to accept the stresses of motherhood and be realistic about its difficulties as well as its rewards.

The exhaustion and frustration described by Huffman are amplified by the long-hours culture which makes bearing the 'dual burdens' impossible for many young mothers. But a long-hours culture is bad for all of us and takes a terrible toll on men's health as well as causing stress to working mothers. Men and women both, especially those in professional and managerial positions, need to reflect on how our own choices are propping up the oppressive system of flexible capitalism.

We also need to challenge the 'icon of the perfect mother' and the privatized version of motherhood, which presents it as an individual lifestyle choice, and view it through the lens of socially necessary labour. Children, it is often said, are the future of the nation. We need mothers to do a good job not just in terms of continuing the species but also in raising children who make positive contributions to society. Effective motherhood benefits us all. We should give support to those who perform this vital social task, whether it be in terms of enabling them to stay at home with their children without jeopardizing their chances of labour market success when they return, or of ensuring that the conditions of labour make it possible for mothers to continue working. Men's further involvement in the reproductive sphere will also help lift the weight from mothers' shoulders.

Lucy Sargisson in her discussion of Utopian feminism (1996) quotes a spine-chilling extract from Michele Roberts's novel *The Book of Mrs Noah*, which articulates a version of possessive privatized motherhood as it appears under current social conditions:

> Is this the mother then, this horror? This hold? This great gloomy imprisoning embrace that hangs on, that won't let the child step out free?
> To become a mother is to become unfree; tied down . . .
> To become a mother is to own up to having a female body and the social consequences of that; invisibility . . .
> Therefore motherhood is a woman's mythical destiny, her fulfilment puts her in touch with the rhythms of the cosmos, a glory men cannot aspire to. . . . Therefore to become a mother is to accept death . . . therefore it is better not. . . . Therefore women are not men. Therefore mothers can't invent their own lives. . . . Therefore women are not. (1996: 196–7)

This stifling, annihilating vision of 'unfree' motherhood contrasts dramatically with the positive view of co-mothering as a happy, shared, free relationship in Piercy's Mattapoisett. A social function that should be positive and life-enhancing can become, for some unsupported women, a nightmare.

It doesn't have to be this way . . .

Conclusion: What the Future Holds – Gender, Theory and Politics

In this book I have combined a discussion of the major theoretical approaches to the concept of gender with an exploration of the processes of gendering in three aspects of social life: production, reproduction and consumption. The aim was to show the centrality and pervasiveness of gendered relations in contemporary societies and thus the continued need for a critical exploration of gender, both theoretically and empirically. I sought to pull theoretical and empirical discussion together because I believe that highly abstracted theory which is removed from discussion of lived reality can become a sterile exercise, the more so because there are so many burning gender issues which need addressing. Sadly, we live in neither a 'post-feminist' world nor a feminist Utopia. As we progress into the twenty-first century, gender inequities obstinately persist. Sarah Delamont concludes her 2001 study of gender and change in Britain with a sceptical and depressing assessment:

> Have women changed their behaviour and attitudes since 1883 or 1951 while men have not? A cool-headed review of the evidence suggests that British men and women are behaving much like their great-grandparents in 1951. . . . Women still do most of the domestic work and emotional work of households; men in every social class still command the best jobs at that socio-economic level. . . . Men have not changed, but women have not changed either. Adolescent girls have

higher aspirations and more credentials, but for most of these young women their credentials are not transferred into labour market success or egalitarian marriage. When Beck (1994: 27) argued that 'a society in which men and women were really equal would without doubt be a new modernity' he was describing some far distant future, not Britain in 2001. We can hope that he is describing 2008, but I doubt it. (2001: 111)

Even in the wealthiest societies of the West, women have not achieved economic equality and have as yet only dented the structures of power which hold men in dominant positions. Yet, if there are inequalities in Britain, things are much worse elsewhere. The life of many women in poorer parts of the world is oppressive, constricted and wretched. Patriarchal family relations mean that women are treated as the possessions and servants of men. Around the globe, in every type of society, male power is viciously inscribed on women's bodies.

In this final chapter I sketch out some ideas and priorities for the future study of gender. First I consider prospects for the theoretical analysis of gender, especially in relation to power. A second priority is to develop a fuller account of the intersectionality of gender and other forms of social difference and inequality. Finally I consider policy approaches and the key issues for a contemporary politics of gender. As I have argued throughout, gender relations exist in particular political contexts. I have suggested that in Britain a 'climate of equality' exists. How can we capitalize on this rhetorical moment to build a society which removes the negative aspects of gender for women and for men?

Theorizing gender: a radical agenda

Chapters 1–3 pointed to three broad approaches to conceptualizing gender. Liberal feminism viewed gender as a form of discrimination practised against individuals on the basis of sex; radical and Marxist feminisms analysed it as a structural base of inequality and oppression, while post-structuralists and postmodernists analysed it as a social category of difference. One could justifiably say that it is all three at the same time. Indeed, my own view of gender is that it can be approached simultaneously as both structure and category. I have chosen to describe it, however, as a social dynamic, a term that I prefer because it conveys the sense of movement and change, while the term 'structure' has connotations of fixity.

Social dynamics could also be conceptualized as a shifting nexus of social relationships, and in my earlier book, *Fractured Identities* (1996), I attempted to explore the interrelation of four different social dynamics: gender, class, ethnicity and age. I argued that gender, class, ethnicity and age should be conceptualized as *both* social constructs *and* sets of social relations. On the one hand, these are all terms (constructs) which we use to represent ways in which members of human societies differ from each other. We can view them as a number of different ways of representing sameness and difference, constructing some social categories as the Other. Where I differ from some post-structuralists is that they suggest that these terms *alone* actually constitute the Other as different. But I would argue, on the other hand, that there are real structures of difference 'out there' to which these terms correspond, if often rather crudely and inadequately. These differences should be seen as 'lived relationships', which involve different access to social resources and power. Thus difference mutates into inequality.

How do the various dynamics listed above (and there are of course others) relate to each other? I suggest that each of them is best seen as having a different 'existential location' – that is, they relate to a different aspect of the way societies are organized, especially in terms of resource allocation and power. Gender, then, is the way we arrange things between people identified as 'women' or as 'men'; that is, the way we divide society's members up into two (or more) biologically distinguished sexes and then allocate to them different social roles, attributes and patterns of behaviour, which we have explored in this book in terms of production, reproduction and consumption. Gender covers both the material aspects of the division of labour and the cultural definitions and ascriptions of femininity and masculinity.

The two other dynamics which I have touched on in these chapters are those of class and of ethnicity or 'race'. The existential location of the latter is spatial, and it refers to relationships deriving from territorial arrangements (involving the ownership of land and the division of land into 'countries', 'territories' occupied by 'tribes' and 'nations') and from the migrations of people from different territorially based groups. On the basis of these relationships, which have in the past been conceived of genetically as opposed to territorially, ascriptions of 'race' have been made. One could say that 'race' corresponds to ethnicity as gender does to sex. 'Racialized groups' are commonly seen as inferior and excluded or marginalized within societies where they are in a minority.

Class is generally acknowledged to consist of relationships derived from the way we produce, exchange, distribute and consume goods and services. This encompasses the organization of production, the operation of labour markets and the evolution of different patterns of consumption or lifestyles. But class is also about ascriptions of behaviour and attributes, with some groups stigmatized and seen as inferior. The distrust and disdain shown by dominant class groups towards the other has resulted in an increasingly class-segregated society in Britain and elsewhere (for example, the children of the wealthier class groups are likely to attend private secondary schools to protect them from contact with the despised 'chavs').

Each of these dynamics or sets of relationships should therefore be seen as having both material and cultural aspects. Material factors include the distribution of power, wealth, income and other social resources (such as healthcare, education or citizen rights). But they also have 'meaningful' or symbolic aspects in terms of the way we identify ourselves as members of the social and of particular collectivities within it, the way that individuals and groups are represented in social and cultural imagery and in the way that particular lifestyles and ways of living are associated with particular social groups. This is part of my insistence that we should take a both/and rather than an either/or approach to explanation.

Although each of these sets of relations occupies a different existential location, in any given time and place the dynamics are bound up with one another. That is what is currently being termed 'intersectionality'. Accordingly, as individuals, each of us is placed in a particular point where these various relations encompass us in differing ways. I have referred to this as 'multiple positioning' (Bradley 1999b). This in turn exposes each of us to a number of different possible sources of identification, as we saw earlier.

There is some sense that the analysis of gender has rather lost its way as a result of the postmodern and cultural turns, which have shifted the focus away from gender relations as a form of inequality to discussion of discourses and texts. Some of this work has been quite abstract and theoretical and off-putting to activist women who work through trade unions, NGOs, women's self-help groups and elsewhere to confront problems of inequality, poverty, abuse, ill-health and violence. To say this is not to condemn postmodern feminism in its entirety. On the contrary, I believe that the gender analysis inspired by the second wave had rather run out of steam by the end of the 1980s. It had become entangled in internal disputes and was over-influenced by a monolithic type of neo-Marxist structuralism. It was, perhaps, time for a paradigm shift. The postmodern turn was a breath of fresh air and brought new topics to the fore, such as the stress on the body, sexuality, selves and subjectivities. Above all, it focused our attention on the complexity and variability of gender and of power relations, especially through the conceptualizing of multiple identities, and in so doing effectively transcended the sterile political battles as to which form of difference (gender, class, ethnicity, disablement, etc.) was the most oppressive.

One can interpret the progress of social analysis in terms of shifts in theory-building between the search for simplicity and unifying concepts and a corrective insistence on complexity and multiplicity. Feminism followed this common tendency. But now I think there is a need to swing back towards a search for commonalities and generalizations. What unites women is as marked as what divides women. To say that is *not* to espouse any kind of essentialism about men and women, but merely to say that in a given time and place those placed in a particular nexus of relationships are likely to have experiences in common. It does not mean that this is true in all times or places, though some social phenomena are remarkably widespread. This should not surprise us, given the facts of both economic and cultural globalization.

One of the major tenets of post-structuralism and post-modernism has been the critique of 'totalizing' theories or grand narratives. This has led to the view of societies as fragmented and chaotic and a belief that one can do little more than explore particular localized phenomena within specific contexts. But of course this cuts at the very heart of the sociological endeavour. As many have pointed out, the notion of postmodernity is itself a kind of totalizing theory, as are the ideas of post-industrialism and globalization, which are frequently used by postmodernists. As curious as it may seem, despite complexity and diversity, societies do work and the parts of the social whole do, somehow, fit together. To explain social phenomena accurately, it will not do to take things out of context; we must have some kind of holistic view of social reality. It seems to me perfectly reasonable and possible to have an account of the social totality which is not a totalizing theory. The attempt should not be to explain everything, but to specify links of the studied part of society to the social entirety which is its context. In this way we can hold on to some of the important truths of modernist feminism while giving credit to the post-structural critique. As Freedman has it:

> Although the postmodern and post-structuralist critique has pointed to the errors of searching for overarching explanatory theories of domination and power inequality, I would argue that this does not mean that feminism should abandon its search for causality, and that feminists must continue to try to explain the causes of power inequalities in our society in order to prevail against them. (2001: 92)

The context in which we now operate is an increasingly competitive global market generated by consumer capitalism. This is the frame which shapes and structures current relations of gender. This is what I find lacking in the work of Butler and her followers. Thus I suggest that we still need to integrate an account of capitalist structures into our gender analysis. In this book I have sought to do this by utilizing Glucksmann's notion of the 'total social organization of labour'. I have discussed how the three related spheres of production, reproduction and consumption are gendered, and used Acker's four-tiered approach to explore these processes.

What I am espousing here, then, is what one might call a new political economy of gender. This is not the only way to approach the analysis of gender, but I have found it helpful to anchor and embed my discussion of gender. However, as I have suggested, one cannot develop a single model to explain everything. I have drawn on Glucksmann's theory of labour as a way to frame the discussion of the processes of gendering, but there are other frames and concepts which can also be used. To conclude this theoretical discussion I want to turn briefly to three of these.

Power

I have argued throughout that gender must be seen in a political context. Gender relations are relations of power, as are the other social dynamics. The way power has been conceptualized has shifted as a result of the 'postmodern turn', and the issue of precisely how power operates is still an issue of debate, but must be, as in the preceding quotation, a central question.

Modernist feminist theories drew upon Marxist models of power, which located power in the hands of the bourgeoisie or capitalist class and its ally the state. Power derived from the ownership of the means of production and thus the control of the social surplus in the form of profits. The state took its share of the profits and used it to finance its own instruments of power: the state bureaucracy, the legal process and the armed forces. As Weber argued, a key characteristic of a properly modernized nation-state is its monopoly over the legal means of violence. But although this could be seen as an independent source of power, Marxists argued that the state, famously described by Marx and Engels as a committee for handling the affairs of the bourgeoisie, actually operated to preserve capitalist interests in order to maintain economic stability. Looking at contemporary western democracies and their fondness for the free market and neo-liberal economic practices, it is rather hard to dissent from this latter view.

However, Marx and the neo-Marxists had nothing to say about gendered power and this led the radical feminists to develop the theory of patriarchy as a way of explaining male domination. As we saw in chapter 2, Marxist feminists often tried to combine theories of patriarchy and capitalism. For example, in Walby's version of dual system theory there was a tension between capitalist and patriarchal power: capitalists liked to employ women as labourers not only because they were cheap, but because they were seen as more docile and less prone to industrial action. However, as wives and daughters earned their own wage and gained independence, private patriarchy in the home was gradually weakened.

Feminists also discussed the issue of state power, although their views were often divergent. Some saw the state as oppressive to women, for example in the way it handled issues of domestic violence and rape which seemed to promote stereotypical views about male and female sexual behaviour (Edwards 1981; Hanmer and Maynard 1987). It was particularly brutal in its approach to minority female citizens, often attempting to curb their fertility (Mama 1984). However, Scandinavian feminists coined the idea of 'state feminism', citing how social security arrangements helped women who had been abandoned by their husbands, the excellent state provision of childcare and the growing European support for equal opportunities legislation (Borchorst and Siim 1987). A problem was that while the state might aid women, this could result in it becoming a kind of paternalistic quasi-husband with the woman trapped into dependence on its support.

These approaches to power were criticized for being too simplistic and monolithic. Patriarchal power implied a unidirectional relationship, all men dominating all women, whereas it was pointed out that in many cases middle-class women commanded the labour of working-class men. Patriarchy was seen to portray women as passive victims, whereas postmodernists wished to explore women as active agents: certainly many non-academic women objected to this aspect of feminist theory, proclaiming that women were indeed powerful and this position was insulting to them. Thus post-structuralists turned to Foucault for an alternative approach to power, which has proved highly popular. Foucault's account of power was developed in direct response to Marxist and other theories of state power. He rejected any notion of a central agency of power and, as we noted in chapter 3, for Foucault everybody was implicated in relations of power as it filtered its way through the social body. Foucault also rejected the idea that power is a possession of any particular individuals or groups; rather, it is dispersed and exercised through the whole society (Bryson 1999).

Key aspects of the exercise of power were the use of discourses embodying certain ideas of human subjects and their manifestation in an array of disciplinary regimes which were designed to work on bodies and render them docile and useful for the state. Here, Foucault developed an account of power as not merely repressive but enabling (Sawicki 1991). For example, dietary and exercise regimes are freely chosen and even enjoyed, though they may be a part of the way power is exercised on female (and increasingly male) bodies. It can easily be seen why feminist work on the body and sexuality has drawn heavily on Foucault's ideas.

However, Foucault offers a micro-level theory which is helpful in showing how we are all enmeshed in webs of power, but fails to answer two important questions for those interested in gendered power: who holds power; and in whose interests is it exercised? From his own empirical writings we might extrapolate that it is held by experts and operates on behalf of the nation-state, but Foucault himself resists, even rejects, this conclusion. Or simply is not interested in it. This makes it a politically unhelpful theory, because without knowing who in a polity or economy holds power we cannot hope to remove inequality. Foucault's theory does not tell us anything about hierarchies of gender, class or ethnicity. Thus feminists like Bordo and Bartky have tended to combine the analysis of disciplinary regimes with a theory of patriarchal domination, which I suspect Foucault himself would deem invalid.

This has led other analysts on to look for other approaches to power which can answer these questions. Current favourite is the work of Pierre Bourdieu, who has produced a post-materialist take on the concept of capital. Bourdieu (1984) expands on Marx to distinguish a number of different capitals, beside the economic form discussed by Marx and

Engels. 'Social capital' refers to social contacts and networks ('who you know, not what you know'); 'cultural capital' refers to knowledge and know-how, especially that used to procure educational and cultural success; and 'symbolic capital' refers to the development of an ideology which embodies these forms of cultural knowledge and legitimates their dominance. Different groups have differential access to these kinds of capital and the dominant social groups are able to use them to maintain their dominance and keep others out. Beverly Skeggs (1997) used this framework to explore the position of working-class women by demonstrating how these various capitals could take gendered forms.

Bourdieu's ideas can prove fruitful in exploring gendered power. However, given that his approach was developed specifically to analyse class, I myself have preferred to use a model of power drawn from the theories of Giddens, because it is more open-ended and can be applied to any kind of social hierarchy. Giddens discusses power in terms of rules and resources which can be employed by groups and individuals to achieve their ends.

In *Gender and Power in the Workplace* (1999a), I set out a model of different types of power resource which could be used by women and men to secure dominance. The advantage of this model is that it is multidimensional; thus, although men control the majority of power resources, there are some that I have mentioned in this book (for example, sexual power and domestic power) which women can use to their advantage. However, I argue that men as a group are able to control some of the most crucial power resources: physical power (used against women as discussed in the last vignette), positional power (holding of posts involved in decision-making and authority), economic power (greater resources of both income and wealth) and symbolic power (the power to define meanings, such as the discourses and imagery discussed throughout this book). In my view, a resource-based approach, such as those of Bourdieu or Giddens, is more useful than that of Foucault, as it allows us to explore how women may be empowered to resist dominations of gender, class or 'race'. This avoids the pessimistic view of overwhelming power, which often arises from readings of Foucault's texts.

Intersectionality

This brings us neatly to consider the perennial issue of how different aspects and difference are related to one another. In her assessment of gender and change, quoted earlier in the chapter, Delamont (2001) observed that women were sharply divided by class and that in Britain deprivations of class were currently greater than those of gender. I agree with both those statements and believe that feminist sociologists have increasingly recognized a need for a return to exploration of how class intersects with gender. This must not, however, mean a return to the older forms of Marxism with their tendency to reduce everything to the economic and to see gender as a second-order phenomenon. Instead, we need to give the different social dynamics, as I defined them above, their due weight, and accept that different social logics may be at play in each case. To explore this issue, I have chosen to explore the currently fashionable idea of intersectionality.

This term is used in a variety of contexts, and is particularly popular among women's rights activists and in the fields of equality law. The United Nations defines intersectionality in the following terms:

> An intersectional approach to analysing the disempowerment and marginalisation of women attempts to capture the consequences of the interaction between two or more forms of subordination. It addresses the manner in which racism, patriarchy, class oppression and other discriminatory systems create inequalities that structure the relative positions of women, races, ethnicities, class and the like. . . . Racially subordinated women are often positioned in the space where racism or xenophobia, class and gender meet. (UN 2001, quoted in Miller 2005)

Intersectionality, then, corresponds to what I call 'multiple positioning' and 'multiple disadvantage', as discussed in earlier sections of the book. It relates to the way in which 'multiple forms of subordination interlink and compound to result in a multiple burden' (Kanyoro 2001). The key points are, first, that looking at a single aspect of disadvantage in isolation may lead to distortions and also may mask other forms of oppression (as was the claim of black feminists about the work of white second-wave theorists). Secondly, since in any given context different social dynamics will be in operation together, the most complete and thorough understanding of inequalities will need to consider intersectionality. Thirdly, the intersection of differences may produce the most extreme cases of exploitation and discrimination. If we consider these points in relation to the theory of patriarchy, for example, we can see that the difficulty of using a totalistic theory based on only one dynamic is that it presents a distorted view of all women as victims. In fact, male power intersects with class power and racially founded power, so that, for example, upper- and middle-class women are in a position to employ white working-class women cleaners or Filipino and Mexican maids to help them with housework and childcare; they may employ men of lower class standing as employees in their businesses, or be in authority over them as managers in their high-level jobs. In this way, class power enables many women, including those from minority backgrounds, to 'buy themselves out' of many of the problems of gender. However, they in turn may be subject to domestic violence from their husbands or harassed in the streets.

There has been a long-standing tradition of research in the UK exploring these kinds of intersections. The influence of Marxism on British second-wave researchers (see chapter 2) ensured that they were interested in the issue of the mutual interaction of class and gender. Although they were subsequently accused of ignoring ethnicity, that was rather unfair. A good example is the study *Women on the Line* written by Miriam Glucksmann under the pseudonym of Ruth Cavendish (1982). Glucksmann gave up her academic job for a while to work in an electric components factory. The book describes the intricate hierarchies of class, gender and ethnicity within the factory. Similarly, Westwood's study (1984) of hosiery workers explores the different position of white and Asian women workers in the factory where she did her fieldwork. At a more general and theoretical level, the work of Floya Anthias and Nira Yuval-Davis (1983; 1991) built on the black critique to explore the intersections of class, race and gender and the different types of exclusion and marginalization faced by women in racialized groups.

However, the term 'intersectionality' itself has not necessarily or exclusively been used as a marker for this kind of exploration. One exception is an interesting paper by Brah and Phoenix, which calls for a return to these issues following the global impact of the second Iraq war. They argue that the need to understand 'the complexities posed by intersections of different axes of differentiation is as pressing' as ever (2004: 75). They insist on the need to continue the critique of essentialist notions of 'woman' in light of the complexities and variable effects resulting from such intersections in different contexts, asserting that 'different dimensions of social life cannot be separated out into discrete and pure strands' (ibid.: 76). The complex effects of intersectionality are explored through a number of examples of women's autobiographical writings, starting with the powerful words of African-American feminist Sojourner Truth at the Akron Women's Rights conference in 1851, which highlighted the hard physical work performed by women like herself and contrasted it with the view of women as fragile creatures in need of male protection: 'that man over there says that women need to be helped into carriages, and lifted over ditches and to have the best place everywhere. Nobody helps me any best places. And ain't I a woman?' (quoted in ibid.: 77).

While I agree with most of Brah and Phoenix's arguments, I don't accept their view that links intersectionality to the 'disruption of modernist thinking' produced by post-structuralism (ibid.: 82). It is perfectly possible, as the examples above indicate, to use this approach within a modernist framework. To do so, indeed, is necessary, it seems to me, if we are to avoid falling back into the 'infinite regress' of specific differences and thus lose any sense of structuration and regularity. Intersectionality is useful in revealing specificities: but a politically useful gender analysis must also look for regularities and recurring patterns of intersection: for example, the persistent assignment of women of colour to jobs seen as dirty by white society (Young 2005).

Identities

The same problem of regress relates to the interest in social identities and processes of identity, which has been such a major topic in the social sciences over the past 20 years. I have discussed identities at length earlier in this book and I only want to make a few points here. I do not expect the interest in identity to go away. It is a popular topic across a range of disciplines and appeals strongly to students and younger scholars. This at times almost obsessive interest might result from the growth of individualism and the ethos of self-interested striving which can be seen as a legacy of the Thatcher years. Giddens sees individualism as a key feature of late-modern, reflexive societies (Giddens 1991). It is indubitably true that the interest in identities, seen as plural and multiple, was precipitated by the spread of postmodernist and post-structural ideas. Some fascinating work, especially round issues of race, ethnicity and nation, has resulted. Given the nature of modern multicultural societies, the growth of inter-marriage, the controversies around the nature of Islam and the proliferation of hybrid or hyphenated identities, the topic has not yet been exhausted and retains its utility.

However, there is a danger that the focus on identities will lead into a relativist regression, as ever smaller, more specific slots on the grid of multiple positionings are identified and explored. Thus, once again, we are in danger of overlooking the regularities introduced by social dynamics and the opera-tion of power. It seems to me that we now need to move to the formulation of some generalizations about the processes of identification; for example, what are the circumstances in which active identities emerge? how do identities become politicized? what are the generational differences? and what are the effects of interethnic marriages?

I will refer here to a very interesting article by Iris Marion Young (2005) in which she advocates a politics of positional difference as opposed to one of cultural difference as espoused, for example, by Charles Taylor (1994) and Will Kymlicka (1995). At core, this is an argument for an approach which sees difference as related to structural inequalities of various types and not just to matters of cultural distinctiveness. As Young states: 'The politics of positional difference theorizes gender as a set of structural social positions' (2005: 42). Thus, she is calling for a politics based on justice and material well-being, rather than identity politics which calls for acknowledgement of the cultural rights and freedoms of various minority groups. In the paper she discusses three types of structural inequality: disability, racial inequality and gender; it is noticeable that, being American, she does not mention class! But I welcome her stress on structuration and a return to material aspects such as the division of labour and violence. As this book has shown, these are the factors that lie at the heart of gender equality.

Policy and progress: ideas for the future

How, then, might we proceed to develop such a politics based on justice and material equality? I will start by very briefly talking about some aspects of current social policy, and then conclude with some general points about feminism and a contemporary politics of gender.

An important force for achieving gender equality has been the involvement of concerned women in the policy-making process. This can take two forms. First, women politicians (such as Clare Short and Tessa Jowell in Britain) and women working in the civil service and local government and a range of other agencies can make crucial interventions. Cadres of such women have built up since the 1970s; in Australia they were nicknamed the 'femocrats'. Secondly, women researchers and academics can work with governments to assess, evaluate and study the implementation of policy to see how it may be improved. In the UK the advent of the New Labour government, which has a good record on gender, and the current fashion for 'evidence-based' policy have been key developments. Many women are now in the position of giving advice to the Cabinet Office about equality and women's issues.

This can be seen as a form of gender mainstreaming – that is, the process whereby gender considerations are brought into all aspects of policy-making service delivery and decision-making. This principle has been widely adopted across Europe and is sponsored by the European Union. For example, in my own university every agenda for each meeting has an item at the end calling for the gender implications of any decisions or actions to be considered.

The EU has been an important driver for all this. A review by Heide (2004) points out that the right to equal pay for work of equal value is a fundamental EU principle to which member states must sign up. It was under pressure from the EU that Britain developed and then amended its own Equal Pay (EPA) and Sex Discrimination (SDA) legislation. Of course, having a law on the statute books does not mean it is enforced, and the practices of case law mean the intention of legislation can be subverted or even overturned. Since the passing of the EPA and SDA in the 1970s, the Equal Opportunities Commission (EOC) has been constantly lobbied by feminists urging it to take a more active role in pursuing group cases and issuing review orders against non-compliant employers. Heide in her review (which covers social security, pensions and retirement as well as equal pay) concludes that EU equality law is a powerful tool but is not sufficiently utilized. She states that even legal experts and the judiciary seem unaware of the range of procedural mechanisms for attacking discrimination.

Apart from its direct role in enforcing constitutional compliance, the EU also serves as a space where member states can learn from each other's experiences. It is helpful here that Sweden, Denmark and Finland are members, since it is generally acknowledged that the Scandinavian or Nordic countries have the most developed policies on gender (one reason why the citizens of Norway have voted in their referenda against joining the EU). Nordic welfare states have a long record of commitment to gender equality. Their welfare policies are designed to help women's advancement, with generous state provision of childcare facilities, longstanding and substantial allowances of maternity and paternity leave, commitment to egalitarian pay and taxation schemes and ample social security payments for those not in employment. They also have the highest levels of representation of women in national political assemblies, running at around 40 per cent and targeted at parity (Siim 2005). Norway has just set quotas for female membership of executive boards. However, the Nordic countries are committed to the 'adult worker' model, meaning that for successful citizenship all adults should be in employment. Hence the nursery provision. Although the system is not perfect, the universal right to state childcare is a key issue in helping women towards a constructive motherhood, and the example of Scandinavia sets a model to which the other countries can aspire.

In the course of this book I have identified two issues at the core of gender divisions: the penalty for motherhood and male violence. It is worth looking at policy issues in these two areas. Hantrais (2000) and colleagues have traced an important shift in the orientation of EU policies on gender away from equal pay to what they term the reconciliation of employment and family life, the European version of work–life balance. This is a key shift, as it recognizes that inequalities of income cannot be addressed within the labour market alone. This follows persistent findings by researchers, including myself (Bradley 1999a), that family responsibilities and motherhood are the main blocks to equality in the workplace. As we have seen, this is difficult to address, since legislation cannot easily intrude into the family sphere. As we say, the 'Englishman's' home is his castle! We cannot legislate men to take on equal shares of domestic labour; we can only educate them.

There are things that legislation can achieve. The Scandinavian 'daddy weeks', when men are required to look after young children while women return to work, are a good idea and seem to have had an impact. This means making paternity leave compulsory, not perhaps easily achieved in Britain, though a tide of opinion is turning; it was reported by the Policy Studies Institute that the number of new fathers changing their hours to accommodate time with their children had tripled since 2002 (*Guardian*, 1 April 2006). Increased paid leave for both parents is an important gain. There is also a range of options that can be adopted by organizations to minimize the effects of motherhood on women's career chances, many of which are in place in progressive organizations (career breaks, return-to-work training, job shares, adjustments to promotions requirements, and so forth). But there are three major changes needed which are likely to be heavily resisted by employers: tackling low pay (for example, raising the minimum wage and re-evaluating the economic rewards for care work, in which women so predominate), raising pay rates for part-time work and cutting work hours. Though not in the interests of capitalist profit-making, these moves are otherwise for the general social good. The long-hours culture is apparently causing stress even for those who seem to be its greatest sponsors and proponents: the Institute of Chartered Management reported that more than half of managers they surveyed were suffering from stresses including tiredness and insomnia, muscular tensions and relationship problems; 92 per cent were working more than their con-tracted hours, 40 per cent were working more than 60 hours per week and many were on temporary contracts. In addition, 64 per cent said their social lives were affected and 59 per cent said relationships were suffering (Carvel 2006). This is the impact of what has been called 'turbo-capitalism' upon some of its best-paid servants. At the other end of the occu-pational hierarchy, fighting low pay would help young couples in the struggles touched upon in this book and counter poverty among women and children. As so often with gender equality, everyone (bar the shareholders and 'fat cat' directors) gains.

Even more intractable is the problem of male violence. Canada has led the way in policies on domestic violence, pioneering the 'no tolerance' approach: all cases are acted on. Further changes in the way cases of domestic and sexual violence are handled by the police, and particularly by the courts, have been the persistent focus of feminist campaigns and research. More vigorous and imaginative action against bullying in schools is a very good point at which to start tackling the issue of youth cultures of aggressive masculinity. But there are major issues about drug abuse and long-term unemployment among young males, especially from minority ethnic backgrounds, which governments in western societies have tried desperately to address and consistently failed. The attacks on low pay and long hours (leading to a wider dis-tribution of the total amount of available work) might help. But there are deeper cultural issues to address: the glamoriza-tion of violent action, men's proprietary attitudes to sex and women's bodies, deeply embedded patriarchal views and values, which are adhered to by some women as well as men.

Policy alone can have a limited impact. This is where a broader politics of gender, enshrining ideals of peace, justice and human rights, is needed. A tall order, when we look at the international situation and the militaristic machismo of so many of the world's political leaders (including women). We have, however, to start somewhere. And we can start small.

The politics of gender: the individual and the collective

> The private lives of men and women are political. There is no aspect of our lives that is not caught up by the political. How we spend and negotiate our time in relationships is political. How we exercise our power at work and home is political. How we exercise our sexuality is political. How we educate is political. How we contribute to the myths of gender is political. The very language we use is political. To be gendered is to be political. It is not necessary to be a feminist or a member of the Christian promise-keepers to engage in this political condition. Such associations are simply a more direct expression of what goes on across all societies between all men and women in all cultures – daily. (Whitehead 2002: 148)

I very much like Stephen Whitehead's eloquent account of the micro-politics of gender, which reminds us both of the ubiquity of gender and of the inextricable link between gender and power. In all our daily interactions as men and women, we are, as Whitehead suggests, involved in innumerable acts of negotiation as we perform being a man or a woman. Sometimes these small acts confirm the status quo, sometimes they challenge it. It does not necessarily have to involve the major transgressions suggested by Butler: refusing to be cowed by the shouting of a male superior or volunteering to change the baby's nappy while the mother relaxes in front of the television are ways in which we can begin the slow erosion of gender stereotypes and inequitable divisions of labour. In her discussion of what a postmodern feminist politics might look like, Diana Coole extends Butler's ideas of subversion to suggest these struggles can be played out culturally through attacks on 'malestream' thinking or men's grand narratives, by processes including 'humour, pastiche, parody, misquotation, decontextualisation, bizarre juxtapositions, excess' in order to challenge dominant representations to render them 'laughable, unnatural, unworkable' (1998: 121). Coole sees this kind of playful subversion not as the formation of a separate female counter-culture, but as an undermining of dominant masculinity from within.

However, while change can be seen as growing incrementally through these myriad acts which challenge and question hierarchy, and through the negotiations which take place constantly between individual women and men, this is a slow and gradual process which on its own may not be enough to bring about radical change. Here we must turn to more focused and collective activity. We considered above the important role of feminists as a lobbying force within social policy circles. This, as I argued, has been very important within the EU, forcing member states to consider issues of equality and diversity. But legislation alone cannot always succeed in doing things. Moreover, the case of the USA shows that legislative reform can be reversed. In the 1970s and 1980s American feminists led the world in lobbying work to promote equal opportunities legislation, including affirmative action programmes (Gelb and Palley 1982). But with the coming to power of the neo-conservatives in their alliance with Christian fundamentalism, some of these programmes have been dismantled. To avoid the vicissitudes of changes in government, a broader social movement is needed which keeps up the struggle to change 'hearts and minds'. Lovenduski and Randall, in their discussion of British gender politics (1993), made the telling point that feminists in positions of power within the system can operate more effectively when backed by an autonomous movement outside the formal political institutions. What, then, is the future for a revitalized and renewed feminist movement? Can there be a 'third wave'?

The signs are mixed and hard to read. On the one hand, many of the generation of women who responded to second-wave ideas are still actively pursuing feminist goals and fighting for equality. Some are now in positions of authority, where they are able to influence the course of events within organizations. Some have passed their ideas on to their daughters (and sons), who continue to fight for equal rights. But at present it seems unlikely that in the UK this continued quest for gender equality will take the form of a centrally coordinated coherent political movement. It is more likely that it will persist in struggles over single issues and focused campaigns for reform.

In a controversial book released in America, Phyllis Chesler, a long-time radical, speaks of the 'death of feminism', which she believes has been caused by its timidity and uncertainty on the issue of 'gender apartheid' in some Islamic societies and the failure of women to speak out against it.[1] In effect, Chesler thinks that respect for cultural difference has blunted the ability of feminists to identify gender oppression. This highlights the tendency of mass-based political movements to be split and weakened by difficult and complex issues where a simple consensus view is unlikely to emerge. In earlier chapters, we discussed how the issues of pornography and ethnic difference had divided the second wave. However, disagreements do not have to end in divorce. It is a sign of maturity in an institution or movement, as in a relationship, that differences can be debated and absorbed. As Bryson says, 'diversity and disagreement can be seen as sources of strength and vitality; rather than a sign of feminism's decline, they show that it is still alive' (1999: 222).

I take Bryson's more optimistic view, and share with Yuval-Davis, Young and others the hope for a politics of justice which could embrace the notion of intersectionality and work upon it. The notions of 'transversal politics', 'rainbow alliances' and 'dialogic democracy' hold the promise of achieving unity across divisions that is based on respectful listening and developing an understanding of other people's problems, needs and priorities. Yuval-Davis has constantly advocated and worked with the notion of transversal politics, which she describes as 'based on dialogue that takes into account the different positionings of women, or people in general, but does not grant any of them a priori privileged access to the truth' (1997: 204). Integral to this dialogic process are ideas

---

[1] Chesler was interviewed in the *Guardian* by John Sutherland on 4 April 2006. Her book, *The Death of Feminism?*, is published by Palgrave but is not, at the time of writing, available in the UK.

of 'rooting' – that is, the firm adherence to one's own position and values, whilst also allowing a 'shifting' to empathize with women in different positions with different values. One can see how this would provide a basis for dialogic exchange between secular and Islamic women, assuming that both sides are able to root and shift. As argued in the last vignette, Utopian thinking can act as a tool for envisaging change. But we have to share our dreams and visions before we can develop these tools.

If we turn away from Europe to the developing world, we get a different perspective. The conferences organized by UNCHR (the United Nations Commission for Human Rights), such as the 1995 Fourth World Conference on Women in Beijing and the 2001 World Conference Against Racism in Durban, have been important platforms for equality issues, with growing numbers of NGOs participating in them. The conferences have provided a framework for activists in Africa, Asia and South America to pursue claims for human rights and women's rights. The Beijing Conference affirmed the UN and participating states' commitment to the 'advancement and empowerment' of women and 'their full participation on the basis of equality in all spheres of society, including participation in the decision-making process and access to power', and saw these as fundamental to democracy and economic development (Beijing Declaration and Platform for Action 1995).

If any jaded feminist wishes to renew the faith, I can recommend a visit to India. The energy, enthusiasm and commitment of women of all ages who have come together to fight for gender justice is the best tonic one could hope for. This is paradoxical in view of the increasing levels of poverty and inequality in India, which have created terrible living conditions for millions of rural women. Academic women have built links with NGOs and government agencies to develop projects to bring literacy, employment and health education to deprived women in villages across the sub-continent. A network of teachers of Women's Studies has been established, with support from the British Council and some funding from the Department for International Development, which promotes a variety of projects, including, for example, training in gender awareness for the police and other agencies, developing learning resources that can be used in all sorts of educational contexts, and helping rural and tribal women acquire entrepreneurial skills. Whether we would label this a revised feminism is beside the point. This is a strong grass-roots movement to promote women's rights in the context of massive poverty and inequality.

Politics is a strange and contingent business. When I was writing about the movements of the 1960s in chapter 2 of this book, I could never have predicted that in 2006 students and trade unionists would once again take to the streets of Paris in mass protest at the impact of capitalism on young people's lives, notably the insecurity and unemployment that result from the global spread of 'flexible' capitalist competition. So who can guess whether or not, after all, there may be a renewed British or European movement to address some of the inequalities of gender that have been addressed in this book, or what form such a movement might take? Walter (2006) found young women ready to protest about the spread of cultural sexism, discussed in chapter 6. An article in the *Guardian* in March 2006 discussed the recent proliferation of feminist web-logs. It is estimated that some 240,000 exist. The article quotes one blogger, Rebecca Traister, as saying: 'People are always saying feminism is dead but I've never believed that. What I think is that it's taking a modern, technological form, and that, from now on, feminism will be about a multiplicity of voices growing louder and louder online' (Cochrane 2006). For a new generation the Internet and e-space are evolving terrains of political exchange and alternative ideas. Who knows what this generation will come up with?

What we *can* say is that their lives are framed and constrained by processes of gendering just as were those of their parents and grandparents, although the patterns of gendering are different. The sexual division of labour both at work and in the home, the demands of parenthood in the context of long-hours culture, the problems of work–life balance, the pleasures and dangers of sexuality, the unemployment of young men with the loss of so much traditional 'men's work', the corrosive effects of male violence, the abuse and exploitation of women's bodies, the tyranny of slenderness on young women: all are contemporary gender troubles which all of us confront. I disagree with Delamont's view that nothing has changed. Instead, I would endorse the verdict of the Beijing Declaration:

> We recognise that the status of women has advanced in some important respects in the past decade but that progress has been uneven, inequalities between women and men have persisted and major obstacles remain. This situation is exacerbated by the increasing poverty that is affecting the lives of the majority of the world's people, in particular women and children, with origins in both the national and international domains.

We have come quite a long way since the 1940s; but there is still a long road ahead – and still a world to win.

References

Abbott, P. (2000) 'Gender', in G. Payne (ed.), *Social Divisions*. London: Macmillan.

Acker, J. (1990) 'Hierarchies, jobs and bodies: a theory of gendered organisations', *Gender and Society* 4/2: 139–58.

Adkins, L. (1995) *Gendered Work: Sexuality, Family and the Labour Market*. Buckingham: Open University Press.

Amos, V. and Parmar, P. (1984) 'Challenging imperial feminism', *Feminist Review* 17: 3–18.

Andermahr, S., Lovell, T. and Wolkowitz, C. (2000) *A Glossary of Feminist Theory*. London: Arnold.

Anderson, M., Bechhofer, F. and Gershuny, J. (1994) *The Social Economy of the Household*. Oxford: Oxford University Press.

Anthias, F. and Yuval-Davis, N. (1983) 'Contextualising feminism; gender, ethnic and class divisions', *Feminist Review* 15: 62–75.

Anthias, F. and Yuval-Davis, N. (1991) *Racialised Boundaries*. London: Routledge.

Arber, S. and Ginn, J. (1991) *Gender and Later Life*. London: Sage.

Badinter, E. (1981) *The Myth of Motherhood: An Historical View of the Maternal Instinct*. London: Souvenir Press.

Bamberger, J. (1974) 'The myth of matriarchy: why men rule in primitive societies', in M. Rosaldo and L. Lamphere (eds.), *Women, Culture and Society*. Stanford: Stanford University Press.

Banks, O. (1981) *Faces of Feminism*. Oxford: Martin Robertson.

Barrett, M. (1980) *Women's Oppression Today*. London: Verso. Rev. edn 1988.

Barrett, M. (1992) 'Words and things; materialism and method in contemporary feminist analysis', in M. Barrett and A. Phillips (eds.), *Destabilizing Theory*. Cambridge: Polity.

Barrett, M. and Phillips, A. (eds.) (1992) *Destabilizing Theory*. Cambridge: Polity.

Bartky, S. (1990) *Feminism and Domination*. New York: Routledge.

Bauman, Z. (1992) *Intimations of Immortality*. London: Routledge.

Bauman, Z. (1998) *Work, Consumerism and the New Poor*. Cambridge: Polity.

Baxter, J. (1998) 'Moving towards equality? Questions of change and inequality in household work patterns', in M. Gatens and A. Mackinnon (eds.), *Gender and Institutions: Welfare, Work and Citizenship*. Cambridge: Cambridge University Press.

Beadle, P. (2005) 'In every boy there is a bit of "idiot savant"', *Guardian*, 15 November.

Beck, U. (1992) *Risk Society*. London: Sage.

Beck, U. and Beck-Gernsheim, E. (1995) *The Normal Chaos of Love*. Cambridge: Polity.

Beck, U. (1994) 'The reinvention of politics', in U. Beck, A. Giddens and S. Lash (eds.), *Reflexive Modernisation*. Cambridge: Polity.

Becker, H. (1963) *Outsiders*. Glencoe, Illinois: Free Press.

Belsey, C. (1985) *The Subject of Tragedy*. London: Routledge.

Berger, J. (1972) *Ways of Seeing*. Harmondsworth: Penguin.

Berger, P. and Berger, S. (1983) *The War Over the Family*. London: Hutchinson.

Bhachu, P. (1991) 'Ethnicity constructed and reconstructed; the role of Sikh women in cultural elaboration and educational decision-making in Britain', *Gender and Education* 3/1: 45–60.

Bhasin, K. (2003) *Understanding Gender*. New Delhi: Women Unlimited.

Bindel, J. (2005) 'Nowhere near enough', *Guardian*, 24 November.

Birke, L. (1986) *Women, Feminism and Biology*. Brighton: Harvester.

Bocock, R. (1993) *Consumption*. London: Routledge.

Borchorst, A. and Siim, B. (1987) 'Women and the advanced welfare state: a new kind of patriarchal power?', in A. Sassoon (ed.), *Women and the State*. London: Hutchinson.

Bordo, S. (1993) *Unbearable Weight*. Berkeley: University of California Press.

Bourdieu, P. (1984) *Distinction*. London: Routledge and Kegan Paul.

Bowcott, O. (2004) 'Make-up and marketing – welcome to the world of ten-year-old girls', *Guardian*, 8 September.

Bradley, H. (1989) *Men's Work, Women's Work*. Cambridge: Polity.

Bradley, H. (1996) *Fractured Identities*. Cambridge: Polity.

Bradley, H. (1999a) *Gender and Power in the Workplace*. London: Macmillan.

Bradley, H. (1999b) 'Inequalities: coming to terms with complexity', in G. Browning, A. Halcli and F. Webster (eds.), *Theory and Society: Understanding the Present*. London: Sage.

Bradley, H. (2003) 'Catching up? Changing inequalities of gender at work and in the family in the UK', in F. Devine and M. Waters (eds.), *Social Inequalities in Comparative Perspective*. Oxford: Blackwell.

Bradley, H. and Dermott, E. (2006) 'Trying to have it all: the balance of work and family in young adults' lives'. Unpublished paper, Bristol University.

Bradley, H. and Fenton, S. (1999) 'Reconciling culture and economy: ways forward in the analysis of ethnicity and gender', in A. Sayer and L. Ray (eds.), *Culture and Economy*. London: Sage.

Bradley, H. and Hebson, G. (2000) 'Breaking the silence: the need to re-articulate class', *International Journal of Sociology and Social Policy*: 187–214.

Bradley, H., Healy, G. and Mukherjee, N. (2003) 'A double disadvantage: the workplace and union experience of minority ethnic women', *Equal Opportunities Review 2003* 121: 12–15.

Bradley, H., Healy, G. and Mukherjee, N. (2005) 'Multiple burdens: problems of work/life balance for ethnic minority trade union activist women', in D. Houstoun (ed.), *Work–life Balance in the Twenty-first Century*. London: Palgrave.

Brah, A. and Phoenix, A. (2004) 'Ain't I a woman? Revisiting intersectionality', *Journal of International Women's Studies* 5/3: 75–86.

Brake, M. (1980) *Sociology of Youth Cultures and Youth Subcultures*. London: Routledge & Kegan Paul.

Branca, P. (1975) *Silent Sisterhood*. Brighton: Croom Helm.

Brannen, J. and Moss, P. (1991) *Managing Mothers*. London: Unwin Hyman.

Briskin, L. and McDermott, P. (eds.) (1993) *Women Challenging Unions*. Toronto: Toronto University Press.

Brittan, A. (1989) *Masculinity and Power*. Oxford: Basil Blackwell.

Brod, H. (1987) *The Making of Masculinities*. London: Allen and Unwin.

Bryson, V. (1999) *Feminist Debates*. London: Macmillan.

Butler, J. (1990) *Gender Trouble: Feminism and the Subversion of Identity*. London: Routledge.

Butler, J. (1994) 'Gender as performance: an interview with Judith Butler', *Radical Philosophy* 67: 32–7.

Butler, J. (1993) *Bodies that Matter: On the Discursive Limits of Sex*. London: Routledge.

Carby, H. (1982) 'White woman listen! Black feminism and the boundaries of sisterhood', in Centre for Contemporary Cultural Studies, *The Empire Strikes Back*. London: Hutchinson.

Carvel, J. (2006) 'Stressed out bosses suffer in silence as long-hours culture takes its toll', *Guardian*, 29 March.

Carvel, J. and Morris, S. (2005) 'Alarm at acceptance of abuse by teenage girls', *Guardian*, 21 March.

Carver, T. (1996) *Gender is not a Synonym for Women*. Colorado: Lynne Rienner.

Casey, C. (1995) *Work, Self and Society: After Industrialism*. London: Routledge.

Cavendish, R. (1982) *Women on the Line*. London: Routledge.

Chaney, D. (1983) 'The department store as cultural form', *Theory, Culture and Society* 1/3: 22–31.

Chapman, R. and Rutherford, J. (eds.) (1988) *Male Order: Unwrapping Masculinity*. London: Lawrence and Wishart.

Chapman, T. (2004) *Gender and Domestic Life*. London: Palgrave.

Cheal, D. (2002) *Sociology of Family Life*. London: Palgrave.

Chodorow, N. (1978) *The Reproduction of Mothering: Psychoanalysis and the Sociology of Gender*. Berkeley: University of California Press.

Christian, H. (1994) *The Making of Anti-sexist Men*. London: Routledge.

Clark, A. (1982 [1910]) *Working Life of Women in the Seventeenth Century*. London: Routledge & Kegan Paul.

Cochrane, K. (2006) 'The third wave – at a computer near you', *Guardian*, 31 March.

Cockburn, C. (1983) *Brothers*. London: Pluto.

Cockburn, C. (1985) *Machinery of Dominance*. London: Pluto.

Cockburn, C. (1991) *In the Way of Women*. London: Macmillan.

Collinson, D. and Hearn, J. (eds.) (1996) *Men as Managers, Managers as Men*. London: Sage.

Connell, R. W. (1983) *Which Way is Up? Essays on Sex, Class and Culture*. Sydney: Allen and Unwin.

Connell, R. W. (1987) *Gender and Power*. Cambridge: Polity.

Connell, R. W. (2002) *Gender*. Cambridge: Polity.

Coole, D. (1998) 'Master narratives and feminist subversions', in J. Good and I. Velody (eds.), *The Politics of Postmodernity*. Cambridge: Cambridge University Press.

Coontz, S. and Henderson, P. (eds.) (1986) *Women's Work, Men's Property*. London: Verso.

Coote, A. and Campbell, B. (1982) *Sweet Freedom*. London: Pan.

Coward, R. (1992) *Our Treacherous Hearts*. London: Faber.

Cranny-Francis, A., Waring, W., Stavropoulos, P. and Kirkby, J. (2003) *Gender Studies: Terms and Debates*. New York: Palgrave Macmillan.

Crompton, R. (1997) *Women's Work in Modern Britain*. Oxford: Oxford University Press.

Crompton, R. (1999) *Restructuring Gender Relations and Employment: The Decline of the Male Breadwinner*. Oxford: Oxford University Press.

Daly, M. (1978) *Gyn/ecology: The Metaethics of Radical Feminism*. Boston: Beacon Press.

Davies, B. (1989) *Frogs and Snails and Feminist Tales*. Sydney: Allen and Unwin.

De Beauvoir, S. (1973) *The Second Sex*. New York: Vintage.

Deem, R. (1986) *All Work and No Play*. Milton Keynes: Open University Press.

Delamont, S. (2001) *Changing Women, Unchanged Men*. Milton Keynes: Open University Press.

Dermott, E. (2005) 'Time and labour; fathers' perceptions of employment and childcare', in L. Pettinger, J. Parry, R. Taylor and M. Glucksmann (eds.), *A New Sociology of Work?* Oxford: Blackwell.

Devine, F. (1992) 'Gender segregation in the engineering and science professions: a cause of continuity and change', *Work, Employment and Society* 6/4: 557–75.

Duncombe, J. and Marsden, D. (1993) 'Love and intimacy: the gender division of emotion and "emotion work"', *Sociology* 27/2: 221–4.

Dworkin, A. (1981) *Pornography: Men Possessing Women*. London: Women's Press.

Dyhouse, C. (2006) *Students: A Gendered History*. London: Routledge.

Edwards, S. (1981) *Female Sexuality and the Law*. Oxford: Martin Robertson.

Edwards, T. (2000) *Contradictions of Consumption*. Buckingham: Open University Press.

Engels, F. (1972) *The Origin of the Family, Private Property and the State*. New York: Pathfinder (originally printed in 1884).

EOC (2004) *Facts About Women and Men in Britain*. Manchester: Equal Opportunities Commission.

Esping-Andersen, G. (1990) *The Three Worlds of Welfare Capitalism*. Cambridge: Polity.

Featherstone, M. (1991) *Consumer Culture and Postmodernism.* London: Sage.

Fenton, S. and Bradley, H. (eds.) (2002) *Ethnicity and Economy: 'Race and Class' Revisited.* London: Palgrave.

Fenton, S., Bradley, H., Devadason, R., West, J. and Guy, W. (2002) *Winners and Losers: Young Adults' Employment Trajectories.* Report for ESRC.

Firestone, S. (1971) *The Dialectic of Sex.* London: Women's Press.

Foucault, M. (1980) *The History of Sexuality*, vol. 1. New York: Vintage Books.

Freedman, J. (2001) *Feminism.* Buckingham: Open University Press.

Friedan, B. (1963) *The Feminine Mystique.* London: Victor Gollancz.

Frost, L. (2001) *Young Women and the Body.* London: Palgrave.

Fuller, A., Beck, V. and Unwin, L. (2005) *Employers, Young People and Gender Segregation.* Leicester University Centre for Labour Market Studies.

Gelb, J. and Palley, M. (1982) *Women and Public Policies.* Princeton: Princeton University Press.

Giddens, A. (1991) *Modernity and Self-Identity.* Cambridge: Polity.

Giddens, A. (1992) *The Transformation of Intimacy.* Cambridge: Polity.

Gill, R. and Walker, R. (1992) 'Heterosexuality, feminism, contradiction: on being young white heterosexual and female in the 1990s', in C. Kitzinger and S. Wilkinson (eds.), *Heterosexuality: A Feminism and Psychology Reader.* London: Sage.

Gilligan, C. (2002) *The Birth of Pleasure.* London: Chatto and Windus.

Gilman, C. P. (1998 [1915]) *Herland.* New York: Dover Publications.

Gittins, D. (1993) *The Family in Question.* Basingstoke: Macmillan.

Glover, D. and Kaplan, K. (2000) *Genders.* London: Routledge.

Glucksmann, M. (1995) 'Why "work"? Gender and the "total social organisation of labour"', *Gender, Work and Organisation* 2/2: 63–75.

Glucksmann, M. (2005) 'Shifting boundaries and interconnections: extending the "total social organisation of labour"', in L. Pettinger, J. Parry, R. Taylor and M. Glucksmann (eds.), *A New Sociology of Work?* Oxford: Blackwell.

Gregson, N. and Lowe, M. (1994) *Servicing the Middle Classes.* London: Routledge.

Griffin, C. (1985) *Typical Girls.* London: Routledge.

Grosz, E. (1994) *Volatile Bodies*. Sydney: Allen and Unwin.

Hakim, C. (2000) *Work-Lifestyle Choices in the 21st Century: Preference Theory*. Oxford: Oxford University Press.

Halford, S., Savage, M. and Witz, A. (1997) *Gender, Careers and Organisations*. London: Macmillan.

Hall, C. (1980) 'History of the housewife', in E. Malos (ed.), *The Politics of Housework*. London: Allison and Busby.

Hamilton, R. (1978) *The Liberation of Women*. London: George Allen and Unwin.

Hanmer, J. and Maynard, M. (1987) *Women, Violence and Social Control*. London: Macmillan.

Hantrais, L. (ed.) (2000) *Gendered Policies in Europe: Reconciling Employment and Family Life*. London: Palgrave.

Haraway, D. (1990) 'A manifesto for cyborgs: science technology and socialist feminism in the 1980s', in L. Nicholson (ed.), *Feminism/Postmodernism*. London: Routledge.

Harding, L. (2006) 'Germany agonises over 30 per cent childless women', *Guardian*, 27 January.

Harris, J. (2005) 'Driving us nuts', *Guardian*, 10 August.

Hartmann, H. (1986) 'The unhappy marriage of Marxism and feminism: towards a more progressive union', in L. Sargent (ed.), *Women and Revolution*. London: Pluto.

Hartsock, N. (1990) 'Foucault on power: a theory for women?', in L. Nicholson (ed.), *Feminism/Postmodernism*. London: Routledge.

Hays, S. (1996) *The Cultural Contradictions of Motherhood*. New Haven: Yale University Press.

Hearn, J. (1998) *The Violences of Men*. London: Sage.

Hearn, J. and Parkin, W. (1987) *Sex at Work*. London: Sage.

Hebdige, D. (1979) *Subculture: The Meaning of Style*. London: Methuen.

Heide, I. (2004) *Gender Roles and Sex Equality: European Solutions to Social Security Disputes*. Geneva: ILO.

Hochschild, A. (1983) *The Managed Heart*. Berkeley: University of California Press.

Hochschild, A. (1989) *The Second Shift*. London: Piatkus.

Hochschild, A. (1997) *The Time Bind*. London: Metropolitan Books.

Holland, J., Ramazonoglu, C., Sharpe, S. and Thomson, R. (1998) *The Male in the Head*. London: Tufnell Press.

Hollows, J. (2000) *Feminism, Femininity and Popular Culture*. Manchester: Manchester University Press.

Hollway, W. (1996) 'Masters and men in the transition from factory hands to sentimental workers', in D. Collinson and J. Hearn (eds.), *Men as Managers, Managers as Men*. London: Sage.

Huffman, F. (2006) Interview in *Guardian*, 11 March.

Hunt, P. (1980) *Gender and Class Consciousness*. London: Macmillan.

Jackson, D. (1990) *Unmasking Masculinity: A Critical Autobiography*. London: Unwin Hyman.

Jeffreys, S. (1990) *Anticlimax: A Feminist Perspective on the Sexual Revolution*. London: The Women's Press.

Jencks, C. (1986) *What is Postmodernism?* London: Academy Editions.

Jencks, C. (1991) *The Language of Postmodern Architecture*. London: Academy Press.

Kantner, R. (1977) *Men and Women of the Corporation*. New York: Basic Books.

Kanyoro, M. (2001) 'The intersection of race and gender', *Concern*. World WYCA website Quarterly Magazine, September.

Kemp, S. and Squires, J. (1997) *Feminisms*. Oxford: Oxford University Press.

Kerr, M. (1958) *The People of Ship Street*. London: Routledge.

Kimmel, M. (1987) *Changing Men*. Thousand Oaks, CA: Sage.

Kimoto, K. (2005) *Gender and Japanese Management*. Melbourne: Trans Pacific Press.

Kingston, P. (2005) 'Building up barriers', *Guardian*, 2 August.

Kitzinger, C. and Wilkinson, S. (eds.) (1992) *Heterosexuality: A Feminism and Psychology Reader*. London: Sage.

Klein, V. (1965) *Britain's Married Women Workers*. London: Routledge.

Korvajarvi, P. (2004) 'Gender and work-related inequalities in Finland', in F. Devine and M. Waters (eds.), *Social Inequalities in Comparative Perspective*. Oxford: Blackwell.

Kuhn, T. (1970) *The Structure of Scientific Revolutions*. Chicago: University of Chicago Press.

Kumar, K. (1991) *Utopianism*. Milton Keynes: Open University Press.

Kymlicka, W. (1995) *Multicultural Citizenship*. Oxford: Oxford University Press.

Lawler, S. (2000) *Mothering the Self*. London: Routledge.

Lees, S. (1986) *Losing Out*. London: Hutchinson.

Levitas, R. (1990) *The Concept of Utopia*. Hemel Hempstead: Phillip Allan.

Levitas, R. (1998) 'Utopian fictions and political theories: domestic labour in the work of Edward Bellamy, Charlotte Perkins Gilman and William Morris', in V. Gough and J. Rudd (eds.), *A Very Different Story: Studies on the Fiction of Charlotte Perkins Gilman*. Liverpool: Liverpool University Press.

Levy, A. (2005) *Female Chauvinist Pigs: Women and the Rise of Raunch Culture*. New York: Free Press.

Lewis, J. (1992) 'Gender and the development of welfare regimes', *Journal of European Social Policy* 2/3: 159–73.

Llewellyn Smith, J. (2006) 'The marriage option', *Sunday Telegraph*, 19 February.

Lovenduski, J. and Randall, V. (1993) *Contemporary Feminist Politics*. Oxford: Oxford University Press.

Lury, C. (1996) *Consumer Culture*. Cambridge: Polity.

Lyotard, J.-F. (1984) *The Postmodern Condition*. Manchester: Manchester University Press.

Mac an Ghaill, M. (1994) *The Making of Men: Masculinities, Sexualities and Schooling*. Buckingham: Open University Press.

Mahony, P. and Zmroczek, C. (1997) *Class Matters: Working-Class Women's Perspectives on Class*. London: Taylor and Francis.

Malinowski, B. (1922) *Argonauts of the Western Pacific*. London: Routledge.

Malos, E. (1980) *The Politics of Housework*. London: Allison and Busby.

Mama, A. (1984) 'Black women, the economic crisis and the British State', *Feminist Review* 17: 21–36.

Mansfield, P. and Collard, J. (1988) *The Beginning of the Rest of Your Life?* London: Macmillan.

Marshall, B. (1994) *Engendering Modernity: feminism, social theory and social change*. Cambridge: Polity.

Marshall, J. (1995) *Women Managers Moving On*. London: Routledge.

Martin, E. (1987) *The Woman in the Body*. Milton Keynes: Open University Press.

Maushart, S. (2002) 'The truth about babies', *Guardian*, 27 June.

Mazariegos Garcia, D. (2005) 'Landscape of Guatemalan women'. Paper delivered at Fourth International Conference on Work, Women and Health, New Delhi.

McDougall, D. (2006) 'Desperate British Asians fly to India to abort baby girls', *Observer*, 22 January.

McDowell, L. (1997) *Capital Culture*. Oxford: Blackwell.

McDowell, L. (2003) *Redundant Masculinities*. Oxford: Blackwell.

McLean, G. (2004) 'Sisters under the skin', *Guardian*, 24 September.

McRobbie, A. (1991) *Feminism and Youth Culture*. Basingstoke: Macmillan.

Miller, C. (2005) UK Gender and Development Network website <www.gadnetwork.org.uk>.

Millett, K. (1971) *Sexual Politics*. London: Sphere.

Mitchell, J. (1971) *Women's Estate*. Harmondsworth: Penguin.

Mitchell, J. (1985) *Feminism and Psychoanalysis*. Harmondsworth: Penguin.

Mokades, R. (2005) 'Modern identity is not all black or white – it's a beige thing', *Guardian*, 29 December.

Morgan, R. (1980) 'Theory and practice: Pornography and rape', in L. J. Lederer (ed.), *Take Back the Night*. New York: William Morrow.

Mort, F. (1996) *Cultures of Consumption*. London: Routledge.

Moylan, T. (1986) *Demand the Impossible: Science Fiction and the Utopian Imagination*. London: Methuen.

Murgatroyd, L. (1981) 'The production of people and domestic labour revisited', in P. Close and R. Collins (eds.), *Family and Economy in Modern Society*. London: Macmillan.

Nardi, P. (1999) *Gay Men's Friendships*. Chicago: Chicago University Press.

New, C. (2001) 'Oppressed and oppressors? The systematic mistreatment of men', *Sociology* 35/3: 729–48.

Nixon, S. (1996) *Hard Looks: Masculinities, Spectatorship and Contemporary Consumption*. London: UCL.

Oakley, A. (1972) *Sex, Gender and Society*. London: Temple-Smith.

Oakley, A. (1974) *Housewife*. Harmondsworth: Penguin.

Oakley, A. (1980) *Women Confined*. Oxford: Martin Robertson.

Oakley, A. (1981) *Subject Woman*. Harmondsworth: Penguin.

Ogasawara, Y. (2004) 'The Japanese paradox: women's voices of fulfilment in the face of inequalities', in F. Devine and M. Waters (eds.), *Social Inequalities in Comparative Perspective*. Oxford: Blackwell.

ONS (2004) *Labour Force Survey*. London: Office of National Statistics.

Orbach, S. (2005) 'Body hatred is becoming a major export of the western world', *Guardian*, 20 December.

Ortner, S. (1974) 'Is female to male as nature is to culture?', in M. Rosaldo and L. Lamphere (eds.), *Women, Culture and Society*. Stanford: Stanford University Press.

Packard, V. (1957) *The Hidden Persuaders*. London: Longmans, Green and Co.

Parkin, F. (1979) *Marxism and Class Theory: A Bourgeois Critique*. London: Tavistock.

Parsons, T. and Bales, R. (1956) *Family Socialisation and Interaction Process*. London: Routledge & Kegan Paul.

Pettinger, L. (2005) 'Friends, relations and colleagues: the blurred boundaries of the workplace', in L. Pettinger, J. Parry, R. Taylor and M. Glucksmann (eds.), *A New Sociology of Work?* Oxford: Blackwell.

Phillips, A. (1987) *Divided Loyalties: Dilemmas of Sex and Class.* London: Virago.

Phillips, A. (1991) *Engendering Democracy.* Cambridge: Polity.

Pilcher, J. (1999) *Women in Contemporary Britain.* London: Routledge.

Pollert, A. (1981) *Girls, Wives, Factory Lives.* London: Macmillan.

Purcell, K. (2000) 'Gendered employment insecurity', in E. Heery and J. Salmon (eds.), *The Insecure Workforce.* London: Routledge.

Rich, A. (1980) 'Compulsory heterosexuality and the lesbian continuum', *Signs* 5/4: 631–90.

Riley, D. (1988) *Am I that Name?* London: Macmillan.

Ritzer, G. (1993) *The McDonaldization of Society.* Thousand Oaks, CA: Sage.

Roberts, Y. (2004) 'Face value', *Guardian,* 4 November.

Roberts, Y. (2005) 'The love drug', *Guardian,* 7 January.

Rubery, J., Smith, M. and Turner, E. (1996) *Bulletin on Women and Employment in the European Union.* Brussels: Commission of the European Community.

Rubin, G. (1975) 'The traffic in women: the political economy of sex', in R. Reiter (ed.), *Towards an Anthropology of Women.* New York: Monthly Review Press.

Sargisson, L. (1996) *Contemporary Feminist Utopianism.* London: Routledge.

Sawicki, J. (1991) *Disciplining Foucault: Gender, Power and the Body.* London: Routledge.

Scott, J. W. (1988) *Gender and the Politics of History.* New York: Columbia University Press.

Segal, L. (1990) *Slow Motion.* London: Pluto.

Segal, L. (1994) *Straight Sex.* London: Virago.

Seidler, V. (1985) 'Fear and intimacy', in A. Metcalf and M. Humphries (eds.), *The Sexuality of Men.* London: Pluto.

Seidler, V. (1992) *Men, Sex and Relationships: Writings from Achilles Heel.* London: Routledge.

Seidler, V. (1997) *Man Enough: Embodying Masculinities.* London: Sage.

Shabi, R. (2005) 'Lessons in loneliness', *Guardian,* 1 October.

Sharma, N. (2005) 'Sexual harassment at the workplace'. Paper delivered at Fourth International Conference on Work, Women and Health, New Delhi.

Siim, B. (2005) 'Gender equality, citizenship and welfare state restructuring', in J. G. Andersen, A.-M. Guillemard, P. Jensen and B. Pfau-Effinger (eds.), *The Changing Face of Welfare.* Bristol: Policy Press.

Siltanen, J. (1996) *Locating Gender*. London: UCL Press.

Skeggs, B. (1997) *Formations of Class and Gender*. London: Sage.

Skelton, C. (1989) *Whatever Happens to Little Women?* Milton Keynes: Open University Press.

Smith, L. (1978) 'Sexist assumptions and female delinquency', in C. Smart and B. Smart (eds.), *Women, Sexuality and Social Control*. London: Routledge.

Soper, K. (1990) *Troubled Pleasures: Writings on Gender, Politics and Hedonism*. London: Verso.

Spender, D. (1985) *Man-Made Language*. London: Routledge & Kegan Paul.

Stanko, E. (2000) *The Day to Count: A Snapshot of the Impact of Domestic Violence in the UK*. Economic and Social Research Council.

Stoller, R. (1968) *Sex and Gender: On the Development of Masculinity and Femininity*. London: The Hogarth Press.

Stone, S. (1991) 'The "Empire" strikes back: a post-transsexual manifesto', <www.sandystone.com/empirestrikesback>.

Sudbury, J. (1998) *Other Kinds of Dreams: Black Women's Organisation and the Politics of Transformation*. London: Routledge.

Sullivan, O. (1997) 'Time waits for no (wo)man', *Sociology* 31/2: 221–40.

Sullivan, O. (2000) 'The division of domestic labour: twenty years of change?', *Sociology* 34/3: 437–56.

Talbot, M. (1979) *Women and Leisure*. SSRC/Sports Council.

Taylor, C. (1994) 'The politics of recognition', in A. Gutmann (ed.), *Multiculturalism*. Princeton, NJ: Princeton University Press.

Thompson, D. (1994) 'The self-contradiction of "postmodernist" feminism', in D. Bell and R. Klein (eds.), *Radically Speaking: Feminism Reclaimed*. London: Zed Books.

Tong, R. (1989) *Feminist Thought*. London: Allen and Unwin.

Valentine, G. (1999) 'Eating in', *Sociological Review* 47/3: 491–524.

Vance, C. (1992) *Pleasure and Danger*. London: Pandora.

Veblen, T. (1925) *The Theory of the Leisure Class*. London: Allen and Unwin.

Vincent, N. (2006) *Self-Made Man: My Year Disguised as a Man*. New York: Atlantic Books; excerpted in *Guardian*, 18 March.

Wacjman, J. (1998) *Managing Like a Man*. Cambridge: Polity.

Walby, S. (1986) *Patriarchy at Work*. Cambridge: Polity.

Walby, S. (1990) *Theorizing Patriarchy*. Oxford: Blackwell.

Walby, S. (1997) *Gender Transformations*. London: Routledge.

Walby, S. and Allen, J. (2004) *Domestic Violence, Sexual Assault and Stalking: Findings from the British Crime Survey*. Home Office Research Study 276. London: Home Office.

Walia, N. (2005) 'Far from just middling', *Times of India*, 27 November.

Walkerdine, V. (1990) *Schoolgirl Fictions*. London: Verso.

Walkerdine, V., Lucey, H. and Melody, J. (2001) *Growing Up Girl*. London: Palgrave.

Walter, N. (2006) 'My part in feminism's failure to tackle our Loaded culture', *Guardian*, 26 January.

Ward, L. (2005) 'Doubt and depression burden teenage girls', *Guardian*, 24 February.

Warde, A. and Hetherington, K. (1993) 'A changing domestic division of labour: issues of measurement and interpretation', *Work, Employment and Society* 7/1: 23–45.

Waugh, P. (1992) *Practising Postmodernism/Reading Modernism*. London: Edward Arnold.

Weber, M. (1949) *The Methodology of the Social Sciences*. Glencoe, Illinois: Free Press.

Weeks, J. (1981) *Sex. Politics and Society*. London: Longman.

Westwood, S. (1984) *All Day, Every Day*. London: Pluto.

Wetherell, M., Stiven, H. and Potter, J. (1987) 'Unequal egalitarianism: a preliminary study of discourses concerning gender and employment opportunities', *British Journal of Social Psychology* 26: 59–71.

Whitaker, R. (2006) 'Veil power', *Guardian*, 21 February.

Whitehead, S. (2002) *Men and Masculinities*. Cambridge: Polity.

Williams, C., Giuffre, P. and Dellinger, K. (2004) 'Research on gender stratification in the US', in F. Devine and M. Waters (eds.), *Social Inequalities in Comparative Perspective*. Oxford: Blackwell.

Williamson, E. (2006) *Findings from Survey of Domestic Violence Services*. Women's Aid Federation of Great Britain.

Wilson, A. (1978) *Finding a Voice*. London: Virago.

Wittig, M. (1981) 'One is not born a woman', *Feminist Issues* 1/2: 47–54.

Wolf, N. (1990) *The Beauty Myth*. London: Chatto and Windus.

Wollstonecraft, M. (1975 [1792]) *A Vindication of the Rights of Women*. Harmondsworth: Penguin.

Wolpe, A.-M. (1988) *Within School Walls*. London: Routledge.

Women's Aid (2005) 'Frequently asked questions', <www.womensaid.org.uk>.

Wood, J. (1984) 'Groping towards sexism: boys' sex talk', in A. McRobbie and M. Nava (eds.), *Gender and Generation*. London: Macmillan.

Woodward, K. (1997) 'Motherhood: identities, meanings and myths', in K. Woodward (ed.), *Identities and Difference*. London: Sage.

Yeandle, S. (1999) 'Gender contracts, welfare systems and no-standard working; diversity and change in Denmark, France, Germany, Italy and the UK', in A. Felstead and N. Jewson (eds.), *Global Trends in Flexible Labour*. Basingstoke: Macmillan.

Young, I. M. (1990) *Justice and the Politics of Difference*. Princeton, NJ: Princeton University Press.

Young, I. M. (2005) 'Structural injustice and the politics of difference'. Paper for presentation at Intersectionality Workshop, AHRC Centre for Law, Gender and Sexuality, University of Keele, May.

Young, M. and Willmott, P. (1973) *The Symmetrical Family*. London: Routledge.

Yuval-Davis, N. (1997) 'Ethnicity, gender relations and multiculturalism', in P. Werbner and T. Modood (eds.), *Debating Cultural Hybridity*. London: Zed Books.

Yuval-Davis, N. (1993) 'Beyond difference: women and coalition politics', in M. Kennedy, C. Lubelska and F. Walsh (eds.), *Making Connections*. London: Taylor and Francis.

Index